Required Writing

by Philip Larkin

poetry
The North Ship
XX Poems
The Fantasy Poets No. 21
The Less Deceived
(*The Marvell Press*)
The Whitsun Weddings
High Windows
Collected Poems

The Oxford Book of Twentieth-Century English Verse (Ed.)

fiction
Jill
A Girl in Winter

non-fiction
All What Jazz: A Record Diary 1961–71

Required Writing

Miscellaneous Pieces 1955–1982

PHILIP LARKIN

faber and faber

LONDON · BOSTON

First published in 1983
by Faber and Faber Limited
3 Queen Square London WC1N 3AU

Filmset by Wilmaset, Birkenhead, Merseyside
Printed and bound in England by
Clays Ltd, St Ives plc
All rights reserved

© Philip Larkin, 1983

A CIP record for this book is
available from the British Library

ISBN 0-571-13120-4 Pbk

To
Anthony Thwaite

Contents

Foreword   *page* 11
Acknowledgements   13

RECOLLECTIONS   15

Introduction to *Jill*   17
Introduction to *The North Ship*   27
Single-handed and Untrained   31
Early Days at Leicester   36
Vernon Watkins: an Encounter and a Re-encounter   40

INTERVIEWS   45

An Interview with the *Observer*   47
An Interview with *Paris Review*   57

WRITING IN GENERAL   77

Statement   79
The Pleasure Principle   80
Writing Poems   83
Books   85
Subsidizing Poetry   87
The Booker Prize 1977   93
A Neglected Responsibility   98

WRITING IN PARTICULAR   109

The Savage Seventh   111
Carnival in Venice   117
Hounded   120
What's Become of Wystan?   123
The Blending of Betjeman   129
Missing Chairs   134

10   Contents

Masters' Voices   *page* 136
Mrs Hardy's Memories   142
The Poetry of William Barnes   149
Frivolous and Vulnerable   153
The War Poet   159
Freshly Scrubbed Potato   164
Wanted: Good Hardy Critic   168
The Poetry of Hardy   175
The Apollo Bit   177
The Most Victorian Laureate   182
Grub Village   188
Big Victims   191
Palgrave's Last Anthology   198
It Could Only Happen In England   204
Mr Powell's Mural   219
Supreme Sophisticate   225
The Real Wilfred   228
The World of Barbara Pym   240
The Changing Face of Andrew Marvell   245
Dull Beyond Description   254
The Girls   260
All Right When You Knew Him   263
The Batman from Blades   266
The Great Gladys   271
The Traffic in the Distance   274
Horror Poet   278

ALL WHAT JAZZ   283

Introduction to *All What Jazz*   285
Just a Little While   299
Coverage   302
Blues Bash   303
Law   305
Basie   306
Moment of Truth   307
Wells or Gibbon?   309
Minority Interest   312
Vocals   313
What Armstrong Did   314

Foreword

The pieces collected here were, with one exception, produced on request—mostly, of course, as reviews, for it is an unexpected consequence of becoming known as a writer that you are assumed to be competent to assess other writers. But for every request complied with, several others were declined, for which either the time or the interest or the capability was lacking. It was, of course, flattering to be asked, but only up to a point: newspapers and magazines have to be filled, and if you won't do it someone else will. It is only the very prolific or the very needy who can afford to say yes to everything.

There is little coherence, therefore, in what is here reprinted. I have never proposed to an editor that I should write this article or review that book, so that what I produced was someone else's idea rather than my own. This is not to say that such tasks were undertaken lightly. A good reviewer combines the knowledge of the scholar with the judgement and cogency of the critic and the readability of the journalist, and knowing how far I fell short of this ideal made me all the more laboriously anxious to do the best I could. I have heard it said that anyone who has spent three years writing a weekly essay for his tutor finds literary journalism easy: I didn't. I found reading the books hard, thinking of something to say about them hard, and saying it hardest of all. That I persisted was due to the encouragement of friendly literary editors, in particular Bill Webb of the *Guardian*, Karl Miller of the *Spectator*, the *New Statesman* and the *Listener* (and now, of course, the *London Review of Books*), and Anthony Thwaite of the *Listener*, the *New Statesman* and *Encounter*, and I should like to record my gratitude to them, reluctant though my response may have been at the time.

The piece written on my own initiative was the introduction to *All What Jazz* (1970), the collection of jazz record reviews I had written for the *Daily Telegraph* between 1960 and 1968. I had originally intended to publish that book privately, which is why it was printed by the now defunct firm Hull Printers; my publishers took it over only when I wrote asking if they would be prepared to distribute it. This may also account for the light-heartedly aggressive tone of what I wrote, and the enjoyment with which I wrote it. In fact I went on reviewing records until the end of 1971, and a few pieces from these last three years have been included along with the introduction.

Although I rarely accepted a literary assignment without a sinking of the heart, nor finished it without an inordinate sense of relief, to undertake such commissions no doubt exercised part of my mind that would otherwise have remained dormant, and to this extent they probably did me no harm. They are now reprinted because some of them have begun to be quoted out of context, and I should like to reiterate the latter, especially their dates. They will, I hope, also carry the rest, whose exhumation would otherwise hardly be justified.

Apart from minor verbal amendments, the pieces are reprinted as they first appeared. The order is chronological by date of publication except for the section 'Recollections', where the order is chronological by subject-matter.

P.L.
February 1982

Acknowledgements

I am grateful to Betty Mackereth for her help in converting a wilderness of press cuttings into something resembling an ordered text, to Catherine Carver for patiently freeing that text from inconsistencies, inaccuracies and inelegances, and to Monica Jones for giving the proofs a second, much-needed reading.

For permission to reprint reviews and articles the publishers acknowledge the following with gratitude:

Antiquarian Booksellers' Association, 'Books'; *The Cornhill*, 'It Could Only Happen in England'; *Critical Quarterly*, 'Mrs Hardy's Memories', 'Wanted: Good Hardy Critic'; the *Daily Telegraph*, 'Just a Little While', 'Coverage', 'Blues Bash', 'Law', 'Basie', 'Moment of Truth', 'Wells or Gibbon?', 'Minority Interest', 'Vocals', 'What Armstrong Did'; *Encounter*, 'A Neglected Responsibility', 'The Real Wilfred', 'Dull Beyond Description'; *English Literary Renaissance*, 'The Changing Face of Andrew Marvell'; Faber and Faber, 'Introduction to *Jill*', 'Introduction to *The North Ship*', 'Vernon Watkins', 'Introduction to *All What Jazz*'; FVS Foundation, Hamburg, 'Subsidizing Poetry'; the *Guardian*, 'Freshly Scrubbed Potato', 'Grub Village', 'All Right When You Knew Him'; Kenyusha, Japan, 'Statement'; *Library Association Record*, 'Single-handed and Untrained'; the *Listener*, 'The Poetry of William Barnes', 'The War Poet', 'The Poetry of Hardy'; the Marvell Press, 'The Pleasure Principle' from *Listen II*; *New Fiction*, 'The Booker Prize 1977'; the *New Statesman*, 'Masters' Voices', 'Missing Chairs', 'Frivolous and Vulnerable', 'The Apollo Bit', 'The Most Victorian Laureate', 'Big Victims', 'Mr Powell's Mural'; the *Observer*, 'The Great Gladys', 'Interview with the *Observer*', 'The Girls'; Oxford University Press, 'Palgrave's Last Anthology: A.E. Housman's Copy', from the *Review of English Studies*, vol XXII; *Paris Review*, 'An Interview with Paris Review', © *Paris Review*,1982; *Poetry Book Society Bulletin*, 'Writing Poems'; *Poetry Review*, 'Horror Poet'; *Punch*, 'Supreme Sophisticate';

the *Spectator*, 'The Savage Seventh', 'Carnival in Venice', 'Hounded', 'What's Become of Wystan?', 'The Blending of Betjeman,' 'The Traffic in the Distance'; the *Times Literary Supplement*, 'The World of Barbara Pym', 'The Batman from Blades'; *University of Leicester Convocation Review*, 'Early Days at Leicester'.

RECOLLECTIONS

Introduction to *Jill*

An American critic recently suggested[1] that *Jill* contained the first
example of that characteristic landmark of the British post-war novel,
the displaced working-class hero. If this is true (and it sounds fair
trend-spotter's comment), the book may hold sufficient historical
interest to justify republication. But again, if it is true, I feel bound to
say that it was unintentional. In 1940 our impulse was still to
minimize social differences rather than exaggerate them. My hero's
background, though an integral part of the story, was not what the
story was about.

As a matter of fact, the Oxford of that autumn was singularly free
from such traditional distinctions. The war (American readers may
need reminding) was then in its second year. Conscription had begun
with the twenties and upwards, but everyone knew that before long
the nineteens and the eighteens would take their turn. In the
meantime, undergraduates liable for service could expect three or
four terms at the most: if they wished then to become officers, they
drilled with the ununiformed Officers' Training Corps half a day a
week (later they got uniforms and drilled a day and a half a week).

Life in college was austere. Its pre-war pattern had been dispersed,
in some instances permanently. Everyone paid the same fees (in our
case, 12s a day) and ate the same meals. Because of Ministry of Food
regulations, the town could offer little in the way of luxurious eating
and drinking, and college festivities, such as commemoration balls,
had been suspended for the duration. Because of petrol rationing,
nobody ran a car. Because of clothes rationing, it was difficult to dress
stylishly. There was still coal in the bunkers outside our rooms, but
fuel rationing was soon to remove it. It became a routine after
ordering one's books in Bodley after breakfast to go and look for a
cake or cigarette queue.

With new men coming up every term, too, there was hardly any

[1] James Gindin, *Postwar British Fiction* (1962).

such thing as a freshman, and distinctions of seniority blurred. Traditional types such as aesthete and hearty were pruned relentlessly back. The younger dons were mostly on war service, and their elders were too busy or too remote to establish contact with us— often, in fact, the men of one college would share a tutor with another, whom they would never see socially at all. Perhaps the most difficult thing to convey was the almost complete suspension of concern for the future. There were none of the pressing dilemmas of teaching or Civil Service, industry or America, publishing or journalism: in consequence, there was next to no careerism. National affairs were going so badly, and a victorious peace was clearly so far off, that effort expended on one's post-war prospects could hardly seem anything but a ludicrous waste of time.

This was not the Oxford of Michael Fane and his fine bindings, or Charles Ryder and his plovers' eggs. Nevertheless, it had a distinctive quality. A lack of *douceur* was balanced by a lack of *bêtises*, whether of college ceremonial or undergraduate extravagance (I still remember the shock during a visit to Oxford after the war of seeing an undergraduate in a sky-blue cloak and with hair down to his shoulders, and of realizing that all that was starting again), and I think our perspectives were truer as a result. At an age when self-importance would have been normal, events cut us ruthlessly down to size.

II

I shared rooms with Noel Hughes, with whom I had just spent two disrespectful years in the Modern Sixth, but my tutorial-mate was a large pallid-faced stranger with a rich Bristolian accent, whose preposterous skirling laugh was always ready to salute his own outrages. Norman had little use for self- or any other kind of discipline, and it was not uncommon, on returning from a nine o'clock lecture, to find him still in his dressing-gown, having missed breakfast by some ninety minutes, plucking disconsolately at a dry loaf and drinking milkless tea. To learn where I had been (Blunden, perhaps, on Biography) did nothing to raise his spirits: 'That bugger's a waste of time. . . . I'm better than that bugger.' His eye falling on his empty cup, he would pitch its dregs messily into the grate, further discouraging the fire, before reaching again for the teapot. 'A gentleman', he would aphorize with dignity, 'never drinks the lees of his wine.'

Norman at once set about roughing up my general character and assumptions. Any action or even word implying respect for qualities such as punctuality, prudence, thrift or respectability called forth a snarling roar like that of the Metro-Goldwyn-Mayer lion and the accusation of *bourgeoisisme*; ostentatious courtesy produced a falsetto celestial-choir effect, ostentatious sensibility the recommendation to 'write a poem about it'. For a few weeks I uneasily counter-attacked along predictable lines: all right, suppose it *was* hypocrisy, hypocrisy was *necessary*, what would happen if *everybody* . . . After that I gave it up. Norman treated everyone like this: it made no difference to their liking for him. Indeed, his most hilarious mockeries were reserved for himself. Like the rest of us (excepting perhaps Noel), he was clearer about his dislikes than his likes, but while we were undergoing a process of adjustment Norman's rejection of his new environment was total. At first this strengthened his influence over us: as time went on, it tended to cut him off. Not in fact until he was with a Friends' unit in Poland after the war did he seem to be doing what he wanted.

We quickly invented 'the Yorkshire scholar', a character embodying many of our prejudices, and conversed in his flat rapacious tones in going to and from our tutor, Gavin Bone. 'You're gettin' the best education in the land, lad.' 'Ay, but you must cut your coat according to your cloth.' 'Had tea wi' t' Dean on Sunday—I showed him I'd been reading his book.' 'Never lose a chance to make a good impression.' 'What play have you written about?' '*King Lear*. You see, I've DONE *King Lear*.' 'Ay.' 'Ay.' This comedy probably gave Norman more emotional release than it did me, for he had been through the hands of the late R. W. Moore at Bristol Grammar School, but I was sufficiently acquainted with the climate of the scholarship year to enjoy keeping the game going. I cannot imagine what Gavin Bone thought of us. Already in failing health (he died in 1942), he treated us like a pair of village idiots who might if tried too hard turn nasty. The highest academic compliment I received as an undergraduate was 'Mr Larkin can see a point, if it is explained to him'.

During these first two terms our friends were mostly outside College; Norman had a group in Queen's, while I kept up with other Old Coventrians or enjoyed jazz evenings with Frank Dixon of Magdalen and Dick Kidner of Christ Church. At the beginning of the Trinity term, however, Norman, who had been idly looking over the notice-board in the lodge, hailed the mention of a newcomer, name of Amis.

'I met him at Cambridge on a schol. . . . He's the hell of a good man.'

'How is he?'

'He shoots guns.'

I did not understand this until later in the afternoon when we were crossing the dusty first quadrangle a fair-haired young man came down staircase three and paused on the bottom step. Norman instantly pointed his right hand at him in the semblance of a pistol and uttered a short coughing bark to signify a shot—a shot not as in reality, but as it would sound from a worn sound-track on Saturday afternoon in the ninepennies.

The young man's reaction was immediate. Clutching his chest in a rictus of agony, he threw one arm up against the archway and began slowly crumpling downwards, fingers scoring the stonework. Just as he was about to collapse on the piled-up laundry, however (Oxford laundries were at that time operating a system described by James Agate as collecting every two weeks and delivering every three, so that the place was generally littered with bundles in transit one way or the other), he righted himself and trotted over to us. 'I've been working on this,' he said, as soon as introductions were completed. 'Listen. This is when you're firing in a ravine.'

We listened.

'And this when you're firing in a ravine and the bullet ricochets off a rock.'

We listened again. Norman's appreciative laughter skirled freely: I stood silent. For the first time I felt myself in the presence of a talent greater than my own.

No one who knew Kingsley at that time would deny that what chiefly distinguished him was this genius for imaginative mimicry. It was not a BBC Variety Hour knack of 'imitations' (though in fact he had a very funny imitation of the man who used to imitate a car driving through a flock of sheep doing his imitation); rather, he used it as the quickest way of convincing you that something was horrible or boring or absurd—the local comrade ('Eesa poincher see . . . assa poincher see'), the Irish tenor ('the sarn wass dee-cli-neeng'), the University CSM ('Goo on, seh'), a Russian radio announcer reading in English a bulletin from the Eastern Front ('twelf field mortars'), his voice suffering slow distortion to unintelligibility followed by a sudden reversion to clarity ('aberbera mumf mumf General von Paulus'). As time went on, his scope widened: 'remind me', a post-war letter ended, 'to do *Caesar and Cleopatra* for you.' Films were always excellent material: the gangster film (with plenty of shooting), especially a version entirely peopled with figures from the University Faculty of English; the no-work film (this was largely silent); the U-boat film ('Wir haben sie!'); and one that involved Humphrey Bogart flashing a torch round a cellar. One day after the war Kingsley, Graham Parkes and Nick Russel were strolling along to the Lamb and Flag when a motor cyclist clearly with the same destination propped his machine against the kerb near by. When he had got some distance across the pavement towards the arch, Kingsley (I gather for want of something better to do) made his motor-bike-failing-to-start noise. The man stopped dead in his tracks and stared at his machine narrowly. Then he walked back and knelt down beside it. Some minutes later he entered the pub with a subdued expression on his face. Kingsley's masterpiece, which was so demanding I heard him do it only twice, involved three subalterns, a Glaswegian driver and a jeep breaking down and refusing to restart somewhere in Germany. Both times I became incapable with laughter.

From this time on my friends all seemed to be in College, and a photograph taken on the sunny lawn the following summer reminds me how much our daily exchanges were informed by Kingsley's pantomimes. In the foreground crouches Kingsley himself, his face contorted to a hideous mask and holding an invisible dagger: 'Japanese soldier,' my note says, but I have forgotten why. Edward du Cann is withdrawing the safety pin from an invisible hand-grenade with his teeth (*In the Rear of the Enemy*, one of Kingsley's Russian documentaries); Norman and David Williams are doing the 'first today' routine,[1] Wally Widdowson has a curiously stiff thumbs-in-belt stance ('Russian officer'—was this part of *In the Rear of the Enemy*?), and David West ('Romanian officer') is attempting to represent a contemporary saying that every Romanian private had a Romanian officer's lipstick in his knapsack. The rest are engaged in the eternal gang warfare.

This is not to say that Kingsley dominated us. Indeed, to some extent he suffered the familiar humorist's fate of being unable to get anyone to take him seriously at all. Kingsley's 'serious side' was

[1] Not Kingsley's invention, but see his story, 'The 2003 Claret', in *The Complete Imbiber* (1958).

political. In those days of Help for Russia Week, when the hammer
and sickle flew with the Union Jack in Carfax, he became editor of the
University Labour Club *Bulletin* and in this capacity printed one of my
poems. (A second, much less ambiguously ambiguous, was denoun-
ced by the committee as 'morbid and unhealthy'.) In his contentious
mood he could be (intentionally) very irritating, especially to those
who thought party politics should be suspended until the war was
over. Sometimes he was the target of delighted laughter and violent
abuse in the same evening and from the same people. I shared his
convictions to the extent of visiting the club's social room in the High
once or twice for coffee after closing time.

About jazz we had no disagreement. Jim Sutton and I had built up a
small record collection at home and had brought it to Oxford (he was
at the Slade, then exiled to the Ashmolean), so that we need not be
without our favourite sound. There was not much live jazz to be
heard at Oxford in those days until the Oxford University Rhythm
Club was set up in 1941 and provided public jam sessions, but on the
advice of Frank Dixon I had found a number of scarce deletions in
Acott's and Russell's (then separate shops) and in one or other of our
rooms there was usually a gramophone going. Kingsley's enthusiasm
flared up immediately. I suppose we devoted to some hundred
records that early anatomizing passion normally reserved for the
more established arts. 'It's the *abject entreaty* of that second phrase.
. . .' 'What she's actually singing is *ick-sart-mean*. . . .' 'Russell goes
right on up to the first bar of Waller. You can hear it on Nick's pick-
up.' 'Isn't it marvellous the way Bechet . . .' 'Isn't it marvellous the
way the trumpet . . .' 'Isn't it marvellous the way Russell . . .'
Russell, Charles Ellsworth 'Pee Wee' (b. 1906), clarinet and saxophone player extraordinary, was, *mutatis mutandis*, our Swinburne
and our Byron. We bought every record he played on that we could
find, and—literally—dreamed about similar items on the American
Commodore label. Someone recently conscripted into the Merchant
Navy had reputedly found his way to the Commodore Music Shop in
New York, where the 'proprietor' had introduced him to 'one of the
guys who helped make these records'; yes, leaning against the
counter had actually been . . . Long afterwards, Kingsley admitted he
had once sent Russell a fan letter. I said that funnily enough I had also
written to Eddie Condon. We looked at each other guardedly. 'Did
you get an answer?' 'No—did you?' 'No.'

At the end of every term somebody left. Sometimes it was a false alarm: Edward du Cann disappeared in December 1942, waving cheerfully from the back of a taxi, but he was back next term, when he promptly swallowed a pin and was rushed to hospital. But more often it was permanent. Norman was commissioned in the Artillery and ironically found himself in the kind of regiment where revolvers were fired in the mess after dinner. Kingsley was commissioned in the Signals, where within an hour a major reprimanded him for having his hands in his pockets. Friends remained plentiful, but contemporaries were becoming scarce. I lost touch with the freshmen, among whom it was reported there was 'a man called Wain'. Years afterwards John told me that our acquaintance at this time was limited to a brief bitter exchange at lunch about Albert Ammons's 'Boogie Woogie Stomp' and the poetry of George Crabbe. If so, it was a great opportunity lost.

None the less, it was almost my last term before I met Bruce Montgomery. In a way this was surprising: among the handful of undergraduates reading full Schools in the humanities friendship was generally automatic. In another it wasn't: Bruce's modern languages-Playhouse-classical music-Randolph Hotel ambience conflicted sharply with my own. Of course, I had seen him about, but it hardly occurred to me that he was an undergraduate, not in the same sense that I was. Wearing an air-raid warden's badge and carrying a walking-stick, he stalked aloofly to and fro in a severe triangle formed by the College lodge (for letters), the Randolph bar and his lodgings in Wellington Square. In his first year he had been partnered at tutorials with Alan Ross; having observed that their tutor's first action was to wind up a small clock on his desk, they took advantage of his lateness one morning to wind it up for him. The tutor was an energetic man and I always understood that the result was disastrous. But now Alan had long since gone into the Navy and Bruce, like myself, was something of a survivor. This did not make me less shy of him. Like 'Mr Austen', he had a grand piano; he had written a book called *Romanticism and the World Crisis*, painted a picture that was hanging on the wall of his sitting-room, and was a skilled pianist, organist and even composer. During the vacation that Easter he had spent ten days writing, with his J nib and silver penholder, a detective story called *The Case of the Gilded Fly*. This was published the following year under the name of Edmund Crispin, launching him on one of his several successful careers.

Beneath this formidable exterior, however, Bruce had unsuspected depths of frivolity, and we were soon spending most of our time together swaying about with laughter on bar stools. True, I could make little of Wyndham Lewis, at that time Bruce's favourite writer, and my admiration for *Belshazzar's Feast* was always qualified, but I was more than ready for John Dickson Carr, Mencken and *Pitié pour les femmes*. In return I played him Billie Holiday records and persuaded him to widen his circle of drinking places. One night the proctor entered one of these and I was caught by the bullers at a side door: Bruce, on the other hand, simply stepped into a kind of kitchen, apologized to someone he found ironing there, and waited until the coast was clear. 'When will you learn', he reproved me afterwards, 'not to act on your own initiative?'

I sometimes wonder if Bruce did not constitute for me a curious creative stimulus. For the next three years we were in fairly constant contact, and I wrote continuously as never before or since. Even in that last term, with Finals a matter of weeks away, I began an unclassifiable story called *Trouble at Willow Gables*, which Bruce and Diana Gollancz would come back to read after an evening at the Lord Napier. Possibly his brisk intellectual epicureanism was just the catalyst I needed.

III

Jill was in fact begun that autumn, when I was twenty-one, and took about a year to write. When it was published in 1946 it aroused no public comment. Kingsley, who by that time was back at Oxford, wrote to say he had enjoyed it very much, adding that its binding reminded him of *Signal Training: Telegraphy and Telephony*, or possibly *Ciceronis Orationes*. Later he reported that he had seen a copy in a shop in Coventry Street between *Naked and Unashamed* and *High-Heeled Yvonne*.

On looking through it again in 1963 I have made a number of minor deletions but have added nothing and rewritten nothing, with the exception of a word here and there, and the reinstatement of a few mild obscenities to which the original printer objected. It will, I hope, still qualify for the indulgence traditionally extended to juvenilia.

1963

IV

Looking, after twelve years,[1] at this introduction and the story it

[1] The following section was added for the first American edition (1976).

introduces, I am struck by the latter's growing claims as a historical document—not only on obvious points such as John's thinking that a pound would be sufficient pocket-money for two weeks, but as recording a vanished mode of Oxford life itself. Christopher and his friends would not now have to bother about wearing gowns, or fear molestation by the proctors when on licensed premises, nor would Elizabeth's visits be limited to between two in the afternoon and seven o'clock in the evening. College authorities today have been known to turn a blind eye to girls actually living in college, aware of the outcry disciplinary action would produce; some colleges, indeed, have begun to take women students, in consequence of the lack of places for them in women's colleges. One wonders, in fact, how long the collegiate system will last: legislation by a succession of socialist or quasi-socialist governments has severely diminished college incomes from investment or property, while the rise in labour and other costs in running these academic hotels has been equally damaging. Furthermore, nobody really wants to live in them: dons and students alike prefer domesticity, houses and wives on the one hand and flats and mistresses on the other. Finally, left-wing agitation is striving to unite all Oxford students into a single political force that would be hostile to the collegiate system and the spirit it engenders. Recently a fellow of my own college said he gave it ten years.

My original purpose in writing an introduction of this kind was to make clear that my own Oxford life was rather different from that of my hero; nevertheless, over the years I can see that I have been to some extent identified with him. A later Oxford generation, according to one writer, liked my poems because they 'found a voice for those in the painful process of transforming themselves from *petits bourgeois* to *hauts bourgeois*'. Though this implication of enterprise is flattering, I think the time has come to disclaim it; thanks to my father's generosity, my education was at no time a charge on public or other funds, and all in all my manner of life is much the same today as it was in 1940—bourgeois, certainly, but neither *haut* nor *petit*. Perhaps in consequence I may receive a few more degrees of imaginative credit for my hero's creation.

Lastly, since the book's original publisher is now dead, I can explain that it was probably his imprint that won *Jill* a place in that Coventry Street shop. Reginald Ashley Caton, mysterious and elusive proprietor of the Fortune Press throughout the Thirties and Forties, divided his publishing activity between poetry and what then passed for pornography, often of a homosexual tinge. My dust-jacket advertised titles such as *Climbing Boy*, *Barbarian Boy*, *A Diary of the Teens by A Boy*, and so on; the previous year he had published a collection of my poems (Dylan Thomas and Roy Fuller were also on his list), and I had rather despairingly bunged the novel at him, as no one else seemed interested. He must have accepted it unread, since the printer's objections appeared to take him by surprise; our only meeting was in a tea shop near Victoria Station to discuss this, when he assured me that to find yourself in the dock on a charge of obscenity was 'no joke'. (That cup of tea was my sole payment for both books.) All the same, as a publisher of poetry at a time when such an activity was even less remunerative than usual, he deserves a footnote in the literary history of the time. An interesting study might be written of the crusading activities of the Fortune Press in the Forties, and of the Fantasy and Marvell Presses in the Fifties, and their effect on English verse. It occurs to me that I am probably the only writer to have been published by all three.

1975

Introduction to *The North Ship*

The North Ship would probably not have been published if the late William Bell, then an undergraduate at Merton College, had not set about making up a collection which he eventually called *Poetry from Oxford in Wartime*. Oxford poetry was reputedly in the ascendant again following the scarlet and yellow *Eight Oxford Poets* in 1941 (Keith Douglas, Sidney Keyes, John Heath-Stubbs, Drummond Allison, *et al.*), and Bell no doubt thought it was time for another round-up. When his anthology came out in 1944 it had Allison, Heath-Stubbs and Roy Porter from the earlier collection, and the new names of Bell himself, Francis King, myself, Christopher Middleton and David Wright. How many of the second group had been in hard covers before I don't know: certainly I hadn't.

Before it appeared, however, the proprietor of the small but then well-known house that was producing the book wrote to some of its contributors enquiring if they would care to submit collections of their own work. The letter I received was on good-quality paper and signed with an illegible broad-nibbed squiggle: I was enormously flattered, and typed out some thirty pieces on my father's old portable Underwood. The publisher seemed to like them, saying that he could undertake publication early next year 'and perhaps have the book ready in February'. Since this was already the end of November, my excitement ran high, but I must (with memories of the *Writers' and Artists' Year Book*) have parried with some enquiry about terms, for another letter a month later (two days before Christmas) assured me that no agreement was necessary.

Looking at the collection today, it seems amazing that anyone should have offered to publish it without a cheque in advance and a certain amount of bullying. This, however, was not how I saw it at the time. As February turned to March, and March to April, my anticipation of the promised six copies curdled through exasperation to fury and finally to indifference; my astonishment to find now, on looking up the records, that in fact they arrived almost exactly nine months after dispatch of typescript (on 31 July 1945) shows how completely I subsequently came to believe my own fantasy of eighteen months or even two years. I inspected them sulkily.

It may not have been the best introduction to publication: my Oxford friend, Bruce Montgomery, was writing Edmund Crispin novels for Gollancz, while Routledge had taken up Keyes and Heath-Stubbs. Still, I was on the same list as Dylan Thomas, Roy Fuller, Nicholas Moore and other luminaries, and the book was nicely enough produced, with hardly any misprints; above all, it was indubitably *there*, an ambition tangibly satisfied. Yet was it? Then, as now, I could never contemplate it without a twinge, faint or powerful, of shame compounded with disappointment. Some of this was caused by the contents but not all: I felt in some ways cheated. I can't exactly say how. It was a pity they had ever mentioned February.

II

Looking back, I find in the poems not one abandoned self but several—the ex-schoolboy, for whom Auden was the only alternative to 'old-fashioned' poetry; the undergraduate, whose work a friend affably characterized as 'Dylan Thomas, but you've a sentimentality that's all your own'; and the immediately post-Oxford self, isolated in Shropshire with a complete Yeats stolen from the local girls' school. This search for a style was merely one aspect of a general immaturity. It might be pleaded that the war years were a bad time to start writing poetry, but in fact the principal poets of the day—Eliot, Auden, Dylan Thomas, Betjeman—were all speaking out loud and clear, and there was no reason to become entangled in the undergrowth of *Poetry Quarterly* and *Poetry London* except by a failure of judgement. Nor were my contemporaries similarly afflicted. I remember looking through an issue of *The Cherwell*, one day in Blackwell's, and coming across John Heath-Stubbs's 'Leporello': I was profoundly bewildered. I had never heard of Leporello, and what sort of poetry was this— who was he copying? And his friend Sidney Keyes was no more comforting: he could talk to history as some people talk to porters, and the mention of names like Schiller and Rilke and Gilles de Retz made me wish I were reading something more demanding than English Language and Literature. He had most remarkable brown and piercing eyes: I met him one day in Turl Street, when there was snow on the ground, and he was wearing a Russian-style fur hat. He stopped, so I suppose we must have known each other to talk to—that is, if we had had anything to say. As far as I remember, we hadn't.

The predominance of Yeats in this volume deserves some explanation. In 1943 the English Club was visited by Vernon Watkins, then stationed at an Air Force camp near by; impassioned and imperative, he swamped us with Yeats until, despite the fact that he had not nearly come to the end of his typescript, the chairman had forcibly to apply the closure. As a final gesture Vernon distributed the volumes he had been quoting from among those of us who were nearest to him, and disappeared, exalted, into the black-out. I had been tremendously impressed by the evening and in the following weeks made it my business to collect his books up again—many of them were Cuala Press limited editions, and later Yeats was scarce at that time—and take them to him at Bradwell, where he was staying with some people called Blackburn who kept a goat. This time Vernon read me Lorca.

As a result I spent the next three years trying to write like Yeats, not because I liked his personality or understood his ideas but out of infatuation with his music (to use the word I think Vernon used). In fairness to myself it must be admitted that it is a particularly potent music, pervasive as garlic, and has ruined many a better talent. Others found it boring. I remember Bruce Montgomery snapping, as I droned for the third or fourth time that evening ' "When such as I cast out remorse / So great a sweetness flows into the breast . . ." ', 'It's not his job to cast out remorse, but to earn forgiveness.' But then Bruce had known Charles Williams. Every night after supper before opening my large dark green manuscript book I used to limber up by turning the pages of the 1933 plum-coloured Macmillan edition, which stopped at 'A Woman Young and Old' and which meant in fact that I never absorbed the harsher last poems. This may be discernible in what I wrote.

When reaction came, it was undramatic, complete and permanent. In early 1946 I had some new digs in which the bedroom faced east, so that the sun woke me inconveniently early. I used to read. One book I had at my bedside was the little blue *Chosen Poems of Thomas Hardy*: Hardy I knew as a novelist, but as regards his verse I shared Lytton Strachey's verdict that 'the gloom is not even relieved by a little elegance of diction'. This opinion did not last long; if I were asked to date its disappearance, I should guess it was the morning I first read

'Thoughts of Phena At News of Her Death'. Many years later, Vernon surprised me by saying that Dylan Thomas had admired Hardy above all poets of this century. 'He thought Yeats was the greatest by miles,' he said. 'But Hardy was his favourite.'

III

'F/Sgt. Watkins, V' was the book's kindest and almost only critic. Writing from the Sergeants' Mess, he was generously encouraging (did I recall his Yeats anecdote: 'Always I encourage, always'?), reserving for only one or two pieces his sharpest term of condemnation, 'not a final statement'. 'Yesterday,' he added, 'I destroyed about two thousand poems that mean nothing to me now.' Despite this hint, although with considerable hesitation, the book is now republished, as there seems to be still some demand for it. I have corrected two misprints and one solecism. As a coda I have added a poem, written a year or so later, which, though not noticeably better than the rest, shows the Celtic fever abated and the patient sleeping soundly.

1965

Single-handed and Untrained

In autumn 1943 the Ministry of Labour wrote to ask what I was doing. I could have answered that, having finished with the university and English literature, I was living at home writing a novel, but I rightly judged the enquiry to be a warning that I had better start doing something. Picking up the day's *Birmingham Post* (the paper we took in those days), I soon discovered an advertisement by a small urban district council for a Librarian. The salary was £175 per annum (plus cost-of-living bonus, Whitley Scale, of £45 10s for men, £36 8s for women), and the duties included 'those usual to the operation of a Lending Library (open access), and Reading Room supervision'.

Recourse to a gazetteer revealed that the town was about twelve miles from a school where a college friend of mine had recently taken a job as a temporary assistant master and was also writing a novel. This seemed a good omen, and I applied. In due course I was asked to attend for interview, and it occurred to me I had better find out something about the operation of a lending library (open access). A friendly senior assistant at the local one was kind enough to spend a morning showing me how books were ordered, accessioned and catalogued, and then given little pockets with individual tickets in them that were slipped into borrowers' cards when the book was lent. 'Come back tomorrow,' she said, 'and I'll tell you about inter-library loans.'

My father, with remote amusement, handed me a green-covered report that had come out in the previous year entitled *The Public Library System of Great Britain*, and I took it with me in the train on 13 November, the day of the interview. Rain smashed against the carriage windows as I read the author's summary dismissals of sample libraries serving populations between 20,000 and 30,000: 'Old buildings, drab stocks and bad traditions of support . . . antiquated methods include a really filthy indicator [what was that?]. . . . the reference library consists of two small cases of quite useless items. . . .' The account of library 'I' seemed particularly intimidating: 'the children's books are much dirtier even than those provided for the adults. There is no proper counter; the single-handed librarian is untrained.' I fancied that the authority to which I had applied was in a smaller population category than this: would its library be worse? Certainly its potential Librarian looked like being single-handed, and could hardly have been more untrained.

Mr McColvin, the author of the trenchant sentences just quoted, would not in all probability have been much kinder about it. The council had adopted the Library Acts and built a Library to celebrate the coronation of Edward VII. It was a simple two-storey building, with a reading room and a boiler room on the ground floor and a lending library, with a rudimentary office-cum-reference room, upstairs; its handsome stone façade was inscribed PUBLIC LIBRARY and recorded why it was erected and when (I think the date was 1903). A librarian-caretaker, son of a failed Wolverhampton bookseller, was appointed. When I turned up forty years later (for my application was successful), the astonishing thing was that almost nothing had changed. The librarian-caretaker was still there, by now a courtly old gentleman of at least seventy, who wore a hat indoors and uttered from time to time an absent-minded blowing noise, like a distant trombone. For many years he had washed the floors and lighted the boiler every morning in addition to his professional duties, and may have done so to the end. After leaving he never used the Library, and I saw him only once again; he called when it was shut ('Anyone in? It's only the old blackguard'), and we chatted, mostly about his inadequate pension and his funeral arrangements ('I've told the wife to stay at home and drink whisky'). I wondered uneasily if my life would be anything like his.

In 1903 the Library had, of course, been closed access; in the Thirties an effort had been made to modernize its methods, opening the doors to readers and constructing an issue desk. There had even been purchased a copy of the current edition of Dewey. Otherwise it remained antiquated. The boiler (which I had to stoke, if not light) did little to heat the radiators, which were in any case poorly placed; the real warmth of the building came from the gas lights, that had to be illuminated with long tapers that dropped wax over the floors, and even on myself until I learned how to handle them. There was no telephone. The stock amounted to about 4,000 books, 3,000 of which were fiction and the rest non-fiction and juvenile (the admission of children had been a severe blow to my predecessor). The shelves were high, but even so layers of long-withdrawn books, thick with dust, were piled on top of them. I wish I had taken more detailed notes both of them and of the current stock: in all, it was like the advertisement pages of late nineteenth- and early twentieth-century novels come to life. A substantial body of the readers were elderly people, who found the stairs difficult, but were still prepared to face them for Mrs Henry Wood, Florence L. Barclay, Silas K. Hocking, Rosa N. Carey and many others. The rest were either children or hopeful adults, some of them strangers to the town and used to better things.

My day began with collecting the day's papers and journals and setting them out in the reading room in time to open its doors at 9 a.m. Then I retreated to the closed lending department and dealt with the post, such as it was, making out applications for inter-library loans and parcelling up volumes to be returned (the post office was, fortunately, directly opposite). From then until 3 p.m. when the first of the two-hour lending-library 'operations' began, my time was my own; landladies did not really want to provide fires in the morning, and I wrote my novel in the Library before taking it back with me to work at after lunch. After another session from 6 to 8 p.m. I finished reshelving and sorted the issue in time to close the reading room at 8.30 p.m. It was a long day, and in some respects a tiring one. Quite early on I recorded a week when I issued 928 books in 20 hours, or 1 about every 77 seconds—not much, perhaps, but an equal number had to be reshelved, and some of the shelves could be reached only by ladder. At first my hand was blistered from stamping books.

It was clear that the premises, stock and staff of the Library were totally inadequate for the potential, or even actual, demands of its readers. At the same time it was difficult to know what to do about it—difficult, because I really had no idea of how to come to grips with the council in order to, for instance, appoint a couple of assistants, double or treble the book grant (I don't think, in fact, that there was one), create a catalogue, modernize the building and so on, and even if I had there would have been, in the middle of the war, no money to do so. My committee, however, was sympathetic, chaired by a friendly and forward-looking headmaster, and they did what they could. New books began to appear on the shelves (I heard that I was 'filling the Library with dirty books'—not in the McColvin sense, but with Lawrence, Forster, Joyce, Isherwood, et al.), and after a year and three-quarters I got an assistant, enabling the Lending Library to 'operate' in the mornings. Readership increased to about twice the original number. Issues did likewise, from 3,000 to 6,000 a month. My most dramatic increase was in inter-library loans, from 68 in the year I came to 499 in the year I left: these were chiefly to sixth formers, and those readers with precise interests and courses of study. Most of the books came from the huge and generous Birmingham City Libraries, at that time presided over by H. M. Cashmore, surely one of the most indefatigable correspondents among chief Librarians. Hardly a day passed when I did not receive a letter signed by him correcting me about the details of an application, or pointing out that a parcel had been badly tied. Other librarians I met later confirmed this experience.

The Library should, of course, have been absorbed into the county system, and the county was anxious to do this: it already sent us a consignment of perhaps 300 books that was changed every few months, and these alone kept readers from complete apathy. Since the council had adopted the Library Acts in 1901 or so, however, it could not be compulsorily taken over, and there was enough local patriotism to believe that with 'the new young man' a proper library service could be offered. Of course improvements took place: almost anything one did was an improvement (one of my early reports states 'the Library has joined the official waiting list for *The Times Literary* and *Educational Supplements*'), and readers responded so eagerly in those book-hungry days that I could never stop trying, but in fact little could be done compared with what was needed. I consoled myself with my novel (having finished the first, I had begun a second), and started a correspondence course for Library Association qualifications.

My appointment there lasted two and three-quarter years. About three years after I left, the council did, in fact, surrender its powers, and 'my' Library became a county branch. Subsequently it was remodelled and enlarged, and in 1962 became a headquarters; to my surprise, I was asked to open it. Usually I avoid such undertakings, but the implication that I was not regarded by those concerned as an unfortunate episode best forgotten was so gratifying that I gladly accepted. The architect had done his work well, so that it was impossible to see where the boiler room had been, or the poky stairs, or the cobwebbed and dingy lavatory, on the walls of which my aged predecessor had pencilled a series of dates, a reference to a brand of pills, and a name that looked like 'Marley Mount'. Split-level and splendid, the Library now had proper staff quarters, a record listening room, a separate children's library and an electric book lift.

As I listened to the other speakers (my old chairman among them, still in office), I wondered what I had done to justify my presence at the ceremony. I had achieved nothing lasting: union with the county system had been delayed only a few years, and it might be said that I had made it inevitable. I found myself thinking of individual readers: the boy I had introduced to the Sherlock Holmes stories, the old lady who sent a messenger for her books and whose final note I still have: 'Owing to failing sight, I have decided no longer to be a Member of the "Free Library". Please accept of my grateful thanks for kindness choosing books for me during the past years . . .' and others, such as the lady who gave me ten 'Cogent' cigarettes at Christmas (product of the Scottish Co-operative Wholesale Society). I thought, too, of the knowledgeable 'graduate trainees' of today, with their year in a university library followed by a year at library school, and wondered further if there were any libraries left as backward as this one had been, or any librarians as unqualified as myself when appointed to it. If not, as seemed probable, this was no doubt the most comforting reflection available.

1977

Early Days at Leicester

I started work in the Library of the University College on 9 September 1946. The town was new to me: my sister had been at the College of Art, and indeed had been inside the YWCA on Victoria Park when the land-mine fell (the hole was still there when I arrived); a distant cousin, John Cuthbert Larkin, came from Shrewsbury to be headmaster of the Wyggeston Boys' School about the same time as I had come from Wellington, some twelve miles away; but although I had heard of Adderley's and the Midland Educational and Dryads' I had to learn my way about. For the first three weeks I stayed with my sister in Loughborough, then I found a room on the London Road overlooking the park, past which trams ground on their way to Stoneygate (they were discontinued in 1949). The room was at the top of the house (a familiar situation to me: I have lived most of my working life in rooms at the top of houses—I am in one now), and if the extremely suspect wiring had misbehaved my situation would have been unenviable. Happily, despite the fearful overloading that so often happens in bed-sitters, it didn't.

The University College was entirely contained in its original building (now, I believe, called the Fielding Johnson Building), and under the brass bell-push was a small brass plate reading 'University College Leicester Ltd.', as despite its recent enrolment as a beneficiary of the University Grants Committee it was still a limited company. The building's earlier role as a lunatic asylum is well known. As can be seen, it was none the less extremely handsome. Its main rooms were large and graceful, but the wings were for obvious reasons constructed on a pattern of tiny cells. In the Library these constituted a kind of elementary carrel. The Library occupied an L-shaped wing on the first floor over the Physics Department: its entrance was at the end of the main corridor that ran the length of the central block.

The College's recurrent grant for 1945–6 was £12,000; 'there is obviously a period of expansion ahead,' the annual report predicted. I should like to think that I was part of it, but in fact I was appointed to replace Leila Bishop, who was moving to Reading University Library.

I have always been grateful to the Librarian, Miss Bennett, for taking a chance on what cannot have been a promising-looking candidate. Her only stipulation was that I should continue to use my spare time to obtain professional qualifications (this was still possible in those days). How much gratitude, indeed, the middle-period university colleges in general owed to their women librarians, Miss Bennett of Leicester, Miss Henderson of Southampton, Miss Kirkus of Reading, Miss Cuming of Hull! Understaffed, underequipped, underfinanced, they battled on through the lean years, reckoning no task beneath them: the sheer numbers of books they ordered, accessioned, catalogued, classified, issued, kept track of, sent for binding and all the rest of it would make—does make—a latter-day chief Librarian blench. The Library staff consisted of Miss Bennett, Molly Bateman and myself. Our hours in term were six mornings, three afternoons and one evening (over by 7.15 p.m.), and we took it in turns to serve the readers, reshelve the books, and in between times catalogue in medieval fashion such books as the Library acquired, every card being written by hand. My salary was £350. Early in 1947 it was increased—everyone's salary was increased—to £450.

On my first morning I accessioned, in a ledger, some of the E. Lewis Lilley Collection. Dr Lilley was a music lover who was gradually transferring to the Library his magnificent collection of scores and books: his book-plate bore the ironic quotation, 'Is it not strange that sheeps' guts should hale souls out of men's bodies?' Molly watched me as I worked, no doubt assessing my handwriting. She told me later that on her first day in Cambridge University Library she had been similarly overlooked by a senior who after ten minutes enquired in a thin voice if her pen suited her. Standards must have been impossibly high at Cambridge. There were no typewriters in the Library; in 1948 I bought a second-hand one in the market for £30, and the Library refunded me. Miss Bennett wrote all her letters by hand. Later on I became familiar with Dr Lilley: he used green ink, and signed his loan cards (we used cards rather than slips) with a signature that would have made Elizabeth I's look like board-school copperplate. At lunchtime we went to a small restaurant on the London Road called the Tatler: I believe it is still there. At one time it had a ginger kitten named Marmaduke.

In about a month the autumn term began and I was able to see what kind of an institution I had joined. There were 218 full-time students, all of them engaged in preparing for University of London external degrees. Most departments were staffed by a professor or head of department with one or two lecturers to support him: in the inter-war period, most heads of department had been single-handed. (Young lecturers today who are particular about their 'fields' might like to imagine sharing the teaching of a complete syllabus with one other person, for examinations set and marked by an outside body.) Everyone knew everyone else. The atmosphere was almost familial. The staff lunched together in what was then called the Outer Hall. The first two courses were brought by waitresses, but the two puddings were put in front of the Principal and Vice-Principal, who sat at opposite ends of the table, and served their colleagues. The conversation was genial. 'What's in that jug?' one senior member of staff asked. 'Not what you hope,' replied another.

Many of the younger staff were unmarried, and social life—tennis on the long-vanished courts, dances and theatricals—flourished. By today's standards we were unsophisticated. I had never heard of the AUT.[1] I never saw the minutes of the Library Committee, or knew what went on at Senate. I had no idea of the size of the Library grant or where it came from, or what could be done to improve the Library's inadequate and often absurd accommodation. Workmen used to appear unannounced and begin alterations: one day in November 1947 I was just leaving after lunch for my free afternoon when a carpet-laying gang appeared and asked for six huge bookcases to be emptied. I gave up my half-day without a moment's thought. Assistants today would not be so meek.

There was no students' union, but they were a cohesive body. At the end of my first term they called a three-day strike; this was not to further their own interests but to protest when some extremely popular heads of department were not elevated to newly created chairs. This was my first experience of militancy; on the second morning of the strike I was accosted in the empty entrance hall by a reporter, who asked what the teaching staff were doing when there were no students to teach. I am afraid that I implied that they were relishing their enforced idleness (Molly and I were, of course, working as usual). When this remark appeared in that evening's *Leicester Mercury* it caused great indignation. Fortunately it was given anonymously. The incident was conducted with dignity and quite

[1] Association of University Teachers, the trade union of university academic staff.

without any of today's political overtones: some of the students were ex-servicemen of courteous and responsible manner, who would certainly not have misused 'participation' if it had existed then. In November 1948, when Prince Charles's birth was announced, one of them was scandalized that the College was not flying a flag. Eventually a Union Jack was hoisted. The student said it was upside-down.

By the time I left in September 1950 a great many changes had taken place. The Library had extended along another wing: new Library staff posts, both senior and junior to us, were advertised and filled. Molly and I continued our correspondence courses and were ultimately registered as Associate members of the Library Association. My salary soared to £500, the students' number to 700. New buildings were going up rapidly: a sort of temporary canteen was erected, in which our lunches were no longer dispensed by waitresses in collaboration with the Principal and Vice-Principal. The College as a whole was changing: it was becoming larger, less personal, full of scaffolding and piles of bricks and (once) a long line of water-closets waiting to be installed. Before I left, the Biology Building, or Astley Clarke Laboratory, was in use, and something called the Worthington Building that held a new senior common room: my memory is that both these buildings were a good deal more elegant than the kind of university block that has come later.

When I finally left, my thoughts were on the future rather than the past. It certainly did not occur to me that I had belonged to an academic community of a kind soon to be superseded but with virtues that in time would seem precious. That is the sort of reflection that comes the best part of twenty-five years later.

1974

Vernon Watkins: an Encounter and a Re-encounter

My acquaintance with Vernon Watkins, I now see, fell into two parts. The first part was from about 1943 to 1945, when I was an undergraduate or an unfledged graduate. The second began ten years later, in about 1957, and continued until I saw him last in November 1966.

Our first meeting was in Oxford. As the author of the recently published first collection of poems, *The Ballad of the Mari Lwyd*, Vernon had been invited to address the English Club. This was easy for him, as he was then in the RAF and stationed at Bradwell; he came in uniform, and, in one of those large, rather anonymous women's college common rooms, spoke to us on Yeats. His typescript looked much too long, and he did not make it any shorter by stopping frequently to read from one or other of the pile of books he had by his chair. His reading was a revelation: unashamedly sonorous, it may have been founded on Yeats's own method, for it suited the poems admirably. 'The heart of a phantom is beating! The heart of a phantom is beating!' he intoned, without affectation but equally without the intention of making the smallest concession to his laconic ('Good show/bad show') wartime audience. I saw one or two people smile at each other, but most were rapt. So was Vernon. Past coffee time, past discussion time, he read on and on, until, with awareness of shutting college gates and indeed the stamina of his audience, the chairman gently brought the evening to a close. Vernon bore him no ill will. In response to our expressions of appreciation, he pressed on us the books from which he had been quoting.

A few weeks later I went to visit him at Bradwell, ostensibly to return his books, which I had collected up again from their involuntary borrowers. He greeted me with the same warm, slightly impersonal vivacity that was always to characterize him, and introduced me to the family he was billeted on: we had tea round a large table. The children teased him kindly. Afterwards we went into the back garden, and he showed me the family's pet goat, making me put the flat of my hand on its bumpy forehead. 'Feel it push,' he said. I gave him his books back (he had clearly not had the slightest misgiving about their safety), and he told me about the Cuala Press and the Yeatses. Then he showed me others: the American anthology of the work of Dylan Thomas called *The World I Breathe*, and some translations of Lorca. When it was time for me to go for my train he pressed the latter book on me, and while we were waiting on the station he reclaimed it for an impromptu reading. 'At five in the afternoon! At five in the afternoon!' he chanted, while a huge engine drew hissingly past.

By this time I was deeply impressed by him—or perhaps I should say strongly, for some of my admiration was without doubt very shallow. I found it exciting that he was a poet, and had had a book published, and had been to Cambridge at the same time as Christopher Isherwood (figuring in the latter's fictionalized autobiography, as he said, as 'Percival or someone'), and knew Dylan Thomas. His devotion to poetry was infectious; his likes became my likes, his methods my methods, or attempted methods. At the same time I could never quite expel from my mind a certain dubiety, a faint sense of being in the wrong galley. At that time there was a group of poets known as the Apocalyptics, most of whom had been published in an anthology called *The White Horseman*, and Vernon's name had been associated with them, but in fact his poetry was much more controlled than theirs and reached further back to the Symbolist poets of Europe. All the same, one could see how the association had taken place: they were both—Vernon, of course, much more successfully—aiming at ecstasy.

We talked a good deal about poetry, or rather Vernon talked, in the main, and I listened: it was difficult to avoid the subject in his company. He did listen patiently to my enthusiasm for D. H. Lawrence, remarking simply, 'The shape of a poem by Lawrence is the shape of the words on the page; the shape of a poem by Yeats is the shape of the instrument on which the poem is played.' I saw instantly what he meant, and asked him if he thought form so important. 'Poetry rhymes all along the lines, not only at the ends,' he pointed out. Talking about poetry with Vernon was just that: it wasn't saying how bad so-and-so's last book was, or comparing royalty rates, or swapping gossip about famous drunks or love affairs. He brought an immediate dignity to the subject, or rather he made it dignified simply by assuming it could never be anything else. Even the poets whose work he did not like he never abused, simply seeming to suggest that it was a question of scope, of range. 'Not a final statement, I feel,' would be his typical judgement.

By this time, too, I was beginning to learn something about his life. This, too, impressed me. Having spent all his adult life in a bank, he was now a flight sergeant, no doubt for the duration; after the war he would go back to being a bank clerk again. This in no way hindered his devotion to poetry, which in turn was quite unaffected by ambition: he had waited until what then seemed to me the farthest brink of middle age before publishing his first book. Plainly he had not the slightest intention of 'living by writing'; he was not interested in journalism or reviewing ('I would never review a living writer'), and found banking much more acceptable than pot-boiling. At that time he was not married. The picture this built up was of a genuinely modest, genuinely dedicated person, who had chosen, in Yeats's phraseology, perfection of the work rather than of the life. To anyone who, like myself, was on the edge of the world of employment his example was significant. Indeed, it was almost encouraging.

In due course I left Oxford; we corresponded fitfully, the war ended, and eventually I sent him a small collection of poems I had published. Although not at all sure that this was a good idea ('I'm against premature publication'), he was extremely generous about the contents, though they must have struck him as painfully imitative. 'But my most important news,' he ended, 'is that I have got married.'

About twelve years passed. It is possible that I should never have seen Vernon again if Garnet Rees had not been appointed to the chair of French in the University of Hull, where I was working. Garnet and Dilys Rees were old friends of Vernon and Gwen Watkins, and Garnet soon set about making it possible for Vernon to come up and give a lecture. He stayed at their house, and Garnet brought him to see me: he was just the same, his luxuriant hair rather grey, his face rather more lined, but he was as slim as ever and moved just as quickly.

I forget what the lecture was about: perhaps it was Yeats again. By now Vernon was much better known (partly by reason of the publication of Dylan Thomas's *Letters to Vernon Watkins* that year), and the hall, which held over 300 people, was full. People were standing at the back. Although keyed up both before and after lecturing, Vernon always seemed calm and composed on the rostrum. His voice, without being raised, filled the auditorium; soon the familiar quotations began:

> I have met them at close of day
> Coming with vivid faces . . .

I looked at his audience: members of the University, students from other colleges, schoolteachers, the public. Here and there someone was scribbling. Once again, as at Oxford, I caught a covert smile exchanged: Vernon's delivery was as bardic as ever, and, if possible, even further from the fashion. But there was no doubt that his authority was undiminished: his passionate sincerity compelled complete attention. I wondered if anyone would go off afterwards and read Yeats for three years, as I had. After the lecture he was soon surrounded by eager questioners, some of them asking about Dylan Thomas rather than Yeats: Vernon, though always more than willing to talk about his friend, never to my knowledge gossiped about him to strangers, and I felt pretty confident that any scandal-seekers would be disappointed. Later on, Garnet and Dilys invited a few people in for drinks: Vernon went on talking cheerfully. Once he had wound himself up, he was virtually tireless.

He came a number of times after that: not every year, but often enough for our acquaintance to revive. I began to receive his letters once more, all written in that fascinating hand, at once flourishing and fastidious. We resumed our debate on Lawrence versus Yeats, only now it was Hardy versus Yeats: 'Hardy's poems are often right in relation to fact and anecdote and right because they have a kind of aura belonging to his sensibility, but practically they are often wrong, because they leave the imagination with misgiving, remorse, the opposite of imagination's food. I'm not clear, but it's midnight. . . .' By now I had settled into a poetic tradition very different from Vernon's, and found much of what he said unacceptable, but he retained his power to convince me that he knew what he was talking about. Despite his kindness, his whimsicality, his friendliness, there was something hard and brilliant about his attachment to poetry: he never hesitated. It was something there, tangible and palpable, commanding instant and unending allegiance. He could not read novels—Gwen had to act as interpreter. 'It is people's emotions, particularly those of girls, that I don't often understand.' In Vernon's presence poetry seemed like a living stream, in which one had only to dip the vessel of one's devotion. He made it clear how one could, in

fact, 'live by poetry'; it was a vocation, at once difficult as sainthood
and easy as breathing.

In 1964 I visited him for the first and only time. Sitting in the
upstairs front seats of the bus (like, I believe, some of Dylan Thomas's
characters), we swooped and plunged along the Gower: Vernon
asked me whether I thought he would be able to drive a car if he
bought one. I had never seen his house on Pennard Cliffs before,
where the National Trust property begins magnificently immediately
the road ends; it was smallish and chalet-like, but friendly and full of
character—full, too, of books and children. Again I saw Vernon
sitting at a tea table in a family setting, but this time the family was his
own. It was no longer possible to think of his having rejected
'perfection of the life' in exchange for literary mastery. He was
drawing near the time of his retirement from the bank, and once more
I heard some of the stories of his life there: 'I've seen manager after
manager saying to himself, I'll make a cashier out of Watkins! But it
never worked.'

On his last visit to Hull (towards the end of 1966) he had actually
retired, and there seemed to be a new career opening out for him,
made up of yearly appointments in universities. Currently at
University College, Swansea, he was looking forward to next year at
Seattle, and one could not help feeling that he had at last found a way
of working that was both congenial and successful. Again Garnet
brought us together and I took a photograph he regarded as sombre:
'The man behind the mask never really knows what the mask looks
like. . . .' His last letter, in March 1967, was to ask me to sponsor him
for a Fulbright fellowship ('it doesn't matter what you say'). As I
concocted the recommendation, I thought of what meeting Vernon
had meant to me when I had been a student, and I tried to say how
lucky I thought American universities would be to have him as a
visitor. Almost exactly a year later I am writing this.

1968

INTERVIEWS

An Interview with the *Observer*[1]

Like most of your readers, I suppose, I've been struck by how much your poems are about unhappiness, loss, a sense of missing out. Do you think this is really a fair impression of the way you see life?

Actually, I like to think of myself as quite funny, and I hope this comes through in my writing. But it's unhappiness that provokes a poem. Being happy doesn't provoke a poem. As Montherlant says somewhere, happiness writes white. It's very difficult to write about being happy. Very easy to write about being miserable. And I think writing about unhappiness is probably the source of my popularity, if I have any—after all most people *are* unhappy, don't you think?

Do you think people go around feeling they haven't got out of life what life has to offer?

I should think quite a lot of people do. Whether Lew Grade does, or Harold Wilson, I don't know. But that's what I see. Deprivation is for me what daffodils were for Wordsworth.

Tell me a bit about your childhood. Was it really as 'unspent' as you suggest in one of your poems?

Oh, I've completely forgotten it. My father was a local government official and we lived in quite respectable houses and had a succession of maids and that sort of thing, as one did before the war. It was all very normal: I had friends whom I played football and cricket with and Hornby trains and so forth.

It was perhaps not a very sophisticated childhood, although the house was full of books. My father was keen on Germany for some reason: he'd gone there to study their office methods and fallen in love with the place. And he took us there twice; I think this sowed the seed of my hatred of abroad—not being able to talk to anyone, or read anything.

As for school, I was an unsuccessful schoolboy. You must

[1] Miriam Gross was the interviewer.

remember that I was very short-sighted and nobody realized it, and also that I stammered, so that really classes were just me sitting with bated breath dreading lest I should be called on to say something. Eventually most of the masters understood and I wasn't bothered — just left alone. I cheered up a bit in the sixth form where the classes were smaller and most things were just across a table.

Did you feel as a child you were somehow an outsider?

Well, I didn't much like other children. Until I grew up I thought I hated everybody, but when I grew up I realized it was just children I didn't like. Once you started meeting grown-ups life was much pleasanter. Children are very horrible, aren't they? Selfish, noisy, cruel, vulgar little brutes. And if you've ever stammered, that's enough to make you feel an outsider—though I think shyness is contagious, you know. I remember when I was quite young telling my father I was shy, and he said very crushingly, 'You don't know what shyness is,' implying that he'd been much more shy. Probably both my parents were rather shy people—of each other, of their children.

I was wondering whether in the new *Oxford Dictionary of Quotations* I was going to be lumbered with 'They fuck you up, your mum and dad'. I had it on good authority that this is what they'd been told is my best-known line, and I wouldn't want it thought that I didn't like my parents. I did like them. But at the same time they were rather awkward people and not very good at being happy. And these things rub off.

Anyway, they didn't put that line in. Chicken, I suppose. For the most part the things they did put in I shouldn't have thought were on everybody's lips. If someone asked me what lines I am known for it would be the one about mum and dad or 'Books are a load of crap'—sentiments to which every bosom returns an echo, as Dr Johnson said—or, rising a little in the spiritual scale, 'What will survive of us is love', or 'Nothing, like something, happens anywhere'. They did include that one, actually.

Can you remember when exactly you started writing?

The same age that everybody starts—at puberty, which admittedly was a little later in my day than I understand it is now. Fifteen, sixteen. I remember the first poem I ever wrote was set for homework. We had to write one, about anything. We were all

absolutely baffled and consternation reigned. The poem I turned in
was terrible.

*But did you have an inkling when you wrote it that you might write other
poems?*

No. You must realize I didn't want to write poems at all, I wanted
to write novels. I started writing *Jill* immediately I left Oxford in
1943. It was published by the Fortune Press in 1946, which was
already two years after it was finished, and by that time I had
written my second novel, *A Girl in Winter*. I distinctly remember
racing away at the final revision just about VE day—a very Prousty
way of disregarding external distractions. It was published by
Faber in the great freeze-up of 1946–7, in February—very appropriate in view of the title, almost like a cosmic publicity campaign.
And I thought this was it, I'm made. But I could never write a third
novel, though I must have spent about five years trying to. I felt a
bit cheated. I'd had visions of myself writing 500 words a day for
six months, shoving the result off to the printer and going to live
on the Côte d'Azur, uninterrupted except for the correction of
proofs. It didn't happen like that—very frustrating.

I still think novels are much more interesting than poems—a
novel is so spreading, it can be so fascinating and so difficult. I
think they were just too hard for me. I've said somewhere that
novels are about other people and poems are about yourself. I
think that was the trouble, really. I didn't know enough about
other people, I didn't like them enough.

Tell me about your Oxford days.

Oxford terrified me. Public-school boys terrified me. The dons
terrified me. So did the scouts. And there was the stammer: I still
stammered quite badly up to the age of maybe thirty. I mean
stammered to the point of handing over little slips of paper at the
railway station saying third-class return to Birmingham instead of
actually trying to get it out. Still, I soon had several circles of
friends at Oxford. The college circle, the jazz circle, possibly the
literary circle. And I don't want to give the impression that there
was a great divide between public-school boys and grammar-school
boys. You see nobody had anything in those days, in the war.
Everybody wore the same utility clothes. There was one kind of
jacket, one kind of trousers; no cars; one bottle of wine a term. The

distinctions between different classes of undergraduates were really pruned back.

And what do you think about Oxford now?

Well, I don't know much about it. Of course the big change since my day is the invasion of women in men's colleges.

'Invasion' seems rather a loaded word. Does that mean you don't approve of it?

I don't know. I suppose I'm a little suspicious of it: one's always suspicious of change. One wonders what the effect will be on what is, after all, the ostensible purpose of universities—learning, teaching, research and so on. On the other hand I see nothing against it in theory, and I'm a little envious, too: it would have been nice to have been part of the experiment. But I'd like to know what the result is in ten years' time: whether they will have settled down into a kind of unisex community or whether it will boil up into shootings and tears and failed exams and nervous breakdowns. Probably something cheerful and non-academic, like an American college musical.

You mentioned jazz. How did your interest in it start?

It started as soon as I heard anything with four beats to the bar, which was, in my early days, dance music. Jack Payne, Billy Cotton, Harry Roy. I listened to bands like that for an awfully long time without realizing that there was such a thing as *American* jazz.

I must have learned dozens of dance lyrics simply by listening to dance music. I suppose they were a kind of folk poetry. Some of them were pretty awful, but I often wonder whether my assumption that a poem is something that rhymes and scans didn't come from listening to them—and some of them were quite sophisticated. 'The Venus de Milo was noted for her charms / But strictly between us, you're cuter than Venus / And what's more you've got arms'—I can't imagine Mick Jagger singing that; you know, it was witty and technically clever.

I always think of Ray Noble's 'Tiger Rag' as my first jazz record: not really very jazzy but it was a jazz number; and the second one I bought was the Washboard Rhythm Kings' 'I'm gonna play down by the Ohio', which I've still got. And the third was Louis Armstrong's 'Ain't Misbehavin''. Of course once I'd got that the way was clear.

Did you dance as well as listen to jazz?

Dance, you mean dance? Dancing was very much more formal in those days. Not a jazz thing. For one thing you had to do it with somebody else, you couldn't dance alone. That presented problems for a start if you hadn't got somebody else. Secondly, it was very difficult. I never learned to dance in a conventional sense: those books you learned from, with black feet and white feet and dotted lines, baffled me completely.

What about your being a librarian? What made you become one?

I came on to the labour market in the middle of the First—Christ, I mean the *Second* World War. Owing to bad eyesight I wasn't called up for military service, and the number of jobs available were few and far between.

I tried twice to get into the Civil Service but the Civil Service didn't want me, and I was sitting at home quietly writing *Jill* when the Ministry of Labour wrote to me asking, very courteously, what I was doing exactly. This scared me and I picked up the *Birmingham Post* and saw that an urban district council in Shropshire wanted a Librarian, so I applied and got it. But looking back it was an inspired choice. Librarianship suits me—I love the feel of libraries —and it has just the right blend of academic interest and administration that seems to match my particular talents, such as they are. And I've always thought that a regular job was no bad thing for a poet. Indeed, Dylan Thomas himself—not that he was noted for regular jobs—said this; you can't write more than two hours a day and after that what do you do? Probably get into trouble.

I'm fond of saying [broad Yorkshire] *I started at the bottom.* I had to do everything in that Shropshire library: I drew the line at cleaning the floor, but I stoked the boiler and kept it going through the day, served the children, put up the papers and so on. And in the evenings I took a correspondence course to get my professional qualifications. I'm still a member of the Library Association: I bought its tie the other day.

In any case, I could never have made a living from writing. If I'd tried in the Forties and Fifties I'd have been a heap of whitened bones long ago. Nowadays you *can* live by being a poet. A lot of people do it: it means a blend of giving readings and lecturing and spending a year at a university as poet in residence or something. But I couldn't bear that: it would embarrass me very much. I don't want to go around pretending to be me.

Can you tell me something about the way you write a poem?

It varies a great deal. A poem can come quickly. You just write it all out and then the next evening you alter a word or two and it's done. Another time it will take longer, perhaps months. What is always true is that the idea for a poem and a bit of it, a snatch or a line—it needn't be the opening line—come simultaneously. In my experience one never sits down and says I will now write a poem about this or that, in the abstract.

Do you feel terribly pleased when you've written one?

Yes, as if I've laid an egg, and even more pleased when I see it published. Because I do think that's a part of it: you want it to be seen and read, you're trying to preserve something. Not for yourself, but for the people who haven't seen it or heard it or experienced it.

What about your politics? For example, you talk in one poem about troops being brought home from various parts of the world. . . .

Well, that's really history rather than politics. That poem has been quoted in several books as a kind of symbol of the British withdrawal from a world role. I don't mind troops being brought home if we'd decided this was the best thing all round, but to bring them home simply because we couldn't afford to keep them there seemed a dreadful humiliation. I've always been right-wing. It's difficult to say why, but not being a political thinker I suppose I identify the Right with certain virtues and the Left with certain vices. All very unfair, no doubt.

Which virtues and vices?

Well, thrift, hard work, reverence, desire to preserve—those are the virtues, in case you wondered: and on the other hand idleness, greed and treason.

What do you think about Mrs Thatcher?

Oh, I adore Mrs Thatcher. At last politics makes sense to me, which it hasn't done since Stafford Cripps (I was very fond of him too). Recognizing that if you haven't got the money for something you can't have it—this is a concept that's vanished for many years. I'm delighted to see it surfacing again. But I'm afraid I don't think she will succeed in changing people's attitudes. I think it's all gone too far. What will happen to this country I can't imagine.

Tell me what you like reading.

I read everything except philosophy, theology, economics, sociology, science, or anything to do with the wonders of nature, anything to do with technology—have I said politics? I'm trying to think of all the Dewey decimal classes. In point of fact I virtually read only novels, or something pretty undemanding in the non-fiction line, which might be a biography. I read almost no poetry. I always thought the reading habits of Dylan Thomas matched mine—he never read anything hard.

I tend to go back to novelists, like Dick Francis, for instance; I've just been through his early novels again which I think are outstandingly good for what they are. And Barbara Pym, of course, whom I've written about. Dickens, Trollope—sometimes you go back to them for about three novels running. And detective stories: Michael Innes—I don't know why there has never been a serious study of him: he's a beautifully sophisticated writer, very funny and, now and then, very moving. Anthony Powell, Rex Stout, Kingsley Amis, Peter de Vries.

And what about poetry?

I read Betjeman, Kingsley again, Gavin Ewart (who I think is extraordinarily funny). Among the illustrious dead, Hardy and Christina Rossetti. Shakespeare, of course. Poetry can creep up on you unawares. Wordsworth was nearly the price of me once. I was driving down the M1 on a Saturday morning: they had this poetry slot on the radio, 'Time for Verse': it was a lovely summer morning, and someone suddenly started reading the Immortality ode, and I couldn't see for tears. And when you're driving down the middle lane at seventy miles an hour . . . I don't suppose I'd read that poem for twenty years, and it's amazing how effective it was when one was totally unprepared for it.

A bibliography of your work has just been published. What do you feel about being bibliographed?

On the whole, very flattered, as long as no one thinks I thought all these things worth exhuming. Barry Bloomfield is a first-class bibliographer, and it's surprising what he dug out.

Do you get much out of reading criticism of your work?

Well, there isn't an awful lot of it. I may flatter myself, but I think in one sense I'm like Evelyn Waugh or John Betjeman, in that there's not much to *say* about my work. When you've read a poem, that's it, it's all quite clear what it means.

What about the themes that run through your poetry—not getting married, for instance?

Is that one of my themes? I don't think it is anything very personal. I find the idea of always being in company rather oppressive; I see life more as an affair of solitude diversified by company than an affair of company diversified by solitude.

I don't want to sound falsely naïve, but I often wonder why people get married. I think perhaps they dislike being alone more than I do. Anyone who knows me will tell you that I'm not fond of company. I'm very fond of people, but it's difficult to get people without company. And I think living with someone and being in love is a very difficult business anyway because almost by definition it means putting yourself at the disposal of someone else, ranking them higher than yourself. I wrote a little poem about this which was never collected so perhaps you never saw it. Do you know it? 'The difficult part of love / Is being selfish enough / Is having the blind persistence / To upset someone's existence / Just for your own sake— / What cheek it must take.' End of first verse. 'Then take the unselfish side— / Who can be satisfied / Putting someone else first , / So that you come off worst? / My life is for me: / As well deny gravity.' There is a third verse, but that's the gist of it. I think love collides very sharply with selfishness, and they're both pretty powerful things.

Do you like living in Hull?

I don't really notice where I live: as long as a few simple wants are satisfied—peace, quiet, warmth—I don't mind where I am. As for Hull, I like it because it's so far away from everywhere else. On the way to nowhere, as somebody put it. It's in the middle of this lonely country, and beyond the lonely country there's only the sea. I like that.

I love all the Americans getting on to the train at King's Cross and thinking they're going to come and bother me, and then looking at the connections and deciding they'll go to Newcastle and bother Basil Bunting instead. Makes it harder for people to get at you. I think it's very sensible not to let people know what you're like. And Hull is an unpretentious place. There's not so much crap around as

there would be in London, at least as I imagine it, or in some other
university cities.

*So you don't ever feel the need to be at the centre of things? You don't want to
see the latest play, for instance?*

Oh no, I very much feel the need to be on the periphery of things. I
suppose when one was young one liked to be up to date. But I very
soon got tired of the theatre. I count it as one of the great moments of
my life when I first realized one could actually walk out of a theatre. I
don't mean offensively—but go to the bar at the interval and not come
back. I did it first at Oxford: I was watching *Playboy of the Western World*
and when the bell rang at the interval I asked myself: 'Am I enjoying
myself? No, I've never watched such stupid balls.' So I just had
another drink and walked out into the evening sunshine.

What about travel? Wouldn't you like to visit, say, China?

I wouldn't mind seeing China if I could come back the same day. I
hate being abroad. Generally speaking, the further one gets from
home the greater the misery. I'm not proud of this, but I'm singularly
incurious about other places. I think travelling is very much a
novelist's thing.

A novelist needs new scenes, new people, new themes. The
Graham Greenes, the Somerset Maughams, travelling is necessary
for them. I don't think it is for poets. The poet is really engaged in re-
creating the familiar, he's not committed to introducing the
unfamiliar.

Do you think much about growing older? Is it something that worries you?

Yes, dreadfully. If you assume you're going to live to be seventy,
seven decades, and think of each decade as a day of the week, starting
with Sunday, then I'm on Friday afternoon now. Rather a shock, isn't
it? If you ask why does it bother me, I can only say I dread endless
extinction.

Do you feel you could have had a much happier life?

Not without being someone else. I think it is very much easier to
imagine happiness than to experience it. Which is a pity because
what you imagine makes you dissatisfied with what you experience,
and may even lead you to neglect it. 'Life, and the world, and mine
own self, are changed/For a dream's sake,' to quote Christina

Rossetti. Though I think that a point does come in life when you realize that there's a limit to what you can get from other people and there's a limit to what your own personality is in itself. That's really the story of A Girl in Winter.

Do you feel worried about people not reading poetry in the future?

No, I'm much more worried about poetry becoming official and subsidized. I think we got much better poetry when it was all regarded as sinful or subversive, and you had to hide it under the cushion when somebody came in. What I don't like about subsidies and official support is that they destroy the essential nexus between the writer and the reader. If the writer is being paid to write and the reader is being paid to read, the element of compulsive contact vanishes.

I should hate anybody to read my work because he's been told to and told what to think about it. I really want to hit them, I want readers to feel yes, I've never thought of it that way, but that's how it is.

1979

An Interview with *Paris Review*[1]

Can you describe your life at Hull? Do you live in a flat or own a house?

I came to Hull in 1955. After eighteen months (during which I wrote 'Mr. Bleaney'), I took a University flat and lived there for nearly eighteen years. It was the top flat in a house that was reputedly the American Consulate during the war, and though it might not have suited everybody, it suited me. I wrote most of *The Whitsun Weddings* and all of *High Windows* there. Probably I should never have moved if the University hadn't decided to sell the house, but as it was I had to get out and find somewhere else. It was a dreadful experience, as at that time houses were hard to find. In the end friends reported a small house near the University, and I bought that in 1974. I haven't decided yet whether or not I like it.

How many days a week do you work at the library, and for how many hours a day?

My job as University Librarian is a full-time one, five days a week, forty-five weeks a year. When I came to Hull, I had eleven staff; now there are over a hundred of one sort and another. We built one new library in 1960 and another in 1970, so that my first fifteen years were busy. Of course, this was a period of university expansion in England, and Hull grew as much as, if not more than, the rest. Luckily the Vice-Chancellor during most of this time was keen on the Library, which is why it is called after him. Looking back, I think that if the Brynmor Jones Library *is* a good library—and I think it is—the credit should go to him and to the Library staff. And to the University as a whole, of course. But you wouldn't be interested in all that.

What is your daily routine?

My life is as simple as I can make it. Work all day, then cook, eat, wash up, telephone, hack writing, drink and television in the evenings. I almost never go out. I suppose everyone tries to ignore the passing of time: some people by doing a lot, being in California one year and

[1] Robert Phillips was the interviewer.

Japan the next; or there's my way—making every day and every year exactly the same. Probably neither works.

You didn't mention a schedule for writing . . .

Yes, I was afraid you'd ask about writing. Anything I say about writing poems is bound to be retrospective, because in fact I've written very little since moving into this house, or since *High Windows*, or since 1974, whichever way you like to put it. But when I did write them, well, it was in the evenings, after work, after washing-up (I'm sorry: you would call this 'doing the dishes'). It was a routine like any other. And really it worked very well: I don't think you can write a poem for more than two hours. After that you're going round in circles, and it's much better to leave it for twenty-four hours, by which time your subconscious or whatever has solved the block and you're ready to go on.

The best writing conditions I ever had were in Belfast, when I was working at the University there. Another top-floor flat, by the way. I wrote between eight and ten in the evenings, then went to the University bar till eleven, then played cards or talked with friends till one or two. The first part of the evening had the second part to look forward to, and I could enjoy the second part with a clear conscience because I'd done my two hours. I can't seem to organize that now.

Does, or did, writing come easily for you? Does a poem get completed slowly or rapidly?

I've no standards of comparison. I wrote short poems quite quickly. Longer ones would take weeks or even months. I used to find that I was never sure I was going to finish a poem until I had thought of the last line. Of course, the last line was sometimes the first one you thought of! But usually the last line would come when I'd done about two-thirds of the poem, and then it was just a matter of closing the gap.

Why do you write, and for whom?

You've been reading Auden: 'To ask the hard question is simple.' The short answer is that you write because you have to. If you rationalize it, it seems as if you've seen this sight, felt this feeling, had this vision, and have got to find a combination of words that will preserve it by setting it off in other people. The duty is to the original experience. It doesn't feel like self-expression, though it may look like it. As for *whom* you write, well, you write for everybody. Or anybody who will listen.

Do you share your manuscripts with anyone before publishing them? Are there any friends whose advice you would follow in revising a poem?

I shouldn't normally show what I'd written to anyone: what would be the point? You remember Tennyson reading an unpublished poem to Jowett; when he had finished, Jowett said, 'I shouldn't publish that if I were you, Tennyson.' Tennyson replied, 'If it comes to that, Master, the sherry you gave us at lunch was downright filthy.' That's about all that can happen.

But when we were young, Kingsley Amis and I used to exchange unpublished poems, largely because we never thought they could be published, I suppose. He encouraged me, I encouraged him. Encouragement is very necessary to a young writer. But it's hard to find anyone worth encouraging: there aren't many Kingsleys about.

In his Paris Review *interview, Kingsley Amis states you helped him with the manuscript of* Lucky Jim. *What was the nature of that working relationship? Is part of that novel based upon your own experiences on staff at Leicester University?*

Well, it's all so long ago, it's hard to remember. My general conviction was that Kingsley was quite the funniest writer I had ever met—in letters and so on—and I wanted everyone else to think so too. I know he says he got the idea of *Lucky Jim* from visiting me when I was working at University College Leicester. This has always seemed rather tenuous to me: after all, he was working at University College Swansea when he was writing it, and the theme—boy meets apparently nasty girl, but turns her into a nice girl by getting her away from nasty environment—is one I think has always meant a lot to Kingsley. He used it again in *I Want It Now*. When I read the first draft I said, Cut this, cut that, let's have more of the other. I remember I said, Let's have more 'faces'—you know, his Edith Sitwell face, and so on. The wonderful thing was that Kingsley could 'do' all those faces himself—'Sex Life in Ancient Rome' and so on. Someone once took photographs of them all. I wish I had a set.

How did you come to be a librarian? Had you no interest in teaching? What was your father's profession?

Oh dear, this means a lot of autobiography. My father was a City

Treasurer, a finance officer. I never had the least desire to 'be' anything when I was at school, and by the time I went to Oxford the war was on and there wasn't anything to 'be' except a serviceman or a teacher or a civil servant. In 1943 when I graduated I knew I couldn't be the first, because I'd been graded unfit (I suppose through eyesight), nor the second because I stammered, and then the Civil Service turned me down twice, and I thought, Well, that lets me out, and I sat at home writing *Jill*. But of course in those days the government had powers to send you into the mines or on to the land or into industry, and they wrote quite politely to ask what in fact I was doing. I looked at the daily paper (the *Birmingham Post*: we were living at Warwick then) and saw that a small town in Shropshire was advertising for a librarian, applied for it, and got it, and told the government so, which seemed to satisfy them.

Of course, I wasn't a real librarian, more a sort of caretaker—it was a one-man library—and I can't pretend I enjoyed it much. The previous librarian had been there about forty years, and I was afraid I should be there all my life too. This made me start qualifying myself professionally, just in order to get away, which I did in 1946. By then I'd written *Jill*, and *The North Ship*, and *A Girl in Winter*. It was probably the 'intensest' time of my life.

Is Jorge Luis Borges the only other contemporary poet of note who is also a librarian, by the way? Are you aware of any others?

Who's Jorge Luis Borges? The writer-librarian *I* like is Archibald MacLeish. You know, he was made Librarian of Congress in 1939, and on his first day they brought him some papers to sign, and he wouldn't sign them until he understood what they were all about. When he did understand, he started making objections and counter-suggestions. The upshot was that he reorganized the whole Library of Congress in five years simply by saying, I don't understand and I don't agree, and in wartime, too. Splendid man.

What do you think of the academic world as a milieu *for the working creative writer—teaching specifically?*

The academic world has worked all right for me, but then, I'm not a teacher. I couldn't be. I should think that chewing over other people's work, writing I mean, must be terribly stultifying. Quite sicken you with the whole business of literature. But then, I haven't got that kind of mind, conceptual or ratiocinative or whatever it is. It would be death to me to have to think about literature as such, to say why one poem was 'better' than another, and so on.

We've heard that you don't give readings from your own work. In America, this has become a business for poets. Do you enjoy attending the readings of others?

I don't give readings, no, although I have recorded three of my collections, just to show how *I* should read them. Hearing a poem, as opposed to reading it on the page, means you miss so much—the shape, the punctuation, the italics, even knowing how far you are from the end. Reading it on the page means you can go your own pace, taking it in properly; hearing it means you're dragged along at the speaker's own rate, missing things, not taking it in, confusing 'there' and 'their' and things like that. And the speaker may interpose his own personality between you and the poem, for better or worse. For that matter, so may the audience. I don't like hearing things in public, even music. In fact, I think poetry readings grew up on a false analogy with music: the text is the 'score' that doesn't 'come to life' until it's 'performed'. It's false because people can read words, whereas they can't read music. When you write a poem, you put everything into it that's needed: the reader should 'hear' it just as clearly as if you were in the room saying it to him. And of course this fashion for poetry readings has led to a kind of poetry that you *can* understand first go: easy rhythms, easy emotions, easy syntax. I don't think it stands up on the page.

Do you think economic security an advantage to the writer?

The whole of British post-war society is based on the assumption that economic security is an advantage to everyone. Certainly *I* like to be economically secure. But aren't you, really, asking about *work*? This whole question of how a writer actually gets his money—especially a poet—is one to which there are probably as many answers as there are writers, and the next man's answer always seems better than your own.

On the one hand, you can't live today by being a 'man of letters' as easily as a hundred or seventy-five years ago, when there were so many magazines and newspapers all having to be filled. Writers' incomes, as writers, have sunk almost below the subsistence line. On the other hand, you *can* live by 'being a writer', or 'being a poet', if you're prepared to join the cultural entertainment industry, and take hand-outs from the Arts Council (not that there are as many of them as there used to be) and be a 'poet in residence' and all that. I suppose I could have said—it's a bit late now—I could have had an agent, and said, Look, I will do anything for six months of the year as long as I can be free to write for the other six months. Some people do this, and I suppose it works for them. But I was brought up to think you had to have a job, and write in your spare time, like Trollope. Then, when you started earning enough money by writing, you phase the job out. But in fact I was over fifty before I could have 'lived by my writing'— and then only because I had edited a big anthology—and by that time you think, Well, I might as well get my pension, since I've gone so far.

Any regrets?

Sometimes I think, Everything I've written has been done after a day's work, in the evening: what would it have been like if I'd written it in the morning, after a night's sleep? Was I wrong? Some time ago a writer said to me—and he was a full-time writer, and a good one—'I wish I had your life. Dealing with people, having colleagues. Being a writer is so lonely.' Everyone envies everyone else.

All I can say is, having a job hasn't been a hard price to pay for economic security. Some people, I know, would sooner have the economic insecurity because they have to 'feel free' before they can write. But it's worked for me. The only thing that does strike me as odd, looking back, is that what society has been willing to *pay* me for is being a Librarian. You get medals and prizes and honorary-this-and-thats—and flattering interviews—but if you turned round and said, Right, if I'm so good, give me an index-linked permanent income equal to what I can get for being an undistinguished university administrator—well, reason would remount its throne pretty quickly.

How did you come to write poems? Was time a factor in choosing poetry over the novel form?

What questions you ask. I wrote prose and poems equally from the age of, say, fifteen. I didn't choose poetry: poetry chose me.

Nicely put. Your last novel, A Girl in Winter—*which is a small masterpiece—was published twenty-five years ago. Do you think you will ever write another?*

I don't know: I shouldn't think so. I tried very hard to write a third novel for about five years. The ability to do so had just vanished. I can't say any more than that.

Jill was written when you were about twenty-one, and your second novel only a year or so later. Was it your intention, then, to be a novelist only?

I wanted to 'be a novelist' in a way I never wanted to 'be a poet', yes. Novels seem to me to be richer, broader, deeper, more enjoyable than poems. When I was young, *Scrutiny* ran a series of articles under the general heading of 'The Novel as Dramatic Poem'. That was a stimulating, an exciting conception. Something that was both a poem and novel. Of course, thinking about my own two stories means going back nearly forty years, and at this distance I can't remember what their genesis was.

I seem to recall that *Jill* was based on the idea that running away from life, John's fantasy about an imaginary sister, might lead you straight into it—meeting the real Jill, I mean. With disastrous results.

A Girl in Winter, which I always think of as *The Kingdom of Winter*, which was its first title, or *Winterreich*, as Bruce Montgomery used to call it—well, that was written when I was feeling pretty low, in this first library job I told you about. It's what Eliot would call an objective correlative. When I look at it today, I do think it's remarkably . . . I suppose the word is *knowing* . . . not really mature, or wise, just incredibly clever. By my standards, I mean. And considering I was only twenty-two. All the same, some people whose opinion I respect prefer *Jill*, as being more natural, more sincere, more directly emotional.

In your preface to the reprint of Jill, *you say it is 'in essence an unambitious short story'. What is your definition of a novel?*

I think a novel should follow the fortunes of more than one character.

At least one critic has cited Jill *as the forerunner of the new British post-war novel—the literature of the displaced working-class hero which spawned later works by Alan Sillitoe, John Wain, Keith Waterhouse, Amis and others. Do you feel a part of any of this?*

I don't think so, no. Because *Jill* has none of the political overtones of that *genre*. John's being working-class was a kind of equivalent of my stammer, a built-in handicap to put him one down.

I'm glad you mention Keith Waterhouse. I think *Billy Liar* and *Jubb* are remarkably original novels, the first very funny, the second harrowing. Much better than my two.

You're extremely modest. Wouldn't you say that an open assumption of the British sense of class is important to your work—Jill, A Girl in Winter, a poem like 'The Whitsun Weddings'?

Are you suggesting there's no sense of class in America? That's not the impression I get from the works of Mr O'Hara.

O'Hara overstated. Did you prefigure a shape to your two novels, or did they evolve? You've stated your mentors in poetry, especially Hardy. But who in fiction early on did you frequently read and admire?

Hard to say. Of course I had read a great many novels, and knew the mannerism of most modern writers, but looking back I can't say I ever imitated anyone. Now don't think I mind imitation, in a young writer. It's just a way of learning the job. Really, my novels were more original than my poems, at the time. My favourite novelists were Lawrence, Isherwood, Maugham, Waugh—oh, and George Moore. I was on a great Moore kick at that time: probably he was at the bottom of my style, then.

A Girl in Winter reminds me stylistically of Elizabeth Bowen's fiction, particularly The Death of the Heart and The House in Paris. Is Bowen a writer you've also admired?

No, I hadn't read Elizabeth Bowen. In fact, someone lent me *The Death of the Heart* when *A Girl in Winter* came out—two years after it was finished. I quite liked it, but it was never one of my personal favourites.

Let's talk about the structure of A Girl in Winter for a moment: did you write it chronologically? That is, did you write 'Part Two' first, then shuffle the pack for effect and counter-point? Or did you actually conceive the novel as present-to-past-to-present?

The second way.

Letters are an important and integral part of both novels, as plot and as texture. Are you a voluminous letter-writer?

I suppose I used to write many more letters than I do now, but so did everyone. Nowadays I keep up with one or two people, in the sense of writing when there isn't anything special to say. I love *getting* letters, which means you have to answer them, and there isn't always time. I had a very amusing and undemanding correspondence with the novelist Barbara Pym, who died in 1980, that arose simply out of a fan letter I wrote her and went on for over ten years before we actually met. I hope she liked getting my letters: I certainly liked hers. I talk about our correspondence in a foreword I provided for the UK edition of her posthumous novel, *An Unsuitable Attachment*.

Can you describe your relationship with the contemporary literary community?

I'm somewhat withdrawn from what you call 'the contemporary literary community', for two reasons: in the first place, I don't write for a living, and so don't have to keep in touch with literary editors and publishers and television people in order to earn money; and in the second, I don't live in London. Given that, my relations with it are quite amicable.

Is Hull a place where you are likely to stay put? If so, have you as a person changed since the writing of the poem 'Places, Loved Ones'—or is the speaker of that poem a persona?

Hull is a place where I *have* stayed. On my twenty-fifth anniversary, I held a little luncheon party for the members of my staff who'd been there as long as I had, or almost as long, and they made me a presentation with a card bearing the very lines you mean. *Touché*, as the French say.

As a bachelor, have you sometimes felt an outsider? Or, like the speaker of your poems 'Reasons for Attendance', 'Dockery & Son', and 'Self's the Man', have you enjoyed being single and remained so because you like and preferred living that way?

Hard to say. Yes, I've remained single by choice, and shouldn't have liked anything else, but of course most people do get married, and divorced too, and so I suppose I am an outsider in the sense you mean. Of course it worries me from time to time, but it would take too long to explain why. Samuel Butler said, Life is an affair of being spoilt in one way or another.

Is the character John Kemp in any way based upon your own youth? Were you that shy?

I would say, yes I was and am extremely shy. Anyone who has

stammered will know what agony it is, especially at school. It means you never take the lead in anything or do anything but try to efface yourself. I often wonder if I was shy because I stammered, or vice versa.

Was your childhood unhappy?

My childhood was all right, comfortable and stable and loving, but I wasn't a happy child, or so they say. On the other hand, I've never been a recluse, contrary to reports: I've had friends, and enjoyed their company. In comparison with some people I know I'm extremely sociable.

Do you feel happiness is unlikely in this world?

Well, I think if you're in good health, and have enough money, and nothing is bothering you in the foreseeable future, that's as much as you can hope for. But 'happiness', in the sense of a continuous emotional orgasm, no. If only because you know that you are going to die, and the people you love are going to die.

After 'Trouble at Willow Gables', did you write any other short stories or tales?

No. I think a short story should be either a poem or a novel. Unless it's just an anecdote.

Have you ever attempted a truly long poem? I've never seen one in print. If not, why?

I've written none. A long poem for me would be a novel. In that sense, *A Girl in Winter* is a poem.

What about a play or a verse play?

I don't like plays. They happen in public, which, as I said, I don't like, and by now I have grown rather deaf, which means I can't hear what's going on. Then again, they are rather like poetry readings: they have to get an instant response, which tends to vulgarize. And of course the intrusion of *personality*—the actor, the producer—or do you call him the director?—is distracting.

All the same, I admire *Murder in the Cathedral* as much as anything Eliot ever wrote. I read it from time to time for pleasure, which is the highest compliment I can pay.

Did you ever meet Eliot?

I didn't know him. Once I was in the Faber offices—the old ones, '24,

Russell Square', that magic address!—talking to Charles Monteith, and he said, 'Have you ever met Eliot?' I said no, and to my astonishment he stepped out and reappeared with Eliot, who must have been in the next room. We shook hands, and he explained that he was expecting someone to tea and couldn't stay. There was a pause, and he said, 'I'm glad to see you in this office.' The significance of that was that I wasn't a Faber author—it must have been before 1964, when they published *The Whitsun Weddings*—and I took it as a great compliment. But it was a shattering few minutes: I hardly remember what I thought.

What about Auden? Were you acquainted?

I didn't know him, either. I met Auden once at Stephen Spender's house, which was very kind of Spender, and in a sense he was more frightening than Eliot. I remember he said, Do you like living in Hull? and I said, I don't suppose I'm unhappier there than I should be anywhere else. To which he replied, Naughty, naughty. I thought that was very funny.

But this business of meeting famous writers is agonizing: I had a dreadful few minutes with Forster. My fault, not his. Dylan Thomas came to Oxford to speak to a club I belonged to, and we had a drink the following morning. *He* wasn't frightening. In fact, and I know it sounds absurd to say so, but I should say I had more in common with Dylan Thomas than with any other 'famous writer', in this sort of context.

You mention Auden, Thomas, Yeats and Hardy as early influences in your introduction to the second edition of The North Ship. *What in particular did you learn from your study of these four?*

Oh, for Christ's sake, one doesn't *study* poets! You *read* them, and think, That's marvellous, how is it done, could I do it? and that's how you learn. At the end of it you can't say, That's Yeats, that's Auden, because they've gone, they're like scaffolding that's been taken down. Thomas was a dead end. What effects? Yeats and Auden, the management of lines, the formal distancing of emotion. Hardy, well . . . not to be afraid of the obvious. All those wonderful *dicta* about poetry: 'the poet should touch our hearts by showing his own', 'the poet takes note of nothing that he cannot feel', 'the emotion of all the ages and the thought of his own'— Hardy knew what it was all about.

When your first book, The North Ship, *appeared, did you feel you were going to be an important poet?*

No, certainly not. I've never felt that anyway. You must remember *The North Ship* was published by an obscure press—the Fortune Press — that didn't even send out review copies; it was next door to a vanity press. One had none of the rewards of authorship, neither money (no agreement) nor publicity. You felt you'd cooked your goose.

How can a young poet know if his work is any good?

I think a young poet, or an old poet, for that matter, should try to produce something that pleases himself personally, not only when he's written it but a couple of weeks later. Then he should see if it pleases anyone else, by sending it to the kind of magazine he likes reading. But if it doesn't, he shouldn't be discouraged. I mean, in the seventeenth century every educated man could turn a verse and play the lute. Supposing no one played tennis because they wouldn't make Wimbledon? First and foremost, writing poems should be a pleasure. So should reading them, by God.

How do you account for the great maturity and originality which developed between your first and second poetry collection, The Less Deceived?

You know, I really don't know. After finishing my first books, say by 1945, I thought I had come to an end. I couldn't write another novel, I published nothing. My personal life was rather harassing. Then in 1950 I went to Belfast, and things reawoke somehow. I wrote some poems, and thought, These aren't bad, and had that little pamphlet *XX Poems* printed privately. I felt for the first time I was speaking for myself. Thoughts, feelings, language cohered and jumped. They have to do that. Of course they are always lying around in you, but they have to get together.

You once wrote that 'The impulse to preserve lies at the bottom of all art.' In your case, what is it you are preserving in your poems?

Well, as I said, the experience. The beauty.

Auden admired your forms. But you've stated that form holds little interest for you—content is everything. Could you comment on that?

I'm afraid that was a rather silly remark, especially now when form is so rare. I read poems, and I think, Yes, that's quite a nice idea, but why can't he make a *poem* of it? Make it memorable? It's no good just writing it down! At any level that matters, form and content are indivisible. What I meant by content is the experience the poem preserves, what it passes on. I must have been seeing too many poems that were simply agglomerations of words when I said that.

In one early interview you stated that you were not interested in any period but the present, or in any poetry but that written in English. Did you mean that quite literally? Has your view changed?

It has not. I don't see how one can ever know a foreign language well enough to make reading poems in it worthwhile. Foreigners' ideas of good English poems are dreadfully crude: Byron and Poe and so on. The Russians liking Burns. But deep down I think foreign languages irrelevant. If that glass thing over there is a window, then it isn't a *Fenster* or a *fenêtre* or whatever. *Hautes Fenêtres*, my God! A writer can have only one language, if language is going to mean anything to him.

In D. J. Enright's Poets of the Nineteen-Fifties, published in 1955, you made several provocative statements about archetypes and myth which have become wellknown. Specifically: 'As a guiding principle I believe that every poem must be its own sole freshly created universe, and therefore have no belief in "tradition" or a common myth-kitty . . . To me the whole of the ancient world, the whole of classical and biblical mythology means very little, and I think that using them today not only fills poems full of dead spots, but dodges the writer's duty to be original.' Does this mean you really do not respond to, say, the monstrous manifestation of the Sphinx in Yeats's 'The Second Coming'? Or were you merely reacting against bookishness?

My objection to the use in new poems of properties or personae from older poems isn't a moral one, but simply because they don't work, either because I haven't read the poems in which they appear, or because I have read them and think of them as part of that poem and not a property to be dragged into a new poem as a substitute for securing the effect that is desired. I admit this argument could be pushed to absurd lengths, when a poet couldn't refer to anything that his readers might not have seen (such as snow, for instance), but in fact poets write for people with the same background and experiences as themselves, which might be taken as a compelling argument in support of provincialism.

The use of archetypes can weaken rather than buttress a poem?

I am not going to fall on my face every time someone uses words such as

Orpheus or Faust or Judas. Writers should work for the effects they want to produce, and not wheel out stale old Wardour Street lay figures.

What do you mainly read?

I don't read much. Books I'm sent to review. Otherwise novels I've read before. Detective stories: Gladys Mitchell, Michael Innes, Dick Francis. I'm reading *Framley Parsonage* at the moment. Nothing difficult.

What do you think of the current state of poetry in England today? Are things better or worse in American poetry?

I'm afraid I know very little about American poetry. As regards England, well, before the war, when I was growing up, we had Yeats, Eliot, Graves, Auden, Dylan Thomas, John Betjeman—could you pick a comparable team today?

You haven't been to America, have you?

Oh no, I've never been to America, nor to anywhere else, for that matter. Does that sound very snubbing? It isn't meant to. I suppose I'm pretty unadventurous by nature, partly that isn't the way I earn my living—reading and lecturing and taking classes and so on. I should hate it.

And of course I'm so deaf now that I shouldn't dare. Someone would say, What about Ashbery, and I'd say, I'd prefer strawberry, that kind of thing. I suppose everyone has his own dream of America. A writer once said to me, If you ever go to America, go either to the East Coast or the West Coast: the rest is a desert full of bigots. That's what I think I'd like: where if you help a girl trim the Christmas tree you're regarded as engaged, and her brothers start oiling their shotguns if you don't call on the minister. A version of pastoral.

How is your writing physically accomplished? At what stage does a poem go through the typewriter?

I write—or used to—in notebooks in pencil, trying to complete each stanza before going on to the next. Then when the poem is finished I type it out, and sometimes make small alterations.

You use a lot of idioms and very common phrases—for irony, I'd guess, or to bear more meaning than usual, never for shock value. Do these phrases come late, to add texture or whatever, or are they integral from the beginning?

They occur naturally.

How important is enjambement for you? In certain lines, you seem to isolate lives by the very line break. . . .

No device is important in itself. Writing poetry is playing off the natural rhythms and word-order of speech against the artificialities of rhyme and metre. One has a few private rules: never split an adjective and its noun, for instance.

How do you decide whether or not to rhyme?

Usually the idea of a poem comes with a line or two of it, and they determine the rest. Normally one does rhyme. Deciding *not* to is much harder.

Can you drink and write? Have you tried any consciousness-expanding drugs?

No, though of course my generation are drinkers. Not druggers.

Can you describe the genesis and working-out of a poem based upon an image that most people would simply pass by? (A clear road between neighbours, an ambulance in city traffic?)

If I could answer this sort of question, I'd be a professor rather than a librarian. And in any case, I shouldn't want to. It's a thing you don't want to think about. It happens, or happened, and if it's something to be grateful for, you're grateful.

I remember saying once, I can't understand these chaps who go round American universities explaining how they write poems: it's like going round explaining how you sleep with your wife. Whoever I was talking to said, They'd do that, too, if their agents could fix it.

Do you throw away a lot of poems?

Some poems didn't get finished. Some didn't get published. I never throw anything away.

You only included six of your own poems in The Oxford Book of Twentieth-Century English Verse *(as opposed, say, to twelve by John Betjeman). Do you consider these to be your half-dozen best, or are they merely 'representative'? I was surprised not to find 'Church Going', arguably your single most famous poem.*

My recollection is that I decided on six as a limit for my generation and anyone younger, to save hurt feelings. Mine were representative, as you say—one pretty one, one funny one, one long one, and so on. As editor, I couldn't give myself much space, could I?

In your introduction to that anthology, you make a fine point of saying you didn't include any poems 'requiring a glossary for their full understanding'. Do you feel your own lucid work has helped close the gap between poetry and the public, a gap which experiment and obscurity have widened?

This was to explain why I hadn't included dialect poems. We have poets who write in pretty dense Lallans. Nothing to do with obscurity in the sense you mean.

Okay, but your introduction to All What Jazz? *takes a stance against experiment, citing the trio of Picasso, Pound, and Parker. Why do you distrust the new?*

It seems to me undeniable that up to this century literature used language in the way we all use it, painting represented what anyone with normal vision sees, and music was an affair of nice noises rather than nasty ones. The innovation of 'modernism' in the arts consisted of doing the opposite. I don't know why, I'm not a historian. You have to distinguish between things that seemed odd when they were new but are now quite familiar, such as Ibsen and Wagner, and things that seemed crazy when they were new and seem crazy now, like *Finnegans Wake* and Picasso.

What's that got to do with jazz?

Everything. Jazz showed this very clearly because it's such a telescoped art, only as old as the century, if that. Charlie Parker wrecked jazz by—or so they tell me—using the chromatic rather than the diatonic scale. The diatonic scale is what you use if you want to write a national anthem, or a love song, or a lullaby. The chromatic scale is what you use to give the effect of drinking a quinine martini and having an enema simultaneously.

If I sound heated on this, it's because I love jazz, the jazz of Armstrong and Bechet and Ellington and Bessie Smith and Beiderbecke. To have it all destroyed by a paranoiac drug-addict made me furious. Anyway, it's dead now, dead as Elizabethan madrigal singing. We can only treasure the records. And I do.

Let's return to the Oxford anthology for a moment. Some of its critics said your selections not only favoured traditional poetic forms, but minor poets as well. How do you respond to that?

Since it was *The Oxford Book of Twentieth-Century English Verse*, I had of course to represent the principal poets of the century by their best or most typical works. I think I did this. The trouble is that if this is all you do, the result will be a worthy but boring book, since there are quite enough books doing this already, and I thought it would be diverting to put in less familiar poems that were good or typical in themselves, but by authors who didn't rank full representation. I saw them as unexpected flowers along an only-too-well-trodden path. I think they upset people in a way I hadn't intended, although it's surprising how they are now being quoted and anthologized themselves.

Most people make anthologies out of other anthologies; I spent five years reading everyone's complete works, ending with six months in the basement of the Bodleian Library handling all the twentieth-century poetry they had received. It was great fun. I don't say I made any major discoveries, but I hope I managed to suggest that there are good poems around that no one knows about. At any rate, I made a readable book. I made twentieth-century poetry sound nice. That's quite an achievement in itself.

Not many have commented upon the humour in your poetry, like the wonderful pun on 'the stuff that dreams are made on' in 'Toads'. Do you consciously use humour to achieve a particular effect, or to avoid an opposite emotion?

One uses humour to make people laugh. In my case, I don't know whether they in fact do. The trouble is, it makes them think you aren't being serious. That's the risk you take.

Your most recent collection, High Windows, *contains at least three poems I'd call satirical—'Posterity', 'Homage to a Government', and 'This Be the Verse'. Do you consider yourself a satirist?*

No, I shouldn't call myself a satirist, or any other sort of -ist. The poems you mention were conceived in the same way as the rest. That is to say, as poems. To be a satirist, you have to think you know better than everyone else. I've never done that.

An American poet-critic, Peter Davison, has characterized yours as a 'diminutional talent'—meaning you make things clear by making them small—England reduced to 'squares of wheat', and so forth. Is this a fair comment? Is it a technique you're aware of?

It's difficult to answer remarks like that. The line, 'Its postal districts packed like squares of wheat' refers to London, not England. It doesn't seem 'diminutional' to me, rather the reverse, if anything. It's meant to make the postal districts seem rich and fruitful.

Davison also sees your favourite subjects as failure and weakness.

I think a poet should be judged by what he does with his subjects, not by what his subjects are. Otherwise you're getting near the totalitarian attitude of wanting poems about steel production figures rather than *'Mais où sont les neiges d'antan?'* Poetry isn't a kind of paint-spray you use to cover selected objects with. A good poem about failure is a success.

Is it intentional that the form of 'Toads' is alternating uneven trimeters and dimeters, with alternating off-rhymes, whereas 'Toads Revisited' is in trimeters and off-rhymed couplets? What determines the form of a poem for you? Is it the first line, with its attendant rhythms?

Well, yes: I think I've admitted this already. At this distance I can't recall how far the second Toad poem was planned as a companion to the first. It's more likely that I found it turning out to be a poem about work, but different from the first, and so it seemed amusing to link them.

How did you arrive upon the image of a toad for work or labour?

Sheer genius.

As a writer, what are your particular quirks? Do you feel you have any conspicuous or secret flaws as a writer?

I really don't know. I suppose I've used the iambic pentameter a lot: some people find this oppressive and try to get away from it. My secret flaw is just not being very good, like everyone else. I've never been didactic, never tried to make poetry *do* things, never gone out to look for it. I waited for it to come to me, in whatever shape it chose.

Do you feel you belong to any particular tradition in English letters?

I seem to remember George Fraser saying that poetry was either 'veeshion'—he was Scotch—or 'moaral deescourse', and I was the second, and the first was better. A well-known publisher asked me how one punctuated poetry, and looked flabbergasted when I said, The same as prose. By which I mean that I write, or wrote, as everyone did till the mad lads started, using words and syntax in the normal way to describe recognizable experiences as memorably as possible. That doesn't seem to me a tradition. The other stuff, the mad stuff, is more an aberration.

Have you any thoughts on the office of Poet Laureate? Does it serve a valid function?

Poetry and sovereignty are very primitive things. I like to think of their being united in this way, in England. On the other hand, it's not clear what the Laureate is, or does. Deliberately so, in a way: it isn't a job, there are no duties, no salary, and yet it isn't quite an honour, either, or not just an honour. I'm sure the worst thing about it, especially today, is the publicity it brings, the pressure to be involved publicly with poetry, which must be pretty inimical to any real writing.

Of course, the days when Tennyson would publish a sonnet telling Gladstone what to do about foreign policy are over. It's funny that Kipling, who is what most people think of as a poet as national spokesman, never was Laureate. He should have had it when Bridges was appointed, but it's typical that he didn't—the post isn't thought of in that way. It really is a genuine attempt to honour someone. But the publicity that anything to do with the Palace gets these days is so fierce, it must be really more of an ordeal than an honour.

Your poetry volumes have appeared at the rate of one per decade. From what you say, though, is it unlikely we'll have another around 1984? Did you really only complete about three poems in any given year?

It's unlikely I shall write any more poems, but when I did, yes, I did write slowly. I was looking at 'The Whitsun Weddings' [the poem] just the other day, and found that I began it sometime in the summer of 1957. After three pages, I dropped it for another poem that in fact was finished but never published. I picked it up again, in March 1958, and worked on it till October, when it was finished. But when I look at the diary I was keeping at the time, I see that the kind of incident it describes happened in July 1955! So in all, it took over three years. Of course, that's an exception. But I did write slowly, partly because you're finding out what to say as well as how to say it, and that takes time.

For someone who dislikes being interviewed, you've responded generously.

I'm afraid I haven't said anything very interesting. You must realize I've never had 'ideas' about poetry. To me it's always been a personal, almost physical release or solution to a complex pressure of needs—wanting to create, to justify, to praise, to explain, to externalize, depending on the circumstances. And I've never been much interested in other people's poetry—one reason for writing, of course, is that no one's written what you want to read.

Probably my notion of poetry is very simple. Some time ago I agreed to help judge a poetry competition—you know, the kind where they get about 35,000 entries, and you look at the best few thousand. After a bit I said, Where are all the love poems? And nature poems? And they said, Oh, we threw all those away. I expect they were the ones I should have liked.

1982

WRITING IN GENERAL

Statement[1]

I find it hard to give any abstract views on poetry and its present condition as I find theorizing on the subject no help to me as a writer. In fact it would be true to say that I make a point of not knowing what poetry is or how to read a page or about the function of myth. It is fatal to decide, intellectually, what good poetry is because you are then in honour bound to try to write it, instead of the poems that only you can write.

I write poems to preserve things I have seen / thought / felt (if I may so indicate a composite and complex experience) both for myself and for others, though I feel that my prime responsibility is to the experience itself, which I am trying to keep from oblivion for its own sake. Why I should do this I have no idea, but I think the impulse to preserve lies at the bottom of all art. Generally my poems are related, therefore, to my own personal life, but by no means always, since I can imagine horses I have never seen or the emotions of a bride without ever having been a woman or married.

As a guiding principle I believe that every poem must be its own sole freshly created universe, and therefore have no belief in 'tradition' or a common myth-kitty or casual allusions in poems to other poems or poets, which last I find unpleasantly like the talk of literary understrappers letting you see they know the right people. A poet's only guide is his own judgement; if that is defective his poetry will be defective, but he had still better judge for himself than listen to anyone else. Of the contemporary scene I can say only that there are not enough poems written according to my ideas, but then if there were I should have less incentive to write myself.

1955

[1] When D. J. Enright was compiling *Poets of the 1950s* (published in Japan in 1956), he wrote to his contributors asking for a brief statement of their views on poetry. I assumed he would use their replies as raw material for an introduction; I was rather dashed to find them printed *verbatim*.

The Pleasure Principle

It is sometimes useful to remind ourselves of the simpler aspects of things normally regarded as complicated. Take, for instance, the writing of a poem. It consists of three stages: the first is when a man becomes obsessed with an emotional concept to such a degree that he is compelled to do something about it. What he does is the second stage, namely, construct a verbal device that will reproduce this emotional concept in anyone who cares to read it, anywhere, any time. The third stage is the recurrent situation of people in different times and places setting off the device and re-creating in themselves what the poet felt when he wrote it. The stages are interdependent and all necessary. If there has been no preliminary feeling, the device has nothing to reproduce and the reader will experience nothing. If the second stage has not been well done, the device will not deliver the goods, or will deliver only a few goods to a few people, or will stop delivering them after an absurdly short while. And if there is no third stage, no successful reading, the poem can hardly be said to exist in a practical sense at all.

What a description of this basic tripartite structure shows is that poetry is emotional in nature and theatrical in operation, a skilled re-creation of emotion in other people, and that, conversely, a bad poem is one that never succeeds in doing this. All modes of critical derogation are no more than different ways of saying this, whatever literary, philosophical or moral terminology they employ, and it would not be necessary to point out anything so obvious if present-day poetry did not suggest that it had been forgotten. We seem to be producing a new kind of bad poetry, not the old kind that tries to move the reader and fails, but one that does not even try. Repeatedly he is confronted with pieces that cannot be understood without reference beyond their own limits or whose contented insipidity argues that their authors are merely reminding themselves of what they know already, rather than re-creating it for a third party. The reader, in fact, seems no longer present in the poet's mind as he used to be, as someone who must understand and enjoy the finished product if it is to be a success at all; the assumption now is that no one will read it, and wouldn't understand or enjoy it if they did. Why should this be so? It is not sufficient to say that poetry has lost its audience, and so need no longer consider it: lots of people still read and even buy poetry. More accurately, poetry has lost its old audience, and gained a new one. This has been caused by the consequences of a cunning merger between poet, literary critic and academic critic (three classes now notoriously indistinguishable): it is hardly an exaggeration to say that the poet has gained the happy position wherein he can praise his own poetry in the press and explain it in the class-room, and the reader has been bullied into giving up the consumer's power to say 'I don't like this, bring me something different.' Let him now so much as breathe a word about not liking a poem, and he is in the dock before he can say Edwin Arlington Robinson. And the charge is a grave one: flabby sensibility, insufficient or inadequate critical tools, and inability to meet new verbal and emotional situations. Verdict: guilty, plus a few riders on the prisoner's mental upbringing, addiction to mass amusements, and enfeebled responses. It is time some of you playboys realized, says the judge, that reading a poem is hard work. Fourteen days in stir. Next case.

The cash customers of poetry, therefore, who used to put down their money in the sure and certain hope of enjoyment as if at a theatre or concert hall, were quick to move elsewhere. Poetry was no longer a pleasure. They have been replaced by a humbler squad, whose aim is not pleasure but self-improvement, and who have uncritically accepted the contention that they cannot appreciate poetry without preliminary investment in the intellectual equipment which, by the merest chance, their tutor happens to have about him. In short, the modern poetic audience, when it is not taking in its own washing, is a *student* audience, pure and simple. At first sight this may not seem a bad thing. The poet has at last a moral ascendancy, and his new clientele not only pay for the poetry but pay to have it explained afterwards. Again, if the poet has only himself to please, he is no longer handicapped by the limitations of his audience. And in any case nobody nowadays believes that a worthwhile artist can rely on anything but his own judgement: public taste is always twenty-five years behind, and picks up a style only when it is exploited by the second-rate. All this is true enough. But at bottom poetry, like all art, is inextricably bound up with giving pleasure, and if a poet loses his pleasure-seeking audience he has lost the only audience worth having, for which the dutiful mob that signs on every September is no substitute. And the effect will be felt throughout his work. He will forget that even if he finds what he has to say interesting, others may not. He will concentrate on moral worth or semantic intricacy. Worst of all, his poems will no longer be born of the tension between what he non-verbally feels and what can be got over in common word-usage to someone who hasn't had his experience or education or travel grant, and once the other end of the rope is dropped what results will not be so much obscure or piffling (though it may be both) as an unrealized, 'undramatized' slackness, because he will have lost the habit of testing what he writes by this particular standard. Hence, no pleasure. Hence, no poetry.

What can be done about this? Who wants anything done about it? Certainly not the poet, who is in the unprecedented position of peddling both his work and the standard by which it is judged. Certainly not the new reader, who, like a partner of some unconsummated marriage, has no idea of anything better. Certainly not the old reader, who has simply replaced one pleasure with another. Only the romantic loiterer who recalls the days when poetry was condemned as sinful might wish things different. But if the medium is in fact to be rescued from among our duties and restored to our pleasures, I can only think that a large-scale revulsion has got to set in against present notions, and that it will have to start with poetry readers asking themselves more frequently whether they do in fact enjoy what they read, and, if not, what the point is of carrying on. And I use 'enjoy' in the commonest of senses, the sense in which we leave a radio on or off. Those interested might like to read David Daiches's essay 'The New Criticism: Some Qualifications' (in *Literary Essays*, 1956); in the meantime, the following note by Samuel Butler may reawaken a furtive itch for freedom: 'I should like to like Schumann's music better than I do; I dare say I could make myself like it better if I tried; but I do not like having to try to make myself like things; I like things that make me like them at once and no trying at all' (*Notebooks*, 1919).

1957

Writing Poems

It would, perhaps, be fitting for me to return the heartening compliment paid by the Selectors[1] to *The Whitsun Weddings* with a detailed annotation of its contents. Unfortunately, however, once I have said that the poems were written in or near Hull, Yorkshire, with a succession of Royal Sovereign 2B pencils during the years 1955 to 1963, there seems little to add. I think in every instance the effect I was trying to get is clear enough. If sometimes I have failed, no marginal annotation will help now. Henceforth the poems belong to their readers, who will in due course pass judgement by either forgetting or remembering them.

If something must be said, it should be about the poems one writes not necessarily being the poems one wants to write. Some years ago I came to the conclusion that to write a poem was to construct a verbal device that would preserve an experience indefinitely by reproducing it in whoever read the poem. As a working definition, this satisfied me sufficiently to enable individual poems to be written. In so far as it suggested that all one had to do was pick an experience and preserve it, however, it was much oversimplified. Nowadays nobody believes in 'poetic' subjects, any more than they believe in poetic diction. The longer one goes on, though, the more one feels that some subjects *are* more poetic than others, if only that poems about them get written whereas poems about other subjects don't. At first one tries to write poems about everything. Later on, one learns to distinguish somewhat, though one can still make enormously time-wasting mistakes. The fact is that my working definition defines very little: it makes no reference to this necessary element of distinction, and it leaves the precise nature of the verbal pickling unexplained.

This means that most of the time one is engaged in doing, or trying to do, something of which the value is doubtful and the mode of operation unclear. Can one feel entirely happy about this? The days when one could claim to be the priest of a mystery are gone: today

---

[1] Of the Poetry Book Society. This was printed in the Society's *Bulletin*.

mystery means either ignorance or hokum, neither fashionable qualities. Yet writing a poem is still not an act of the will. The distinction between subjects is not an act of the will. Whatever makes a poem successful is not an act of the will. In consequence, the poems that actually get written may seem trivial or unedifying, compared with those that don't. But the poems that get written, even if they do not please the will, evidently please that mysterious something that has to be pleased.

This is not to say that one is forever writing poems of which the will disapproves. What it does mean, however, is that there must be among the ingredients that go towards the writing of a poem a streak of curious self-gratification, almost impossible to describe except in some such terms, the presence of which tends to nullify any satisfaction the will might be feeling at a finished job. Without this element of self-interest, the theme, however worthy, can drift away and be forgotten. The situation is full of ambiguities. To write a poem is a pleasure: sometimes I deliberately let it compete in the open market, so to speak, with other spare-time activities, ostensibly on the grounds that if a poem isn't more entertaining to write than listening to records or going out it won't be entertaining to read. Yet doesn't this perhaps conceal a subconscious objection to writing? After all, how many of our pleasures really bear thinking about? Or is it just concealed laziness?

Whether one worries about this depends, really, on whether one is more interested in writing or in finding how poems are written. If the former, then such considerations become just another technical difficulty, like noisy neighbours or one's own character, parallel to a clergyman's doubts: one has to go on in spite of them. I suppose in raising them one is seeking some justification in the finished product for the sacrifices made on its behalf. Since it is the will that is the seeker, satisfaction is unlikely to be forthcoming. The only consolation in the whole business, as in just about every other, is that in all probability there was really no choice.

1964

Books

I am quite the wrong person to write this foreword.[1] I should never call myself a book lover, any more than a people lover: it all depends what's inside them. Nor am I a book collector: when a don asked me how many books I had, I really couldn't reply, but this didn't matter as all he wanted to tell me was that he had 25,000, or 50,000, or some improbable number. I was too polite to deliver a variant of Samuel Butler's 'I keep my books round the corner, in the British Museum', yet at the same time I felt a wave of pity, as if he had confessed to kleptomania or some other minor psychological compulsion.

Yet my life has lain among books: what minor psychological compulsion makes me strike this disclaiming attitude? Perhaps a question of age: I grew up when the written word was ceasing to be a major entertainment industry. Society was turning away from the state of affairs that made it possible to live comfortably in, say, St. John's Wood with a couple of servants, and bring up a family, by reviewing and reporting and writing trivial 'middles'. Then again, the writers one admired—Lawrence, for instance, or Auden—tended to dramatize a Literature v. Life conflict, and leave no doubt which side you should be on. If you weren't careful, you would end up 'with an animal for a friend or a volume of memoirs'. Thirdly, well, books— and particularly the kind designated 'antiquarian'—were politically suspect. The workers didn't bother with them: they were the badge of the *rentier*. The pink-boarded Left Book Club volumes were all right, and the first Penguins, but any hint of 'musing among silent friends' marked you out as an enemy of the people.

Nevertheless, I have always been a compulsive reader, to match one compulsion with another, and this has meant that books have crept in somehow. Only the other day I found myself eyeing a patch of wall in my flat and thinking I could get some more shelves in there. I keep novels and detective stories in my bedroom, so that visitors shan't be tempted to borrow them; the sitting-room houses the higher

[1] To the programme of the Antiquarian Book Fair, 1972.

forms of literature (and my jazz books, a far from exhaustive collection), while the hall I reserve for thoroughly worthy items, calculated to speed the parting guest. None of them can be called remarkable. At best they are items bought on publication which now qualify as 'modern first editions'. At worst they are picked from a bad bunch on a station bookstall. I remember that John Malcolm Brinnin says somewhere that he never saw Dylan Thomas read anything but a paperback shocker. Still, they *are* read, not like Michael Fane's nine-volume Pater 'in thick sea-green cloth' that I doubt ever got opened: read in bed, in the bath, at meals. Within reach of my working chair I have reference books on the right, and twelve poets on the left: Hardy, Wordsworth, Christina Rossetti, Hopkins, Sassoon, Edward Thomas, Barnes, Praed, Betjeman, Whitman, Frost and Owen. True, I reach to the right more often than to the left, but the twelve are there as exemplars. All in all, therefore, I should miss my books. I like to think I could do without them—I like to think I could do without anything—but indubitably I should miss them.

It may be that a writer's attitude to books is always ambivalent, for one of the reasons one writes is that all existing books are somehow unsatisfactory, but it's certainly difficult to think of a better symbol of civilization. Of course the symbol changes: the fine book, its materials, its craftsmanship, its design, was eloquent of a civilization founded on means, leisure and taste; today the symbol is the paperback, hurled in hundreds of thousands against the undeveloped areas (Asia, Africa, the young), spreading what we think is best in our thought and imagination. If our values are to maintain a place in the world, these are the troops that will win it for them, but victory is not a foregone conclusion. And what is won abroad may all too easily be lost at home. Perhaps George Orwell best used the book-as-symbol in a way satisfactory to both sides: you remember how in *1984* he made his hero, Winston Smith, treasure a book that he had acquired from 'a frowsy little junk shop'; it was, Orwell tells us, 'a peculiarly beautiful book' in paper and binding alike. Only, the pages were blank. For a writer, the image is a powerful one: the books the past has given us, the books in which the bookseller deals, are printed; they are magnificent, but they are finite. Only the blank book, the manuscript book, may be the book we shall give the future. Its potentialities are endless.

1972

Subsidizing Poetry

It is a great honour to me, and a great pleasure, to receive this prize,[1] and I thank the Foundation and its jury most warmly for conferring it on me. I offer my deep gratitude also to Professor Dr Haas for his more than handsome *laudatio*, to which I listened with that willing suspension of disbelief recommended by Coleridge in another context, and I know that my scholar, Mr Peter Czornyj, shares my sense of privilege at our participation in so generous and memorable a ceremony.

As you have already heard, the last poet to receive this prize was John Masefield in 1938, and I am delighted to be associated even in this fortuitous way with a writer whose strength and simplicity I have long admired. At the same time, I doubt whether Masefield could be regarded as a typical English poet of the Thirties, and I have been wondering rather uneasily whether I am any more typical of the English poets of today. Of course, in one sense there is no such thing as a typical poet: they go their own ways without reference or resemblance to each other, but all the same every age has its own particular image of poetry, and its own conditions under which poets operate, and there is no doubt that in England in the Seventies these are different from what they were forty years ago. The most striking change is the degree to which poetry has become a public event. One might almost say it has been encouraged to become part of the entertainment world, there has been so decided a shift towards spoken poetry, towards poetry on the platform, instead of allowing it to be read silently from the printed page. For the poet this has meant that he must learn new skills: he must grow used to microphones, and television cameras, and even to musical groups, and be prepared to cultivate his personality as something that mediates between his poem and the reader.

Then again, poetry has been encouraged to move into the

[1] The Shakespeare Prize 1976, presented by the FVS Foundation of Hamburg.

education world. Poetry teaching in schools and universities no longer stops at Tennyson, or 1914; it carries on up to the present, with the implication that today's poetry is as worthy of study as the poetry of the past. And this again involves the poet: he is made welcome on the university campus as a visiting reader or lecturer, or even on a longer-term basis as a resident poet or fellow in creative writing. He is having to adapt himself to the *teaching* of poetry, his own and other people's, to finding at least as many ideas about it as will fill a seminar hour, and in addition he may have to explain to his class how he writes it—and, even worse, how they can write it too.

I have been using the word 'encouraged' advisedly, because these two developments haven't taken place without the third and most important of these recent changes: poetry is now sufficiently well thought of to be subsidized with public, and semi-public, money. This is disposed in several ways: as individual grants to writers, as support for poetry festivals and magazines, as fellowships in universities of the kind I have mentioned. I am sure that the impulse behind all this is both generous and reasonable. If poetry is a good thing, then let as many people as possible have as much of it as possible. If it has living significance, then let us attend to the poetry of our time in the hope that it will give our own lives significance. If the poets of the past starved, or were swindled by booksellers, or had no leisure to write, all the more reason for ensuring that it doesn't happen again by giving them enough to live on.

What this has meant, in short, is that in the Seventies it has become possible, as it so rarely was in the past, to make a living, if not by poetry, then at least by being a poet. And this, like so many other things in life, seems to me potentially both a good thing and a not so good thing. Take poetry readings, for example: what Dylan Thomas called 'travelling 200 miles just to recite, in my fruity voice, poems that would not be appreciated and could, anyway, be read in books'. If by such readings a poet enables his audience to understand his poems more fully, and so to enjoy them more, this is good. But if doing so tempts him to begin writing the kind of poems that succeed only in front of an audience, he may start to deal in instant emotion, instant opinion, instant sound and fury, and this may not be so good. Dylan Thomas, if I may quote him once more, sized up the situation succinctly when he said that he worked on the poem in private, and gave it the works in public, but even so I don't think he always kept these two operations as separate as they should be. And today we are all too familiar with the poem that is rapturously received in the auditorium, but seems on the printed page obvious and unmemorable.

The same kind of danger awaits the poet on the campus. If literature is a good thing, then exegesis and analysis can only demonstrate its goodness, and lead to fresh and deeper ways of enjoying it. But if the poet engages in this exegesis and analysis by becoming a university teacher, the danger is that he will begin to assume unconsciously that the more a poem can be analysed—and therefore the more it needs to be analysed—the better poem it is, and he may in consequence, again unconsciously, start to write the kind of poem that is earning him a living. But a worse danger than this for the campus poet is that by acting like a critic he may come to think like a critic; he may insensibly come to embrace what I think of as the American, or Ford-car, view of literature, which holds that every new poem somehow incorporates all poems that have gone before it and takes them a step further. Now I can see that to earn one's living by weighing one poem against another may well make one imagine a kind of ideal poetry that gathers up what is best from all ages and all languages and asserts it in a new way, but the drawback of such a notion is that it suggests that poems are born of other poems, rather than from personal non-literary experience, and for a poet this is disastrous. He will become obsessed with poems that are already in existence, instead of those it is his business to bring into being by externalizing and eternalizing his own perceptions in unique and original verbal form. In fact I am not sure, once a poet has found out what has been written already, and how it was written—once, in short, he has learnt his trade—that he should bother with literature at all. Poetry is not like surgery, a technique that can be copied: every operation the poet performs is unique, and need never be done again.

But over both the concert hall and the lecture room hangs the common problem of displacement. For if a poet is to live by selling not only his poems but his reading of them and his views on poetry in general, he is bound to follow the market to find fresh audiences and fresh fees, and this will lead him from country to country and from continent to continent until his sense of cultural identity becomes blurred and weakened. Once again comes the question, is this a bad thing? Isn't it better to belong to the world, in any and every sense, rather than to one bit of it? Politically, it may be; poetically, I am not so sure. A constant succession of new environments may be stimulating

to a novelist—as to Somerset Maugham, for example, or your own
prize-winner Graham Greene—because he is always seeking new
characters and situations, but the poet is more likely to find them
exhausting, for the essence of his gift is to re-create the familiar, and it
is from the familiar that he draws his strength. You will remember
Auden's poem 'On the Circuit', describing the miseries of the lecture
tour, and how he says

> Spirit is willing to repeat
> Without a qualm the same old talk,
> But Flesh is homesick for our snug
> Apartment in New York.
>
> A sulky fifty-six, he finds
> A change of mealtime utter hell,
> Grown far too crotchety to like
> A luxury hotel.

And how it ends,

> Another morning comes: I see,
> Dwindling below me on the plane,
> The roofs of one more audience
> I shall not see again.
>
> God bless the lot of them, although
> I don't remember which was which:
> God bless the U.S.A., so large,
> So friendly, and so rich.

This is of course very funny, but I think it is rather dreadful too; the
lecture circuit suddenly comes to resemble one of those other circuits
described in Dante's *Inferno*.

  All this leads me to wonder whether the efforts we in England have
made during the last quarter of a century to help poetry by helping
poets may not be having some less welcome side-effects. Unfortunately I can't contribute to the argument from personal experience: I
said earlier that I doubted whether I was representative of today's
English poets, and I have to admit with some shame that I have never
read my poems in public, never lectured on poetry, never taught
anyone how to write it, and indeed this is only the second time since
1945 that I have been abroad. Perhaps what I have been saying has
been unconsciously influenced by these circumstances. But when I

think of the English poets who along with Masefield were writing in 1938—Yeats, Eliot, Auden, Betjeman, Dylan Thomas—I can't pretend that we in the Seventies can call up a comparable team, even acknowledging that Sir John Betjeman is still with us as Poet Laureate in such undiminished form, and even with Professor Dr Haas's *laudatio* still ringing deliciously in my ears. The ebb and flow of the poetic impulse is as unpredictable in the life of a nation as it is in the life of an individual, but it would be ironic if, to mix my English proverbs, we were to find that we had killed the goose that laid the golden eggs by choking it with cream. Or, if killed is too strong a word, at least sent it off the gold standard.

But despite my shortcomings, I am still much more like today's English poets than Shakespeare was, for one can't avoid reflecting, especially on this auspicious occasion, how devoid Shakespeare's own life was of the kind of help I have been describing. It is easy to assume that today's public subsidy is only a continuation of the patronage of the past, but although the companies that acted Shakespeare's plays were called the Lord Chamberlain's Men in the reign of Elizabeth, and the King's Men under James, this does not mean that they received permanent royal support. As a member of these companies, and a shareholder in them, Shakespeare eventually enjoyed a prosperous career, but this was done by writing plays that pleased his audiences; and if we speculate what his plays would have been like if he hadn't had to please them, it is hard to avoid the conclusion that they wouldn't have been as good. Again, there was no opportunity for Shakespeare to make money simply by being Shakespeare even in his own country, much less in any other. There would, in short, have been no Shakespeare Prize for Shakespeare. The first printed mention of his name in Germany occurs in 1682, more than sixty years after his death, and it wasn't until 1741 that one of his plays was actually translated into German, when Baron von Borck, the Prussian ambassador in London, produced a version of *Julius Caesar*. One might be forgiven for thinking that Shakespeare was unknown in Germany until he had been dead for more than a hundred years, and for concluding from my presence here today that his successors are very much more fortunate. But the astonishing fact is that versions of Shakespeare's plays *were* acted here, in German, throughout nearly the whole of his working lifetime. Germany had public theatres even before England, and bands of travelling English actors played in them, and at the courts, crude but recognizable versions of Shakespeare's plays. Some of these have survived: their language is nothing like the original, and there are numerous farcical or sensational interpolations, but there is no doubt that people in Hamburg in the late sixteenth and early seventeenth centuries knew about the merchant of Venice, and the murder of Julius Caesar in the Capitol, and Bottom the weaver, and the young prince who met his father's ghost at night on the battlements. They didn't know that Shakespeare had written them: they had never heard of Shakespeare. But already, in those garbled clownish travesties, the great good news of his genius was spreading.

I find it enormously exciting to think of Shakespeare's plays making their unofficial way under these conditions, in mutilated form, in a different language, with no grant from the Arts Council, no course of lectures at the local university to say how good they were, no personal appearance of their author on television, in fact with nothing to recommend them but their own power to interest and amuse. It seems to reassert the fundamental nexus between poet and audience, which is something he has to struggle for in the same way that he struggles with his medium of words; indeed, it is from these two simultaneous struggles—that are in reality two halves of the same struggle—that the work of art is born. The basic danger in subsidizing poetry is that it does away with this struggle: the poet is paid to write, and the audience is paid to listen. Something vital goes out of their relation, and I am afraid that something vital goes out of poetry too.

It may be that I am saying no more than that English poets today get more official encouragement than Shakespeare did, but at the same time write less well, to which one can only add, 'There needs no ghost, my Lord, come from the grave to tell us this.' To write less well than Shakespeare is something that poets of all ages and all languages have had to put up with, and as for official encouragement, I have too high an opinion of English poetry to think it can be killed with a little kindness. Very likely prosperity, for the poet, is like poverty: one more technical problem he has to solve. But all the same let us not forget those seventeenth-century German playgoers enjoying Shakespeare's plays without knowing who they were by, putting down their own money, and perhaps asking for it back if they were bored, because this does seem to me the healthiest relation that can exist between artist and audience. And let us remember it all finally for the early unplanned cultural link between our two countries that it constituted, which today your generous prize continues to do so much to foster and support.

1976

The Booker Prize 1977

This is the ninth occasion on which the chairman of the Booker panel of judges has risen to announce the result of its deliberations, and I think the Management Committee may fitly congratulate itself on the progress the Award has made since its inception. I was in fact talking the other day to your first chairman, Mr Bill Webb, who happily is here tonight, and he told me rather wistfully that in his day there were no microphones, and no dinner either. Clearly we have come a long way since then. In fact I can supply a much more recent instance. Only a few months ago our Secretary Mr Martyn Goff assured me that there was no need to buy new evening clothes for this occasion, as dress was informal.[1] In consequence I am forced to appear before you unmistakably as a writer of the Fifties, a man overtaken by the Booker Award's continuing increase in status.

I understand that it is customary on this occasion for the chairman of the judges to refer to Auden's sonnet 'The Novelist', the poem in which he compares the novelist to what he calls 'every poet', much to the latter's disadvantage. 'They can dash forward like hussars,' he says, meaning the poets, while the unfortunate novelists

> must
> Become the whole of boredom, subject to
> Vulgar complaints like love, among the Just
>
> Be just, among the Filthy filthy too,
> And in his own weak person, if he can,
> Must suffer dully all the wrongs of Man.

Now although on the whole I agree with this, as I shall make clear in a few minutes, I doubt if it is 100 per cent accurate. Nobody has ever likened me to a hussar, and I doubt if any novelist has ever quite managed to become the whole of boredom; there is always a little left over for the reader. Finally, if Auden doubts whether poets can be 'among the Filthy filthy too', then all I can say is that his acquaintance among his brothers in the craft must be remarkably circumscribed. It

[1] It was not.

may be that poets are not good judges of novelists. The fact is, we envy them: we suspect them first of all of living by their writing, and secondly of doing so in a peculiarly self-indulgent way, for as another of your former chairmen put it, the late—alas—Cyril Connolly, 'Who would not be the worst of novelists and contrive between November and April a novel from the excesses which he has committed from May to October?'

And if poets are not good judges of novelists, they are not likely to be good judges of novels either, and I am therefore especially grateful to my colleagues on this year's panel whose conscientiousness and percipience has supplemented my own deficiencies. We met twice only, and our relationship was therefore remote yet intense, like people sharing a raft after a shipwreck, but our meetings were characterized by the greatest good humour: nobody raised their voice, or thumped the table, and if one of us did lie on the floor at one point, this was simply to recover strength for fresh discussion: no heels were drummed. When in the summer I had the pleasure of lunching with the Management Committee, I was told that what they wanted was a strong chairman. After our work was over, the Secretary told me that I had been the weakest chairman they had ever had. He didn't put it quite like that, of course; what he said was that never before had members of the panel been encouraged to make so full a contribution. They did, and I am most grateful to them.

I think we did our work well. We read novels set in Africa, Egypt, India, Ireland and Spain as well as in England, Scotland and Wales and various countries of the imagination also. We read about childhoods, middle ages and old ages: about men, women and children, animals and robots. We read about real people in imaginary situations and imaginary people in real situations, as well as about nameless people and people who didn't know themselves who they were. All this was very testing. I think if we had any special virtue as a panel, it was that we came to our work without any preconceived ideas of what a good novel should be, which was just as well when confronted with such diversity. In our discussions I thought we resembled a bunch of terriers looking for a rat: we couldn't describe it, but we should know when we found it. Personally, I found myself asking four questions about every book: Could I read it? If I could read it, did I believe it? If I believed it, did I care about it? And if I cared about it, what was the quality of my caring, and would it last? I came to think that quite a number of novelists—and for that matter poets too—might do well to imagine a reader asking himself such questions about their work, because, to be honest, very few novels I read survived as far as question four. Far too many relied on the classic formula of a beginning, a muddle, and an end. On the question of credibility—'do people really behave like this?'—the Secretary had tactfully warned us that judges in the past had been deeply shocked by some of the novels they had had to read, even to the point of being unable to continue, and there were certainly moments when, to adapt the old country saying, one did wonder whether there was any more to the modern novel than four bare legs in a bed, unless it was six. Of course one doesn't really read in this analytic way: readability to a large extent is credibility, and both are part of the conviction, but if I had to name the most frustrating kind of failure I found in the novels I read it was the good initial situation either not sustained, and falling into tedium, or developed outside the frame of aesthetic credibility altogether, and losing all conviction in the process.

I think it is harder to write a good novel than a good poem. The poem, or the kind of poem we write nowadays, is a single emotional spear-point, a concentrated effect that is achieved by leaving everything out but the emotion itself. But the novel can't do this. In the novel, the emotion has to be attached to a human being, and the human being has to be attached to a particular time and a particular place, and has to do with other human beings and be involved with them. I don't think, in the last analysis, that the novelist and the poet are trying to do different things: they are both using language to say something about life in emotional rather than analytic terms. But whereas the poet relies on the intensity with which he can say it, the novelist relies on the persuasiveness with which he can show it. The poet says old age is sad; the novelist describes a group of old people.

Now this seems to me harder not only in the obvious way of requiring a wider and more detailed knowledge of life as it is lived, and therefore a keener interest in it; it is harder because while the poet has only to say he is in love, or miserable, the novelist has to supply for his characters circumstantial evidence of love and misery, and this, as the Fat Man says in *The Maltese Falcon*, calls for the most delicate judgement. No novel comes to grief more certainly than that in which the reader finds a 'lovable' character unlovable, or reasons for misery unconvincing. The novelist, therefore, has not only to feel emotion and devise a human situation to express it: he has to evaluate its causes and its objects in his readers' terms as well as in his own. Or, to put this in its simplest terms, if you tell a novelist 'Life's not like that', he has to do something about it. The poet simply replies, 'No, but I am.'

Finally, the novelist has to relate these emotions to other things. A poem can be all love, or all misery: a novel cannot. It seems to me that Auden was much nearer to describing the novelist's craft when he wrote of suffering,

> how it takes place
> When someone else is eating or opening a window or just walking
>   dully along

The novelist has to bring in these other people, not for the sake of irony, nor even to heighten the emotion he is invoking by contrast, but to strengthen the credibility of his story by putting it into the perspective of that great part of life that is not his story. And it strengthens it because this is the most difficult thing we have to learn about life: that nothing is absolute, that it is only we who are in love, or miserable, or about to die, and it is appropriate that it should fall to the novel to teach it, for as you will have guessed by now I consider the novel at its best to be the maturest of our literary forms.

The authors of the six books that in the end made up our short list are to be congratulated on the fact that when it came to the crunch there was at least one member of the panel who was prepared to argue that they should get the Award. And I don't think it would be unfair to go a little further and say that the last hour of our discussion revolved round three books only. The first was *Quartet in Autumn* by Barbara Pym. As you will know, this is Miss Pym's first book to be published for sixteen years, although that is not her fault, and is a study of four ordinary people reaching retirement, at once dispassionate and compassionate and at bottom deeply courageous. It's a great pleasure to see a new Barbara Pym in the autumn lists again, and I hope there will be many more.

Then none of us will forget Caroline Blackwood's *Great Granny Webster*, a matter-of-fact account—and all the grimmer for this matter-of-factness—of the temperamental and circumstantial misfortunes of an Ulster family. Although it's deceptively concise, it evokes the spirits of no less than four ages—Victorian, Edwardian, pre- and post-war —in exact and resonant prose, and the way the shadow of Great Granny Webster, like that of some Cromwellian eagle, broods over the miseries and insanities of its setting and characters makes up a unique literary experience in this or any other year.

Finally, however, we decided to recommend that the Award be made to Paul Scott for his novel *Staying On*. It is a matter for great sadness that Mr Scott is prevented by serious illness from being here tonight, and I am sure that we all hope that his recovery will be made even speedier by the announcement I have just made. *Staying On*, the story of an undistinguished ex-Army couple living out their retirement in the new India, has all the characteristics of the novel as I have described it. Around the devious and pig-headed Colonel Smalley and his day-dreaming wife Lucy spreads an India that was home for them once but is now less familiar each day, and behind them stretches their own unsuccessful history, what life has made of them and what they have made of each other. Yet although seemingly a delineation of failure, the book resolves triumphantly into a study of love—inarticulate and unfashionable love, perhaps—but a study in which the end by death of a marriage is linked to the end by history of an Empire, and the love that informs both these areas as Mr Scott evokes them seems for this reason all the stronger and more enduring. Let me conclude by saying that *Staying On* is a most original and moving book, and does honour to the Award for which my colleagues and I now propose it.

1977

A Neglected Responsibility:

Contemporary Literary Manuscripts

I am delighted that this seminar[1] has been arranged, because its subject is a complex and important one that has not, as far as I know, been discussed on this scale before. I am not so delighted at being asked to make the first contribution, because, in contrast with the rest of our speakers, I really know very little about modern literary manuscripts in this particular context. In fact not many people do, unless they are regularly engaged in buying or selling them. These operations most often take place privately and personally, for undisclosed prices; even public auctions are usually conducted through discreet agents, so that, unless one is extremely interested, who paid how much for what is hard to discover. In consequence, one never really knows the going price for any given manuscript: there is no manuscript equivalent of *Book-Auction Records*. Nor is it much easier to find out which libraries have what manuscripts. There is no parallel in this country to the Library of Congress's *National Union Catalogue of Manuscripts*, which in America provides a starting-point for those seeking this kind of information, and even the British Library's *Catalogue of Additions to Manuscripts* is several decades behindhand. It follows that for the average librarian the whole question of literary manuscripts and their acquisition is rather a mystery. I hope that this seminar will go some way towards changing this, and that we shall leave it better equipped to take on what up till now has been a neglected responsibility. I hope too that the group will find it possible to collate and publish the information supplied in response to Jenny Stratford's questionnaire. I know that this is a project she has long had at heart, and it is good to see it a stage nearer realization.

We should remember that when we talk of manuscripts we are likely to mean several different things. Primarily, of course, we mean

[1] On modern literary manuscripts, held by the Manuscripts Group of the Standing Conference of National and University Libraries (SCONUL) at King's College, London, in 1979; this talk was the introduction.

texts produced by the author before a work reaches publication, in a form that shows its genesis and evolution. These may be manuscripts, but they may be typescripts: they may even be corrected proofs. But equally we can mean diaries, notebooks, letters to and from, even photographs and recorded tapes: anything, in fact, that makes up the archive of a creative writer's life and constitutes the background of his works. Even fair copies done for charity or presentation may contain variant readings. So I think we should begin by agreeing that by modern literary manuscripts we don't only mean the worksheets of a poem; we could mean the revised proofs of a novel, or even the engagement diary of a playwright. I make this point because manuscripts in this broad definition tend to fall into two categories: those that might be acquired, and increasingly are being acquired, during a writer's lifetime, and those that we can expect to become available only after his death. It is the first kind that we stand the best chance of getting, and that we should try to get, for we are less likely to have the chance to acquire the second when the time comes.

I hope we can agree, too, that modern literary manuscripts are not intrinsically different from any other kind of literary manuscript, and that we should collect them for the same reasons. All literary manuscripts have two kinds of value: what might be called the magical value and the meaningful value. The magical value is the older and more universal: this is the paper he wrote on, these are the words as he wrote them, emerging for the first time in this particular miraculous combination. We may feel inclined to be patronizing about this Shelley-plain, Thomas-coloured factor, but it is a potent element in all collecting, and I doubt if any librarian can be a successful manuscript collector unless he responds to it to some extent. The meaningful value is of much more recent origin, and is the degree to which a manuscript helps to enlarge our knowledge and understanding of a writer's life and work. A manuscript can show the cancellations, the substitutions, the shifting towards the ultimate form and the final meaning. A notebook, simply by being a fixed sequence of pages, can supply evidence of chronology. Unpublished work, unfinished work, even notes towards unwritten work all contribute to our knowledge of a writer's intentions; his letters and diaries add to what we know of his life and the circumstances in which he wrote. This kind of value has been greatly enhanced by the rise of English studies in our universities during this century, and we probably think of modern literary manuscripts in these terms; all the same, not every manuscript has meaningful value, whereas it is bound to have magical value, if it is worth keeping at all.

Those last half-dozen words bring up what is probably the biggest reservation the average librarian has about modern literary manuscripts. A manuscript, by and large, is as good as its author, but whereas we know whether a nineteenth-century writer is good, we don't know whether a modern writer may not be totally forgotten in ten years' time, or at least whether he will be of sufficient interest to make it important that we should be able to know how his works were written. This of course is an extremely complex question, and raises the whole subject of literary evaluation, but I don't see it as a reason for not collecting manuscripts, any more than not knowing which horse is going to win is a reason for not placing a bet. In any case, we do know which writers are thought to be good, or if we don't our English departments will tell us; if we go beyond accepted reputations, then we do so on the theory that one win will compensate for ninety-nine misses, even in crude terms of cash. This seems to me a quite adequate basis on which to proceed. It is, after all, a poor author who is not worth a thesis at some time or other.

At this point I think I should say that if our proceedings are to be realistic we must talk not only about modern literary manuscripts but about the modern literary manuscript situation, and this situation as I think we all know is that during the last forty or fifty years, and more particularly during the last twenty years, the papers of the major British writers of this century have been intensively collected not by British but by American libraries. It is hardly an exaggeration to say that in so far as future studies of these writers, and definitive editions of their works, depend on direct access to their papers, these studies and these editions are most likely to be undertaken by American scholars in American universities. There are of course exceptions, but in the main the popular view of modern literary manuscripts is that they are all in America, and when one considers the great American university collections one can only agree. A meeting of British national and university librarians to discuss modern literary manuscripts resembles an annual convention of stable-door lockers. However we try to talk objectively, our discussions are bound in the end to come back to what went wrong in the past, and what we can do in the future.

There are of course those who think that nothing much has gone wrong: Britain and America make up one English-speaking community with a common ancestry, and we should be glad that American libraries have taken up the cause of preserving our common heritage so assiduously. You may remember that last year Mr Geoffrey Gorer wrote to *The Times* protesting against the use of the word 'saved' when what was meant was 'retained in England'. 'It is inaccurate as well as discourteous to suggest that these papers and paintings would have been in any peril if they went to their American purchasers; they would probably have been better looked after and would certainly have been as available to interested scholars.' And the late E. M. Forster once wrote to me:

> I fear the transatlantic migration can't be checked. The Americans can't collect medieval manuscripts, for the reason that we and other European countries have got hold of them already. They are therefore collecting the 1850–1950 period instead, and I feel that our librarians and other scholars would do well to keep in friendly touch with them, and promote the exchange of microfilms.

Well, as they say, it's a point of view. I certainly don't mean to imply that American libraries are not responsible custodians of manuscripts, or that they are not better off in them than in private hands. Opinions may differ on their accessibility: for British scholars, of course, they are many thousand miles away, and I am not sure how far 'the exchange of microfilms' proves a satisfactory solution in all cases. On the whole I remain convinced that the best place for a writer's papers is in one of the libraries of his own country. I think they are more likely to be studied there, and studied with greater understanding; I think they are more likely to grow there by the addition of further related collections from his family and friends; I think above all that a country's writers are one of its most precious assets, and that if British librarians resign the collection and care of their manuscripts to the librarians of other countries they are letting one of their most rewarding responsibilities slide irretrievably away.

Why have British libraries allowed themselves to be so comprehensively scooped in this field? Because this is what happened: we have not been beaten in a fair fight, we have not fought at all. In 1960 I wrote to twenty leading British writers to ask what their experience in this field had been, and received a number of revealing comments.

The whole point is that England is not really interested in the manuscripts of anyone not securely dead.

If almost any English university had asked me five years ago to give them my manuscript collection, which happened to be unusually complete, I should certainly have said yes.

A third said that he had never known British libraries take the slightest interest in such collecting. What was the reason for this difference of attitudes? Obviously, at least in part, it relates to the attitudes of our respective universities towards modern writers.

English studies in this country were slow to come to terms with the twentieth century. When I was an undergraduate in the early years of the war, the most recent author I was examined on was Wordsworth; my friends, coming back after 1945, were allowed to advance as far as Tennyson. In the 1950s I worked as a librarian in a university where the head of the English department would not sanction the purchase for the library of texts by living writers (he was eventually compelled to compromise in the case of Bernard Shaw). Although this attitude has largely altered, I suspect that even today a research student is discouraged from working on a living writer. American universities are very different: they see living writers as fit subjects for study, and their papers as raw material for research. C. P. Snow told me in 1960 that there were thirty-one theses about him in America and none in England, and I doubt if his was an isolated case. I am sure that all this helped to bring about what I have called the present manuscript situation. On the whole, as I am fond of saying, libraries are feminine: they respond, they do not initiate. The lack of interest shown in modern literary manuscripts by British libraries reflects an identical lack of interest by British universities.

This analysis may seem to ignore a much more potent and obvious factor: if I may paraphrase the famous Fitzgerald / Hemingway exchange, American librarians are different from us, they have more money. Well, of course, this is true; at the same time, it is galling to recall that the first successful concerted effort to secure modern English manuscripts was based on solicitation. This was the campaign mounted in the late 1930s by the Librarian of the Lockwood Memorial Library in the University of Buffalo, Charles Abbott. Abbott saw the importance of worksheets in the full study of a poem, and started sending letters to poets asking for them. The sheer novelty of the request was so successful that in January 1938 he came over on the *Aquitania* to conduct the operation personally. He stayed for three months, visiting poets or being visited by them. The names he mentions are a strange comment on the mutability of literary reputations: Herbert Read, Hilaire Belloc, James Stephens, Ruth Pitter, Sylvia Townsend Warner, W. J. Turner, Richard Church, Humbert Wolfe, Walter de la Mare, Lord Alfred Douglas, Andrew Young, Alfred Noyes, Martin Armstrong, Gordon Macleod, Bryan Guinness and many others, although there is no mention of Auden, MacNeice, Betjeman or Dylan Thomas. Stephen Spender gave him a big ledger containing the drafts of nearly all the poems in his first collection. Abbott left England reflecting that 'if there had been any doubts about the superiority of the interview method over the begging-letter approach, they were long since dispelled'.

It was receiving this kind of solicitation myself—at first from Mr Abbott, then from others—that awoke my interest in what was going on. It seemed dreadful to me that manuscript material was leaving the country just because American librarians could take the trouble to ask for it, and I wrote several letters to the papers grumbling. Then I held my mini-survey, and put the results in a memorandum to SCONUL's Sub-Committee on Manuscripts in March 1961. Their response was that although they rejected the idea of collective action, and did not favour the earmarking of grants for this particular purpose, and didn't think staff should have special responsibility for it, they thought that national and university libraries could make it better known to living British authors that they were interested in acquiring their manuscripts. No doubt this was not as feeble as it seemed at the time.

But as one door shut, another opened: Eric Walter White, then Assistant Secretary of the Arts Council, had read my letters and had also seen the Lockwood Memorial Library at Buffalo, and he was interested in setting up a similar collection in Britain, possibly as an adjunct to the Arts Council Poetry Library. The negotiations that he set in train resulted in the foundation of the National Manuscript Collection of Contemporary Writers. An Arts Council Committee, armed with a modest grant from the Pilgrim Trust, set about buying manuscripts and reselling them to the British Museum to form a collection with this title. This in itself marked a notable change in Museum policy, as up till then it had not reckoned to accept papers of living authors, even as gifts. Truly, as John Lehmann once wrote, 'English libraries were sleeping till Texas woke them', a scene I should dearly like to see depicted by William Blake, or possibly Max Beerbohm.

Given its small resources, the committee was surprisingly successful. In 1967 it held an exhibition in the British Museum, showing notebooks by Auden, Andrew Young, Peter Porter, David Gascoyne and myself, with worksheets by Vernon Watkins, Ted Hughes, Sylvia Plath, Edmund Blunden, Keith Douglas, Stevie Smith and David Wright. Jenny Stratford compiled a hardback catalogue called *Poetry in the Making*, which is by now a collector's piece. After 1967 the scheme broadened: at first, on the Lockwood pattern, the committee had collected poetry worksheets only; now all kinds of literary manuscripts were purchased, and sold to any SCONUL library at a discount of 25 per cent. In 1974 another exhibition was held, this time with a complete catalogue of the collection up to 1972, again compiled to the highest professional standard by Jenny Stratford. After that, the discount was increased to 50 per cent, parallel to the subsidy given by the Victoria and Albert Museum, but most regrettably the British Museum, or British Library as it had by then become, was ruled by the Department of Education and Science as ineligible to receive it. This seemed to me then a piece of vicious bureaucracy, and still does.

I have dwelt a little on the work of the Arts Council committee for a number of reasons. In the first place, even after nearly twenty years I doubt if it and its work is as well known as it should be. Secondly, what little I know about acquiring manuscripts I owe to being one of its members and latterly its chairman. Thirdly, although of course I don't pretend it has materially altered the overall manuscript situation, it showed what could be done even in the Sixties and Seventies with extremely small resources, if only the will to act were there. And, lastly, in its short life it has demonstrated two different ways of going about the business of finding and conserving on a national basis the kind of material we are discussing. The first was an enthusiastic individual, Eric White, working in conjunction with a single national library, the British Museum. The second was by resigning the initiative of finding manuscripts to the member libraries of SCONUL, and then subsidizing their purchases by up to 50 per cent. My expectation was that the second method would be far more productive than the first. In fact it was not. No more purchases, if as many, were made under the second scheme than under the first, and the committee's grant was reduced in consequence. This was a great disappointment. If half SCONUL's libraries had bought one manuscript a year, the scheme would have boomed.

Why didn't they? Well, it has to be admitted that even for a library prepared to interest itself in literary manuscripts, their collection is not easy. Even if we begin as Charles Abbott began, and write fifty letters to fifty living writers—for instance, fifteen poets, fifteen novelists, fifteen playwrights and five miscellaneous—we can no longer expect the success rate of 1938. Writers are aware that their papers are in demand, and any response we get is likely to be cautious. Time and patience are needed to make contact, to go and see them, to entertain them at the library to show them what has already been acquired, to convince them that we have a knowledge of their work and a real desire to preserve the records of its making. This calls for staff with a knowledge of modern literature, and a genuine liking for it. What is more, our interest must, in this day and age, be supported by funds, and I know from personal experience that for the average university library in these days this is far from easy. Charles Abbott rationalized his begging technique by saying that he had to spend what money he had on first editions (which couldn't be got for nothing), and that it was all right, as writers would only have thrown their manuscripts away if he hadn't asked for them. This would not work today. Writers do not expect British libraries to pay American prices, but they expect something, and we shall not get very far if we seem to be trying to drive an unfairly hard bargain. I wonder how much it is reasonable to expect the average university library to spend on manuscripts in a year. One per cent of its grant? Half one per cent? As much as we spend on journals that are never looked at and could be borrowed from the British Library Lending Division at Boston Spa anyway? I wonder.

On the other hand, British librarians enjoy one enormous advantage over their American colleagues: we are here. We don't have to take the *Aquitania* to establish contact with British writers: increasingly, they are in and out of our universities, giving talks, giving readings, on one-year appointments: contact can be made, meetings arranged, even—in extreme cases—honorary degrees offered. Secondly, although writers differ very much in their reactions, I honestly believe that most of them would prefer their manuscripts to stay in this country, where they can see them from time to time if they want, than have them disappear for ever across the Atlantic. Recognition in one's own country can mean a great deal. In many cases it might lead a writer to sell his papers to a British library for less money than he would have got from America, simply because of this added element of local recognition. Several writers I wrote to in 1960 said this.

I am not envisaging a situation in which Britain's hundred best writers each have fifty honorary degrees and spend their weekdays being driven from university to university in hired Daimlers for champagne lunches. But I do think that university libraries might initiate discussions with their departments of English on the collection of literary manuscripts in general, and, given a favourable response, on which writers it would be sensible to approach. Three classes come to mind immediately: writers born in that area, writers who studied or worked at the university in question, and writers in whom the department is particularly interested, either through research interests or by chance association such as personal friendship. It may be that no response will be forthcoming, but at least I think the attempt should be made, and this kind of approach will minimize the possibility of overlap.

As I said earlier, we should do all we can to collect the papers of living writers, because increasingly we are at a great disadvantage when it comes to acquiring the archives of the recently dead. Once a collection of this kind comes into the sale-room on an international market, I recognize that British libraries simply have not the resources necessary to compete for them. Very occasionally a collection can be located and secured that has not come up for sale: one hears encouraging reports about the University of Sussex and Virginia Woolf, but such negotiation needs a good deal of luck, tact and persistence—perhaps I should say, even, thickness of skin. It is said that the world at large did not believe that Thomas Hardy was dying until it heard that Sir Sydney Cockerell of the Fitzwilliam Museum had arrived at Max Gate. But in general what we do not acquire during a writer's lifetime, we are not likely to acquire after his death. His papers make one melancholy appearance in the pages of Sotheby's catalogue, then yield to that irresistible gravitational westward pull, to end up deep in the heart of one of those institutions for which Mr Gorer has so much respect, as indeed we all have.

Is there a lesson to be learned in this connection from the recent acquisition of the papers of Walter de la Mare by the Bodleian Library, with the assistance of the Victoria and Albert Museum and the Arts Council? The sum involved here was substantial, but it was met by a pooling of resources by bodies that individually could not have met the price asked. If this can happen once, it can surely happen again: the drawback as things stand at present is the time it takes to mobilize the combined support in question. If a consortium of these sources could be organized, and machinery devised for quick consultation when a substantial collection comes on the market, then more successes might be achieved. Otherwise, one can only hope that the proposed National Heritage Fund may be persuaded to take notice of literary archives, if and when it comes into operation.

Mr Chairman, the fact that you have asked me to say the first word on this question means, happily, that you do not expect me to say the last. I am well aware that there are many aspects of the subject I have not mentioned. How far, for instance, has the harvest of twentieth-century literary manuscripts now been gathered in, leaving nothing but the meagre gleanings of the present and future? How far, in short, is there anything left to collect? How far has the world recession halted the transatlantic migration? Will Mrs Stratford's questionnaire and its answers reveal that, despite popular belief, there are substantial modern manuscript holdings in this country after all? These are questions on which I hope succeeding speakers will throw some light.

But let me in closing make one final comment. I have said that I hope our proceedings will be realistic, but I wonder how far I have been realistic in speaking as if we are all agreed that the collection of modern literary manuscripts is a serious and rewarding responsibility. This is what I hope we believe. But when I look at SCONUL's track record over the last decade as I have experienced it, I am forced to the conclusion that the libraries that really do believe it are in a minority. Perhaps it is a pity that we have not included in our programme of speakers a librarian who would say that he has no intention of throwing away money on the waste paper of nonentities to pander to a passing fad, because despite signs of a change of heart in recent years this is what the majority of British librarians have thought in the past, and is what I strongly suspect the majority of them think today. Perhaps one is here today; if so, I hope he will put his point of view in discussion, and the sooner the better. It will help the rest of us to realize the magnitude of our responsibility.

1979

WRITING IN PARTICULAR

The Savage Seventh

It was that verse about becoming again as a little child that caused the first sharp waning of my Christian sympathies. If the Kingdom of Heaven could be entered only by those fulfilling such a condition I knew I should be unhappy there. It was not the prospect of being deprived of money, keys, wallet, letters, books, long-playing records, drinks, the opposite sex, and other solaces of adulthood that upset me (I should have been about eleven), but having to put up indefinitely with the company of other children, their noise, their nastiness, their boasting, their back-answers, their cruelty, their silliness. Until I began to meet grown-ups on more or less equal terms I fancied myself a kind of Ishmael. The realization that it was not people I disliked but children was for me one of those celebrated moments of revelation, comparable to reading Haeckel or Ingersoll in the last century. The knowledge that I should never (except by deliberate act of folly) get mixed up with them again more than compensated for having to start earning a living.

Today I am more tolerant. It's not that I loathe the little scum, as Hesketh Pearson put it; merely that 'the fact is that a child is a nuisance to a grown-up person. What is more, the nuisance becomes more and more intolerable as the grown-up person becomes more cultivated, more sensitive, and more engaged in the highest methods of adult work' (Shaw). I don't know about highest methods of adult work: what makes the contest between them so unequal is that the child is younger and so in better physical shape, life hasn't yet cut it down to size, it's not worried about anything, it hasn't been to work all today and hasn't got to go to work all tomorrow, all of which makes it quite unbearable but for none of which can it fairly be blamed. The two chief characteristics of childhood, and the two things that make it so seductive to a certain type of adult mind, are its freedom from reason and its freedom from responsibility. It is these that give it its peculiar heartless, savage strength.

These few commonplaces are intended to prepare the reader for the unflattering approach of Mr and Mrs Opie in their new book.[1] 'The worldwide fraternity of children', they quote from Douglas Newton, 'is the greatest of savage tribes, and the only one that shows no sign of dying out,' and they lose no time in implanting in their reader's mind the notion that the whole seven-million-strong community of children can be likened to a separate more primitive population suitable for frank anthropological study, like Trobrianders or the nineteenth-century poor. With this assumption, Mr and Mrs Opie suspected that such a self-contained world held a great deal of traditional lore and sayings, and hence enlisted the aid of numerous field-workers who appear to have spent eight years accumulating and reporting what they found. Since these workers included teachers at over seventy schools throughout the British Isles, the coverage was thorough, but the field-work was clearly backed up with extensive reading and private correspondence. The authors' wish, if a large body of oral material was discovered to exist, was to get it down on paper in an accurate, unidealized way. Clearly their expectations were gratified, and they have brought to the task of recording the results the blend of charm and thoroughness already evinced in their nursery rhyme collections. Their 400-page book takes the reader right into the heart of the child country. What does he find there?

Leaving aside games (to be the subject of a second volume later), the mass of sayings and customs here presented refers to almost every aspect of the unofficial social life of childhood between the ages six and fourteen. It is made up of rhymes, parodies, jokes, riddles, nicknames and repartee, together with more practical formulae of promise, barter, friendship, fortune and superstition, and a miscellaneous collection of calendar customs, pranks, and such expertise as the use of lean bacon rashers to deaden caning. The vast majority involve rhyming. Children love rhymes, however pointless, just because they are rhymes:

> Have you seen Pa
> Smoking a cigar
> Riding on a bicycle?
> Ha! Ha! Ha!

[1] Iona and Peter Opie, *The Lore and Language of Schoolchildren* (Oxford: Clarendon Press, 1959).

and a belief or prayer or promise is felt to be truer or more effective or
more binding if in the form of a jingle:

> Touch your head, touch your toes
> Hope I never go in one of those.
>
> (*On seeing an ambulance.*)

The authors claim that this susceptibility goes deeper. 'When on
their own they burst into rhyme, of no recognisable relevancy, as a
cover in unexpected situations, to pass off an awkward meeting, to fill a
silence, to hide a deeply-felt emotion, or in a gasp of excitement?' This
does not mean that children are natural poets. The many lovers of the
Opies' earlier books should be warned not to expect another harvest of
ageless magical-simple ditties of cottage and countryside. The rhymes
children do not let die (as opposed to those preserved for them by their
elders) have no obvious qualifications for immortality:

> I'm a man that came from Scotland
> Shooting peas up a Nannie goat's bottom,
> I'm the man that came from Scotland
> Shooting peas away.

All the same, they frequently have unexpectedly long ancestries. In
1954 children were skipping in York to a rhyme the authors could trace
back in an unbroken line to 1725: this is true oral tradition, exemplifying
the innate conservatism of childhood in these matters that was one of
the authors' chief discoveries. Norman Douglas, writing in *London
Street Games* (1916), thought he was showing 'how wide-awake our
youngsters are, to be able to go on inventing games out of their heads all
the time'. But Douglas was wrong: the Opies report that of the 137
chants and fragments he records, 108 are still being sung today, and
were presumably as traditional then as now. 'Boys continue to crack
jokes that Swift collected from his friends in Queen Anne's time; they
play tricks which lads used to play on each other in the heyday of Beau
Brummel; they ask riddles that were posed when Henry VIII was a
boy.' A verse reported from Regency days by Edmund Gosse's father
was sent in by a twelve-year-old Spennymoor girl 130 years later; in
1952 Wiltshire girls were skipping to:

> Kaiser Bill went up the hill
>   To see if the war was over;
> General French got out of his trench

And kicked him into Dover.
He say if the Bone Man come
Stick your bayonet up his bum.

To come upon the shadowy figure of Kaiser Wilhelm II, and the still more shadowy Napoleon Bonaparte, standing in a children's song like ghosts at midsummer noontide shows as well as anything could the way a particular rhyme will be transmitted unthinkingly from generation to generation until it loses all significance. Yet, paradoxically, the child has a keen sense of the topical. Lottie Collins becomes Diana Dors; Bonnie Prince Charlie becomes Charlie Chaplin; Jack the Ripper becomes Kruger and then Mickey Mouse. There are even purely modern songs:

Catch a Perry Como
Wash him in some Omo
Hang him on a line to dry.

The authors explain this paradox by insisting that 'schoolchild chant and chatter' is made up of two very distinct streams of oral lore: the modern mass of catch-phrases, slang, fashionable jokes and nicknames, and the traditional inheritance of dialect and custom governing such things as playing truant, giving warning, sneaking, swearing, tormenting, fighting, and in general the darker and sterner side of life. This dichotomy receives curious reinforcement from the discovery that while terms of approval (smashing, bang on, flashy, lush, smack on, snazzy, etc.) change rapidly with the fashion, terms of disapproval (blinking awful, bloomin' 'orrible, boring, cheesy, corny, daft, disgraceful, flippin' awful, foul, fusty, frowsty, etc.) show very little alteration. But the persistence of tradition is seen even more clearly in non-verbal ways: in calendar customs, for instance, in superstitions, in mysterious convictions connected with assembling a million milk-bottle tops, of saying 'rabbits' on the first of the month. Many of these are strictly local. Egg-rolling at Easter, widely practised north of the Trent, is quite unknown in the Midlands and the South; Mischief Night (4 November) occupies a belt east to west across the country between, say, Derby and Saltburn. (From my observation this custom is spreading and growing more violent and disagreeable: I suggest a Herod's Eve to coincide with it, on which bands of adults might roam the streets and bash hell out of anyone under sixteen found out of doors.)

Long before the reader finishes the last chapter he will be asking himself what this tumult of rhyming, joking, riddling, jeers and epithets (the extent of which I have done no more than hint at) really amounts to in terms of knowledge about children today. Here the authors are not helpful. No doubt designedly, they have spent their space on recording the greatest possible number of jingles, nicknames, synonyms, customs and conundrums for posterity, rather than trying to draw conclusions from them. The trouble is their material is not sufficiently interesting to stand by itself. To me it demonstrated that on the whole children are quite as boring and nearly as unpleasant as I remember them. To read the chapter 'Wit and Repartee' is to live again those appalling half-hours in playground, corridor or cloakroom when the feeble backchat almost suffocated one by its staleness. And since the authors assure us that they are not concerned with the delinquent, the verses called 'Today's Menu' ('Scab and matter custard . . .') must not be regarded as untypical.

Nevertheless, I can't quite subscribe to the Opies' delineation of all children as an entirely separate race of quasi-savages, or not without some reservations. All their examples are collected from non-private, non-fee-paying schools, which means in practice that, like most folklorists, they are sampling from the least literate section of the community: the title of the book should be modified mentally in consequence. Again, I cannot accept unquestioned the authors' remark that '[childhood] is as unnoticed by the sophisticated world, and quite as little affected by it, as is the culture of some dwindling aboriginal tribe living out its helpless existence in the hinterland of a native reserve.' Children copy adults ceaselessly. In fact, it might be argued that both streams of oral lore, topical and traditional, are largely cast-offs from the grown-up world. The fact that children cross their legs in examinations for luck like eighteenth-century gamblers suggests that customs and superstitions persist in childhood long after maturity has abandoned them. Already we are beginning to call Christmas 'the children's festival'. How long will 'Here's the Bible open, Here's the Bible shut, If I don't tell the truth,' etc., continue to be chanted after the present legal form of taking the oath has vanished?

Above all, though, children are linked to adults by the simple fact that they are in process of turning into them. For this they may be forgiven much. Children are bound to be inferior to adults, or there is no incentive to grow up. But there has been much agitation recently about whether grown-ups themselves are deteriorating by reason of addiction to mass media, loss of traditional self-amusements, and the like. To me (if I may quote *After Many a Summer*) 'they look as if they were having a pretty good time, in their own way of course,' but the question may be asked whether there is any evidence in this book that the hypothetical blight is spreading backwards into childhood. It is not an easy one to answer. During the time that the Opies were collecting their material, television licences increased from 800,000 to 8,000,000. It is possible, therefore, that the lore they record will soon be largely obsolete. On the other hand, we cannot be certain of this until a comparable investigation is made fifty or a hundred years hence. It is likely that the whole traditional corpus is expiring at a slower rate than we can measure, just as it has among adults, and if this is so many will regret it. But I do not think it can be said to matter seriously provided childhood retains the vitality to convert and adapt new material to its obscure and secret ends. Norman Douglas took a pessimistic view of the future: 'the standardisation of youth proceeds endlessly.' The Opies do not: 'we cannot but feel that [this] is a virile generation.' The reader is left feeling, in short, that the old rhymes are not so marvellous that it matters if children forget to sing them. The important thing is that they should sing. And there is no evidence here that they are forgetting how to do that.

1959

Carnival in Venice

It looks as though the artistic life (as distinct from the life of the artist) is back with us again, this time not from Paris (France) but Venice (Calif.). Of course, in one sense it has never been away. There are always people who, on the pretext of having to do with art, choose to live in a way that strikes the rest of society as reprehensible. But every so often they get a militant fit, and come rampaging out of the *Quartier* vilifying and castigating like nobody's business, making it clear that since the artist is the only man cosmically in step it's okay for him to commit adultery, leave the washing-up, and generally *épater* the contemptible dupes of the social Mammon who make up the rest of the world. We had it from the French towards the end of the last century, and now it looks as though we may be going to get it from the Americans. Mr Lipton's raucous book[1] gives a preview of the charge sheet.

The Beat Generation (the 'holy barbarians' of his title) came into prominence during the Fifties as an American-type bohemianism that in addition to the normal syllabus requirements (art, not working, sex) featured Zen Buddhism, jazz, marijuana-smoking and a new slang. The publisher's blurb cautiously describes its adherents as 'a band of non-conformists living a kind of life very different from that of the average American'. Mr Lipton is more expansive: 'This is not just another alienation. It is a deep-going change, a revolution under the ribs. . . . The present generation has passed on to a total rejection of the whole society, and that, in present-day America, means the business civilization.' Himself a veteran beatster, Mr Lipton takes Venice West (a Los Angeles slum where he lives) as his text, introduces us to his neighbours and the life they lead, then explains what they stand for and what it means socially. This is not a history but an epiphany. Chuck Bennison, Chris Nelson, Tanya Bromberger ('I took to them [heroin and marijuana] like a duck to water') and Angel Dan Davies ('to whom nothing is a laughing matter, least of all

[1] Lawrence Lipton, *The Holy Barbarians* (London: W. H. Allen, 1960).

where he is concerned') stand before us in their habits as they live, tapping drums, smoking pot (=pod, marijuana) while they dig the Bird, planning how to cheat the landlord and dodge the draft board, getting married (nothing legal, of course) by chucking a ring (of flowers) into the sea while someone spouts poetry (the couple staying together all of three months), and, above all, explaining to each other how near they are to flipping, but how it's their destiny, like with Dylan Thomas, and how flipping shows they're real far out anyway. Mr Lipton traces their previous histories of buggings and breakdowns in Squaresville, their homosexual mothers and incestuous fathers, until 'one day' they find themselves 'shacked-up with a girl in a store-front pad and pounding away at a typewriter set up on a packing-case'—growing, of course, a beard. 'Not until I came to Venice West', as one of them says, 'was I able to know and be what I am.'

Now one must clear one's mind of cant and admit, firstly, that everyone is free to live as he likes as far as society will let him; secondly, that other people besides Angel Dan Davies enjoy poetry, jazz and sex; and thirdly that, appalling as it would be to have Itchy Dave Gelden coming in one's door 'fidgeting and scratching his crotch' ('Hi, what's cookin'? Are we gonna blow some poetry, maybe?'), he would probably be no worse than a guardee subaltern talking about Buck House, or your father-in-law telling you how his new golf clubs cost more but aren't as good as his old ones. Other people are Hell (I have never seen why Sartre should have been praised for inverting and falsifying this truism), and the self-important spongers of Venice no more so than the rest. But Mr Lipton's point is that they are a lot less so. Once he raises his sights from Los Angeles, the definition of his subjects blurs until it seems to include many quite normal classes such as socialists, homosexuals, opponents of racial segregation, undergraduates, creative artists and mixed-up book-fuddled kids, and the hipster looks much more Aldermastonian and reassuring—he becomes, in fact, anyone who is sick of the rat race of American business civilization (Mr Lipton throws phrases like this around freely) and is prepared to live cheaply in order to do what he likes and be independent. Hence the holiness and the barbarity. Mr Lipton suggests that this kind of withdrawal will 'save' America and probably the rest of the world as well; one catches, infinitely vulgarized, that forlorn hope recurrent through all the later D. H. Lawrence that if only a few people, somewhere, somehow, would 'let go of the social lie', machine civilization would perish of itself.

To be beat is therefore a social as well as an artistic state. But Mr Lipton's book is so cheerful, so sensational, so simple-minded in its simplifications, that it is impossible for a British reviewer to tell whether he really has something or whether he is just writing up a piece of successful bohemian publicity-campaigning. Despite his protests, there seems little new in the Beat Generation unless it is a new degree of hysteria in art or irresponsibility in life, and there is little temptation to take his characters as mentors for either. It would be interesting to have a historical, documented account of this movement from a less partisan viewpoint—a square viewpoint—but in the meantime Mr Lipton's cats would make a cat laugh and his book can be warmly recommended on this basis.

1960

Hounded

This book[1] is fascinating because Thompson is fascinating, with all the fascination of character produced to excess. Born in Ashton-under-Lyne in 1859, the son of a Catholic-convert doctor, he had a happy childhood—indeed, too happy: after the nursery fantasies of dolls and his toy theatre, adult life was an anticlimax. An attempt to enter the priesthood was foiled by the percipient Fathers at St. Cuthbert's, Ushaw, and he was sent instead to study medicine at Owens College. Daily he went by train to Manchester, to please his father, but once there he spent his time wandering about, reading and sleeping in Manchester Public Library, and watching cricket, in this way pleasing, or at least not displeasing, himself. Every so often he failed an examination. Incredibly, he kept this up for six years, and would no doubt have been content to spend the rest of his life travelling backwards and forwards on this misunderstanding if his father had not lost patience, and demanded at last that his son go to work. It was too late. Thompson had already found the answer to growing up: laudanum.

Sooner than work, he quitted Ashton for London. Whether this sole decisive action of his life was simply an evasion, or whether it was in its pitiful, maimed way a gesture of independence, its consequences were terrible. Between 1885 and 1888 Thompson lived as miserably as any English poet before or after. Begging, selling papers or matches, running errands for a kind bootmaker, spending what money he had on laudanum while he ate vegetable refuse in Covent Garden and slept on the Embankment, it is unbelievable that any man of sensibility could have voluntarily endured it—voluntarily, because his father sent him an allowance of seven shillings a week to a reading room in the Strand. But to collect it would have required conscious exercise of the will, a recognition of reality, a degree of self-discipline. Thompson preferred to starve.

There is no suggestion that he was engaged in any systematic

[1] J. C. Reid, *Francis Thompson: Man and Poet* (London: Routledge, 1959).

dérèglement as recommended by more ferocious confrères. He just wanted to escape crushing responsibilities like getting up in the morning. Though there had been some talk of a literary career at home, he wrote nothing—certainly no poetry—and it was not until a tentative and long-disregarded contribution to *Merry England* had aroused the curiosity and compassion of the editor, Wilfrid Meynell, not until Thompson had been persuaded into a private hospital and broken of his addiction, that 'from this man of thirty who had had only two rather mediocre poems printed, poetry now poured in a turbid torrent.' In 1893 Elkin Mathews and John Lane published his first book, *Poems*. From then on he lived the rest of his life—another fourteen years only—in the Meynells' kindly ambience. He was no more efficient, and not much happier, but at least he was never without food and lodging. Laudanum reasserted its hold, perhaps to dull consumption, and he died in 1907, murmuring 'My withered dreams, my withered dreams'.

Thompson, who never referred to his own failings except by deploring them in others, defined his own poetic vices precisely:

> There are word-tasters and word-swillers. Unfortunately the two are confounded. . . . These [i.e. the word-tasters] are connoisseurs in words. The others are drunkards in words. Like the dram drinker, they have swallowed language till their palate has lost all distinction but that of coarse stimulus. Is it intoxicant enough? Is it hot in the mouth? Whether it be the best, the right word, they care nought, so it blisters the tongue.

Mr Reid does not defend this side of Thompson, and admits the frigid inhumanity, the lurid overemphasis, the infantility and philological freakishness that are its characteristics. The poems that go some way towards justifying his reputation Mr Reid nominates as 'The Hound of Heaven', 'The Mistress of Vision', 'All Flesh' and several others, all poetry of religious experience, for Thompson's devotion to the Church never faltered.

One finishes Mr Reid's book almost liking Thompson. If he was work-shy, he was ready to pay the price; and in those days that meant hunger and homelessness, not a dainty progression from foundation to fellowship over the safety net of national assistance. He was no Skimpole. And whose heart would not be softened by a verse like this?

At the Last Trump thou wilt arise Betimes!
Up; for when thou wouldst not, thou wilt shortly sleep long.
The worm is even now weaving thy body its night-shift.
Love slept not a-saving thee. Love calls thee.
Rise, and seek him early. Ask, and receive.

It was Thompson's attempt to get himself out of bed. It did not work.

1960

What's Become of Wystan?

I have been trying to imagine a discussion of Auden between one man who had read nothing of his after 1940 and another who had read nothing before. After an initial agreement by adjective—'Versatile,' 'Fluent,' 'Too smart sometimes'—a mystifying gap would open between them, as one spoke of a tremendously exciting English social poet full of energetic unliterary knock-about and unique lucidity of phrase, and the other of an engaging, bookish, American talent, too verbose to be memorable and too intellectual to be moving. And not only would they differ about his poetic character: there would be a sharp division of opinion about his poetic stature.

Only an experiment of this kind could bring home how little the last twenty years have added to Auden's reputation. Why should this be so? He has remained energetic and productive; his later work shows the same readiness to experiment coupled with new and (in theory) maturer themes; he has not lost his sense of humour. And yet no one is going to justify his place in literary history by *The Shield of Achilles* any more than Swinburne's is justified by *Poems and Ballads: Third Series*.

The appearance of his latest collection, *Homage to Clio*,[1] marks the end of the third decade of Auden's poetic life and does not alter the fact that almost all we value is still confined to its first ten years. We need not remind ourselves of his virtues—the wide-angled rhetoric, the seamless lyricism, the sudden gripping dramatizations—but to understand what succeeded it we must understand to what extent his poetry was of its time. He was, of course, the first 'modern' poet, in that he could employ modern properties unselfconsciously ('A solitary truck, the last / Of shunting in the Autumn'), but he was modern also by embracing a kind of neo-Wordsworthianism which, in an effort to put poetry at the service of the working-class movement, called it 'memorable speech' and made no theoretical distinction between *Paradise Lost* and *'The Young Fellow Called Dave'*.

[1] W. H. Auden, *Homage to Clio* (London: Faber, 1960).

This view held that if the poet were not concerned with the historic necessities of the age and akin to the healer and the explorer (typical figures!) his work would be deservedly disregarded.

Few poets since Pope have been so committed to their period. It is not only that to be at home in Auden's poetry we must recognize Bishop Barnes, Coghlan's coffin, Van der Lubbe and all the personalia of 'Last Will and Testament' (*Letters from Iceland*, with Louis MacNeice); we shall also find the Depression, strikes, the hunger marchers; we shall find Spain and China; and above all we shall encounter not only the age's properties but its obsessions: feeling inferior to the working class, a sense that things needed a new impetus from somewhere, seeing out of the corner of an eye the rise of Fascism, the persecution of the Jews, the gathering dread of the next war that was half projected guilt about the last:

> The chairs are being brought in from the garden,
> The summer talk stopped on that savage coast
> Before the storms, after the guests and birds:
> In sanatoriums they laugh less and less,
> Less certain of cure; and the loud madman
> Sinks now into a more terrible calm.

It is precisely this dominant and ubiquitous unease that lay at the centre of Auden's verse and which he was so apt to express. How quickly, for example, he seized on the symbol of 'the Struggle', 'the game . . . that tends to become like a war'; in other writers as well as Auden this concept of the 'Two Sides' was used time and again to represent the young against the old, the poor against the rich, the healthy against the diseased, the class struggle, Spain, the coming war. And whereas the conflict was originally seen as victorious (*The Orators*), as the Thirties wore on disaster became more and more likely. It was in this atmosphere that Auden's sensitivity was quickened and his perceptions heightened, perceptions not only of

> Ten thousand of the desperate marching by
> Five feet, six feet, seven feet high.

but also how

> In the houses
> The little pianos are closed, and a clock strikes.

I have stressed this identification not for its own sake but to make clear why Auden's outlook was completely dislocated when it ceased. As everyone knows, this came about in two ways—by the outbreak of war in 1939, and by Auden's departure for America a few months earlier. At one stroke he lost his key subject and emotion—Europe and the fear of war—and abandoned his audience together with their common dialect and concerns. For a different sort of poet this might have been less important. For Auden it seems to have been irreparable.

His immediate reaction was to take a header into literature. Previously few writers had been named in his pages—Lawrence, Owen, Katherine Mansfield—which was eloquent of his 'deep abhorrence'

> If I caught anyone preferring Art
> To Life and Love and being Pure-in-Heart.

Now there came a whole flood. One cannot but notice the shift in tone from the disrespectful reference in 1937 to 'Daunty, Gouty, Shopkeeper, the three Supreme Old Masters' to the eulogistic invocation in the *New Year Letter* of 1941:

> Great masters who have shown mankind
> An order it has yet to find, . . .
> Now large, magnificent, and calm,
> Your changeless presences disarm
> The sullen generations, still
> The fright and fidget of the will,
> And to the growing and the weak
> Your final transformations speak, &c., &c.

Auden no longer parries the question 'Who are the great?' with the poet's qualification

> you must ask me who
> Have written just as I'd have liked to do.

He has become a reader rather than a writer, and the 'Notes'—eighty-one pages of James, Kierkegaard, Chekhov, Rilke, Nietzsche, Goethe, Milton, Spinoza and so on against fifty-eight pages of text—gave warning how far literature was replacing experience as material for his verse.

Some critics might think this legitimate. The likely consequences, however—loss of vividness, a tendency to rehearse themes already existing as literature, a certain abstract windiness—were very much the criticisms Auden now invited. His first three American books were long, ambitious, and stylistically variegated, yet held the reader's attention only sporadically if at all. The rambling intellectual stew of *New Year Letter* was hardly more than a vamp-till-ready; *The Sea and the Mirror*, which appeared in 1945, was an unsuccessful piece of literary inbreeding; while although in *For the Time Being*, also 1945, Auden works hard to reinvigorate the Christian myth as a poetic subject, he is too often chilly ('weave in us the freedom of / The actually deficient on / The justly actual') or silly ('It was visiting day at the vinegar works'). As for *The Age of Anxiety* in 1948, I never finished it, and have never met anyone who has.

Now, contrary to what has sometimes been suggested, it is no crime to write dull or even bad poetry. Even if it were, Auden has earned a reprieve many times over. Despite the bitter disappointment of the Forties for his admirers, it was really no more than they could have expected of a poet who had elected to remake his entire poetic equipment. The question was how soon he would get reorganized. His continued productivity, intermittent successes such as the speeches of Caliban and Herod (Auden has always been brilliant at prose parody—did he write 'Hetty to Nancy'?) and the sonnets in *The Quest* gave grounds for hope. If his poetry could once take root again in the life surrounding him rather than in his reading (perhaps *The Age of Anxiety* was a first struggling attempt to do this), then a new Auden might result, a *New Yorker* Walt Whitman viewing the American scene through lenses coated with a European irony.

Ten years and three books later, one has to admit that this hope was over-optimistic. True, with *Nones* (1952), *The Shield of Achilles* (1955) and now *Homage to Clio* Auden has returned to the shorter poem as his medium: the Supreme Old Masters have retreated (though they have been replaced to some extent by the stale personages of classical mythology), and his themes have become more personal and have a greater chance of interesting. He has begun to produce a kind of long reflective poem in a stabilized tone in which every facet of his subject is exhibited at leisure, 'The Bucolics' in *The Shield of Achilles*, 'Ode to Gaea', 'In Praise of Limestone', and now 'Homage to Clio' and 'Goodbye to the Mezzogiorno':

> Out of a gothic North, the pallid children
> Of a potato, beer-or-whiskey

> Guilt culture, we behave like our fathers and come
> Southward into a sunburnt otherwhere
>
> Of vineyards, baroque, *la bella figura*,
> To these feminine townships where men
> Are males, and siblings untrained in a ruthless
> Verbal in-fighting as it is taught
>
> In Protestant rectories upon drizzling
> Sunday afternoons. . . .

These poems are agreeable and ingenious essays, more closely directed than his earlier excursions such as 'August for the people' or 'Here on the cropped grass', but their poetic pressure is not high—nor, indeed, is it intended to be. They read like the reflections of a practised and celebrated writer with no particular worries who is free to indulge his tastes in reading and travel, and as such we can accept them. Auden has not, in fact, gone in the direction one hoped: he has not adopted America or taken root, but has pursued an individual and cosmopolitan path which has precluded the kind of identification that seemed so much a part of his previous successes.

There would be no point in mentioning this if it did not seem to have had regrettable poetic consequences. Firstly, although he has by now recovered a dialect, it is all too often an extraordinarily jarring one, a wilful jumble of Age-of-Plastic nursery rhyme, ballet folklore, and Hollywood Lemprière served up with a lisping archness that sets the teeth on edge:

> Romance? Not in this weather. Ovid's charmer
> Who leads the quadrilles in Arcady, boy-lord
> Of hearts who can call their Yes and No their own,
> Would, madcap that he is, soon die of cold or sunstroke:
> Their lives are in firmer hands: that old grim She
> Who makes the blind dates for the hatless genera
> Creates their country matters.

Such is, explicitly, the kind of thing he likes:

> Be subtle, various, ornamental, clever,
> And do not listen to those critics ever
> Whose crude provincial gullets crave in books
> Plain cooking made still plainer by plain cooks.

This view must be what permits lines like 'Just reeling off their names is ever so comfy' or:

> She mayn't be all She might be but She *is* our Mum.

Are there people who talk this dialect, or is it how Auden talks to himself?

Secondly, one cannot escape the conclusion that in some way Auden, never a pompous poet, has now become an unserious one. For some time he has insisted that poetry is a game, with the elements of a crossword puzzle: it is 'the luck of verbal playing'. One need not be a romantic to suspect that this attitude will produce poetry exactly answering to that description. Here again it seems that Auden was happier when his work had an extraneous social function, and if he feels that poetry is fundamentally unserious otherwise, it is a pity he parted from it, for lack of serious intention too often means lack of serious effect.

In the end that is what our discontent comes down to: Auden no longer touches our imaginations. My guess is that the peculiar insecurity of pre-war England sharpened his talent in a way that nothing else has, or that once 'the next War' really arrived everything since has seemed to him an anticlimax. But these are only guesses. Something, after all, led him to write 'A poet's prayer' in *New Year Letter*: 'Lord, teach me to write so well that I shall no longer want to.' In any case it is our loss.

1960

The Blending of Betjeman

One of the most striking passages in this first instalment of Mr Betjeman's verse autobiography[1] describes how, as a schoolboy in Highgate, he fancied that his poems were 'as good as Campbell now':

> And so I bound my verse into a book,
> *The Best of Betjeman*, and handed it
> To one who, I was told, liked poetry—
> The American master, Mr. Eliot.

The scene is worthy of a nineteenth-century narrative painter: 'The Infant Betjeman Offers His Verses to the Young Eliot'. For, leaving aside their respective poetic statures, it was Eliot who gave the modernist poetic movement its charter in the sentence, 'Poets in our civilization, as it exists at present, must be *difficult.*' And it was Betjeman who, forty years later, was to bypass the whole light industry of exegesis that had grown up round his fatal phrase, and prove, like Kipling and Housman before him, that a direct relation with the reading public could be established by anyone prepared to be moving and memorable.

It is ironic that, up to a point, the poetry of Betjeman (and also that of his contemporary W. H. Auden) is precisely the kind Mr Eliot foresaw. 'Our civilization', the passage continues, 'comprehends great variety and complexity, and this variety and complexity, playing upon a refined sensibility, must produce various and complex results.' So it has! Betjeman does more than genuflect before Victorian lamp brackets and shudder at words like 'serviette': despite the flailing introduction to *First and Last Loves*, he is an accepter, not a rejecter, of our time, registering 'dear old, bloody old England' with robustness, precision and a vivacious affection that shimmers continually between laughter and rage, his sense of the past casting long perspectives behind every observation. And the age has accepted him, in the most unambiguous way possible: it has made him a television personality.

[1] John Betjeman, *Summoned by Bells* (London: John Murray, 1960).

Some awareness of the existence of this personality has no doubt
gone towards the publication of *Summoned by Bells*. For Christmas is
coming, and what more tempting to the trade than Mr Betjeman's
autobiography? And actually handling the book (relentless pre-
publication serialization has made this almost an anticlimax) does
little to allay our fears: the Old Style Antique, the regressive
ornamentation (the endpapers are horrible), and solemn-funny
chapter synopses ('inexplicable desires—attempt to explain them')
make one dread that Betjeman is putting on an act for the gallery.
Fortunately this is not so. *Summoned by Bells* comprises nine chapters
of the kind of reminiscential verse Mr Betjeman has already given us
('Original Sin on the Sussex Coast'), demurely pedestrian, Leica-
sharp in detail, recounting by selective episodic narrative his life from
boyhood to involuntary departure from Oxford, done not in the spirit
of farcical or shocking revelation (much of his material is as familiar as
his manner), but with an eager pleasure in re-creating incidents and
circumstances that still have power to move him. The personality is in
abeyance. And indeed what first emerges from a reading of this poem
is that Betjeman, though an original, is not an egoist: rather, he is that
rare thing, an extrovert sensitive, not interested in himself but in the
experiences being himself enables him to savour, including that of
being himself. He may write:

> An only child, deliciously apart,
> Misunderstood and not like other boys.
> Deep, dark and pitiful I saw myself.

but his handling of 'personal' situations is oddly detached:

> . . . Then what, by God, was this—
> This tender, humble, unrequited love
> For Biddy Walsham? What the worshipping
> That put me off my supper, fixed my hair
> Thick with Anzora for the dance tonight?
> The Talbot-Darracq, with its leather seats
> And Biddy in beside me!

Here the proper names all stand on much the same emotional footing,
and time and again in scenes where interest might be expected to
focus on the author's feelings we find it instead shifting to the details:

> I scraped my wrist along the unstained oak
> And slammed the door against my father's weight—

And ran like mad and ran like mad and ran . . .
'I'm free! I'm free!' The open air was warm
And heavy with the scent of flowering mint,
And beetles waved on bending leagues of grass,
And all the baking countryside was kind.

None the less, the connecting theme of the narrative is highly personal, not dissimilar to Samuel Butler's 'I had to steal my own birthright. I stole it and was bitterly punished. But I saved my soul alive.' Only son of a forceful father and semi-invalid mother, Mr Betjeman was expected to carry on the family business of making luxury articles of fine wood, glass and silver for sale by Asprey and Mappin and Webb. He refused—implicitly, when young, by incompetence; explicitly, when older, with defiance. This was a grave defection for an only son, and Mr Betjeman does not minimize his father's anger ('Bone-lazy, like my eldest brother Jack, / A rotten, low, deceitful little snob') nor his own feelings of remorse ('A sense of guilt increasing with the years') that spread like a discoloration across his whole life. The excuse he gives is single and unvarying: 'I was a poet. That was why I failed.'

The lame self-importance of this attitude must be interpreted by what we know of Betjeman today. Destined to be one of those rare persons who can say, 'Simply the thing I am shall make me live,' he was holding off with an instinctive obstinate wisdom anything that might hinder contact with the factors that were to form his particular nature. And one by one we see them enter—Cornwall and the sea, Oxford and church architecture, London and railway stations; then religion, announced by the strangest of all the bells that summon him throughout the narrative—it hangs on an elm bough, beaten by a bearded book-reading priest outside a ruined church; then, lastly, Magdalen, where for the first time his sullenly smouldering character bursts into violent flame, and the extraordinary blend of interests that we label Betjemania becomes recognizable. Thus although the book ends in ostensible failure ('Failed in Divinity!'), it is really a triumph. Betjeman has made it. He has become Betjeman.

The value of this poem will no doubt be hotly disputed. On chilly battlements the critical sentries are continually aware of the spectre of 90,000 copies of *Collected Poems* ('Shall I strike at it with my *Partisan*?'), and the thought that they have sold without a single subsidized summer-school seminar makes them doubly vigilant. For the moment it is enough to name two of its virtues. First, Betjeman has an astonishing command of detail, both visual and circumstantial. It makes the surface of his flat, *Task*-like blank verse (resigned to swallowing anything, even 'Don't throw old blades into the w.c.') glitter like John Brett's *Stonebreaker*, whether in sustained felicities:

> The lofty entrance hall, the flights of stairs,
> The huge expanse of sunny drawing-room,
> Looking for miles across the chimney-pots
> To spired St. Pancras and the dome of Paul's;

or in accumulation of flotsam from its author's remarkable memory:

> In late September, in the conker time,
> When Poperinghe and Zillebeke and Mons
> Boomed with five-nines, large sepia gravures
> Of French, Smith-Dorrien and Haig were given
> Gratis with each half-pound of Brooke Bond's tea.
> A neighbour's son had just been killed at Ypres;
> Another had been wounded. *Rainbow* came
> On Wednesdays—with the pranks of Tiger Tim,
> And Bonnie Bluebell and her magic gloves.

This imaginative and precise evocation is part of the poem's purpose, and is accomplished with splendid competence.

Secondly, although it remains a mystery how Mr Betjeman can avoid the traps of self-importance, exhibitionism, silliness, sentimentality and boredom, he continues to do so. Why should we accept his teddy bear when we want to stuff Sebastian Flyte's down his throat? How, without embarrassing us, can he write:

> Poor mother, walking bravely on the lawn,
> Her body one huge toothache! Would she die?
> And if she died could I forgive myself?

How, without alienating us, can he confess his social climbing into 'the leisured set in Canterbury Quad', or admit his infatuation with the Firbanky world of Harold Acton ('My dears, I want to rush into the fields / And slap raw meat with lilies') without attracting to himself some of the impatience that today it rouses in us? No doubt sincerity is the answer, a sincerity as unselfconscious as it is absolute, but it is helped by his own attitude to himself, scrupulously free of what they no doubt called 'side' at Marlborough and disinfected by his palpably greater interest in things other than himself. It may irritate us that it should be so marketable. But one finishes the book with a considerable respect for this almost moral tactfulness. It will be interesting to see if it can be maintained as Mr Betjeman's memory, like Poe's pendulum, sweeps closer and closer to the present.

1960

Missing Chairs

Very little comic poetry comes off—very little poetry of any kind comes off, actually, but the success ratio is higher in the straight kind—for preoccupation with the short, escapable, unimportant periods when life is funny to the exclusion of the long, inescapable, important periods when it is serious implies, ultimately (and sometimes immediately), mediocre taste. It is a shock, therefore, to hear that Ogden Nash bears the awesome title of America's Most Quoted Poet. More, he lives by his work. Clearly, he is saying a lot of things that a lot of people are willing to pay to see said, and merits the longer look at his talents which this volume[1] affords.

Most readers will already have met his stylistic patent: the uneven lines shutting suddenly like a pair of lop-sided nutcrackers with half an assonance still hanging out:

> Oh, sometimes I sit around and think, what would you do if you
> were up a dark alley and there was Caesar Borgia,
> And he was coming torgia . . .

Or sometimes the second line is the longer, and one waits suspensefully as the rhyme slowly teeters down the incline like a pin-table ball, knocking into every obstruction before holing up in the 20,000:

> And his host said, Oh yes, and steer away from education when
> you talk to the Senator,
> Because somebody said his seventeen-year-old nephew would
> have to burn down the schoolhouse to get out of the third grade
> and his nephew overheard them and did burn down the
> schoolhouse, including the music master and the janitor . . .

This inherently ludicrous device gathers force when the verse is read in quantity, however, because one begins to sense a parallel between it and Nash's normal subject-matter. 'What is Life?' he asks:

[1] Ogden Nash, *Collected Verse from 1929 On* (London: Dent, 1961).

Life is stepping down a step or sitting in a chair
And it isn't there.
Life is not having been told that the man has just waxed the floor,
It is pulling doors marked PUSH and pushing doors marked PULL and
    not noticing notices which say PLEASE USE OTHER DOOR . . .

Nash's let-down rhymes and wait-for-it metrics are perfect stylistic
equivalents for the missing chairs and slow burns of which civilized
masculine living is compounded: waiting for women, putting up with
children, social boredom and humiliation, having to work, the
agenbite of inwit. In fact, if it is long inescapable etc. periods you
want, Nash couldn't pour them straighter:

Ah woe, woe, woe, man was created to live by the sweat of his brow,
And it doesn't make any difference if your brow was moist yesterday
    and the day before, you've still got to get it moist again right now,
And you know deep in your heart that you will have to continue
    keeping it dewy
Right up to the time when somebody at the Club says, I suppose we
    ought to go to what's-his-name's funeral, who won the fifth at
    Bowie?
That's a nasty outlook to face.
But it's what you get for belonging to the human race.

He is, in fact, in line with those humorists who make you laugh at
things not because they are funny but because laughing at them makes
it easier to stand them—which is, I suppose, the same as calling him a
sort of honorary serious writer after all.

He isn't always as good as this. Whenever he departs from his own
peculiar half-acre he is no better than any anonymous calendar writer
or comic-verse merchant. The collection, too, is made up in that
American way that seems frightened of saying what books the poems
came from and when they were published. But all in all it is an ideal
present for the middle-aged, respectable, hard-working husband and
parent—in fact, for you. And when you have finished the poems you
can go back and read the list of their titles ('Portrait of the Artist as a
Prematurely Aged Man'; 'Ask Daddy, He Won't Know'; 'I'll Eat My
Split-Level Turkey in the Breezeway'; 'Come On In, the Senility Is
Fine'; 'Oafishness Sells Good, Like an Advertisement Should'). It is a
poem in itself.

                                                            1961

Masters' Voices

Had the history of technology meshed a little differently with the history of literature I might now be able to lay reverently on my turntable a thick black 78 r.p.m. with a Globe label reading *Will Shaxsper: Sundrie Sonnets* (recording supervif'd by my Lord Verulam), and, after a vertiginous crackling pause, hear in almost incomprehensible Elizabethan, 'From fairest creatures we desire increase, / That thereby beauty's rose might never die . . .' What should I gain if I could? Concede at once the souvenir value: it would be fascinating as a photograph, or J. P. Morgan's lock of Keats's hair. But would Will's Warwickshire, or for that matter Wordsworth's Westmorland, have any more relevance to my reading of their poems (once my excitement had died down) than Tennyson's Lincolnshire (which in fact we have) to 'The Northern Farmer'?

Perhaps this is to begin in the middle. But when spoken poetry is mentioned, all my antiquarian rage boils at the thought of the legions of pre-1928 tenors and sopranos we preserved when nobody thought to record, say, Hardy or Lawrence. Others feel differently. 'Poets nowadays', as Mr John Wain, director of last summer's 'Poetry at the Mermaid', pointed out in its prospectus, 'make records of their work as naturally as they print it. Does this mean that the printed page will cede first place to the living voice?' Is the poem, as it were, the 'score' that must be brought to life by performance? Or must we share the dubiety with which Dylan Thomas regarded the whole business of 'travelling 200 miles just to recite, in my fruity voice, poems that would not be appreciated and could, anyway, be read in books'?

There are one or two distinctions to be made before an answer can be given. First, however appropriate the medium was for ballads in the rush-strewn hall or Homer smiting his blooming lyre, its public application to modern meditative non-communal poems affects me as the choir of a thousand Boy Scouts reciting 'The Lake Isle of Innisfree' did W. B. Yeats. To readopt it would seem to me regression, like moving one's lips when reading silently. Not that I expect complete agreement: many poets are paranoiac bores, and those impure assemblages known as poetry readings are a wonderful new way of being paranoiacally boring. But as my first axiom I should lay down that the only desirable form of spoken modern poetry is that which whispers in the corner (or corners, these days) in hi-fi.

Secondly, who is to read it? The price of having the poem re-created in the element in which it was conceived (as they say) is the interposing of a new factor, the reader, between me and the poem. He will not read it with the emphases that I should use, and this will irritate me. Or he will have the kind of voice I associate with brown-eyed young men called Frank. Or, if the reader is a lady, she may use that tone so popular among her kind which indicates that in the very act of enunciation she has perceived in the poem an unbelievably obscene acrostic. None of this seems to me an advantage. But suppose it is read by the author? Here a new contention is raised: can one legitimately quarrel with any aspect of an author's reading of his own poem? Isn't he supplying a definitive, authoritative rendering from which it will ever after be 'wrong' to depart?

Yes and no. I should hate to find myself in agreement with the kind of critic who denies the poet supreme authority regarding his work—seeing nothing in his explanation of a poem, for example, but an attempt to limit its suggestiveness—and for this reason I should contend that if an author has read a passage fiercely, ironically, humorously, sadly, then for ever after to read it softly, idealistically, seriously and gaily will be a smart bit of wrong-headedness, like *Hamlet* in space dress. But one's quarrel with the author's reading does not usually take this form. To answer 'yes' to this question too often commits one for ever after to reading the poem as if it were one of the sections of the Sale and Movement of Poultry (Domestic) Act, 1943. Poets, in fact, too often do their poems less than justice, and why shouldn't readers who have flexible and expressive voices and have been trained to use them show what music lies in the cold print? One is forced to admit this is legitimate.

Yet, now we are getting more and more examples of authors' own readings, I doubt whether authors read as badly as they are popularly supposed to do. I remember, for instance, putting on a record of Mr Eliot reading 'The Love Song of J. Alfred Prufrock' to show an Italian visitor what his voice was like, and though I had intended to stop it after perhaps thirty seconds I found myself letting it go to the end. And yet Eliot is not supposed to be a good reader. Again, no one could throw his poems away with more contemptuous dryness than

Mr Graves, but should we prefer them read with more voluptuous intonation? I think not. Earlier ages said: 'The style is the man.' We might add: 'And the voice is the style.'

I am a little taken aback to find that Francis Berry has anticipated me in his new book[1] with a full-scale contention that 'style is voice':

> 'A style' has therefore become synonymous with 'a private idiom'. But the 'style' of an actual speech, of any oral delivery, is as much conditioned by the speaker's voice as by his choice of language and his individual manner of thinking and feeling. Indeed, it can control his choice of language, his manner of thinking, his rhythms . . . .

Mr Berry contrasts the 'oes and aes' of Tennyson with the shrillness of Shelley ('I shall never be able to bear his voice—it would kill me'— Hogg): 'the poetry of Shelley requires for its saying (and hearing) one kind of voice which Shelley had, and the poetry of Tennyson requires for its saying (and hearing) a quite other kind of voice which Tennyson had.' If a man's style changes, it may be because his voice changes: 'what is called Milton's late style, in contrast to his early style, records a change of the physical voice. The voice deepened. . . .' This is because a poet always thinks of his poems as being read in his own voice—that is, unless he is a dramatic poet such as Shakespeare, when the voices he imagines are those of his company. The fact that the 'voice' of the Shakespearian hero ages (Romeo, Hamlet, Lear) may simply be a reflection of the ageing of Burbage.

Like myself, Mr Berry regrets that technology did not give us sound recording earlier: 'What would we not give for a gramophone record of Wordsworth . . . or of Keats saying his odes? or of Hopkins declaiming "The Wreck of the Deutschland"?' But in fact these are unnecessary. For Mr Berry 'the last stage of acquaintance with a poet occurs when one can hear the voice in the absence of the text, when the signs on the page no longer act as intermediary but instantaneously conduct.' Subjective? Not a bit of it. The poem's vowels, mood, pitch and so on 'contribute towards, and compel, a timbre and a series of vocal harmonics, that only one voice could produce.'

If I hesitate to call this boloney, it is partly because I cannot disprove it (any more than he can prove it), and partly because I seem to have said something of the sort myself. It is, indeed, easier to go at least

[1] *Poetry and the Physical Voice* (London: Routledge, 1962).

part of the way with Mr Berry by instinct than to adduce any real evidence for doing so. To read his book, however, is to realize how many of our assumptions about poetry come from always meeting it in printed form and not in the voice of its author.

The question remains, though: is spoken poetry—poems read by their authors in a way that lets us listen to them without distraction— a good thing? Is it better than reading? I still can't believe it is. True, one actually hears the rough mouth-music of vowels and consonants and all that, but he is a poor reader who cannot imagine that for himself. It prohibits skipping, perhaps, but equally allows your mind to wander. And if the poem is unfamiliar, how much harder it is to grasp without its punctuation, stanza shape, and knowing how far one is from the end! These may be the objections of someone hopelessly enslaved by an out-of-date reading technique. Perhaps we should not be regressing if we regained the Elizabethan ability to listen, which enabled them to take in *Macbeth* as we do Maigret. But for me, in the end, it comes down to a certain restless resentment at having the book taken away from me: I want to do it myself.

Is spoken poetry a bad thing, then—a gimmick of the professor just back from America, a toy for the tired schoolteacher, a way of meeting girls? No, equally strongly. Though I remain convinced that the reader's first encounter with the poem must be a silent, active one, an absorption of spelling and stanza arrangement as much as paraphrasable meaning and corrective historical knowledge, there comes a moment with any poem that we have really taken to ourselves when we want to hear its author read it. We want to confirm our conviction that he would quicken the pace here, throw away an irony there, or perhaps our curiosity is just for what his voice can add, something we cannot define until we hear it. Well, for such ages as succeed our own this will be possible in the case of poets writing after 1930, and knowledge of them will be richer in consequence.

The most interesting production in this field lately is Donald Davie's *A Sequence For Francis Parkman*.[1] Here the publisher, Mr George Hartley, has taken Mr Wain at his word and produced a new kind of book: he offers, in conventional printed form, a sequence of seven new poems by Dr Davie, but in addition he includes in a pocket in the back flap a 7" LP (yes, 33⅓ r.p.m.) of the author reading them. This has never been done before to my knowledge, and I therefore

[1] Listenbooks 1 (Hessle: Marvell Press, 1961).

salute a landmark in publishing history. Its only drawback as a medium for publishing new verse is that at present it seems to get sent to the hack that does the records instead of the distinguished critic who notices poetry.

It is, perhaps, a little recherché to inaugurate a series: neither the sleeve nor Dr Davie's mock-archaic marginal notes tell me who Parkman is: one of his American friends, perhaps, as the poems all deal with the early colonial days—British and French—in North America. If the author does not quite escape his own accusation of 'sipping at names', he provides a tough commentary on such ironies as that an Ottawa who once tried to burn Detroit was called Pontiac. His reading is appropriate, perhaps just a little mannered: in places it is rather like having your tutor read you an essay. My copy suffered from some surface noise. The next Listenbook is rumoured to be by Kingsley Amis, which should really be something.

Selected Poems by Louis MacNeice (Argo) gives the author's reading of two dozen of his poems plus a section from *Autumn Journal*. Here the voice is not the style—at least, not if you think of Mr MacNeice, as I do, as poetically a sophisticated, almost dressing-gowned figure, dropping epithets into place effortlessly and exactly. His voice is hard and at times harsh, with a lurking Northern Irish accent (suitably exaggerated for 'Carrickfergus'), and makes such poems as 'The Sunlight on the Garden' and 'Nuts in May' much craggier and more forceful than one remembered them. The *Autumn Journal* extract (mistitled 'Autumn Sequel') is so good that one would welcome a record of the whole poem.

And why not? For if John Betjeman's *Summoned by Bells* (Argo) is not the whole poem, the cutting is so skilful that one hardly notices. I know that Betjeman, like Peter Simple, Ornette Coleman and frilled evening shirts, makes some people swell up and turn black: if you didn't like the book, then probably you won't like the record even more. But for all that this is wonderful reading: even, unhurried, inclining now a little to sanctimony, now to self-reproof; utterly clear; accented at times with a suitable mischievousness. A pity it does not include the actual bells the BBC gave us when he read the poem on the Third, but that is the only criticism that occurs to me: in its quiet way, a virtuoso performance. Dylan Thomas's *Quite Early One Morning* (Caedmon) is equally so in a noisier and more familiar manner; here the voice and the style are indissoluble, and the material four prose pieces, 'Reminiscences of Childhood', 'A Visit to Grandpa's',

'Holiday Memory', and the embryo of *Under Milk Wood* that gives the record its title. Like many Welsh voices, Thomas's has a rich fraudulence that sets you chuckling even before—perhaps I should say even after—the adjectival combination-punching begins, and there are people who think this Sketches-by-Dai-Boz manner his strongest claim on posterity. Certainly Betjeman and Thomas have voices in the platform-entertainer sense, whereas Davie and MacNeice haven't. It all makes for variety.

The one certain thing is that companies are going to go on issuing records of poets and poetry no matter what the aesthetics of the thing are, and I for one am not prepared to grumble. Take *Authopoetry No. 1—British* (Poets Lot), for instance—readings of a few of their own poems each by Christopher Logue, Thomas Blackburn, Jon Silkin, Charles Causley and Roy MacGregor-Hastie. This is a well-produced (except that the sleeve has no details of what is being read) and enterprising record. Whether or not you buy it will depend largely on your estimate of the worth of the poets represented, but I enjoyed Mr Logue's Demon King contributions at any rate. And suppose it had been made in 1598—Thomas Churchyard, Robert Southwell, Thomas Watson, Anthony Munday, and—what was that name again? Will . . . ?

1962

Mrs Hardy's Memories

In *The Early Life of Thomas Hardy* (1928), now admittedly autobiographical, Hardy printed in 'Chapter V: St. Juliot' what he called 'The latter part of Mrs (Emma Lavinia) Hardy's MS, found after her death, and entitled *Some Recollections*'. It described his meeting with Miss Gifford, as she then was, and their subsequent marriage. Now it has been rediscovered by Miss Evelyn Hardy, and printed in its entirety, showing that Hardy chose to print only 18 pages of the total 74, and made a number of omissions from what he did print. This book[1] is therefore a major addition to the scanty biographical materials available about Hardy and his circle.

The figure of the first Mrs Hardy flickers ominously on the cloud of anecdote and hearsay that overhangs the marriage. Despite Hardy's scrupulous destruction of private papers, and his reticence during the fifteen years of his life after her death, it has long been accepted that Hardy's first marriage became unhappy sometime in the 1890s. Opinion has differed on the degree of this unhappiness. The Hardys continued to live under the same roof, to entertain, to visit. But Sir Newman Flower tells us that Hardy built a private entrance to his study so that he could enter and leave the house without hindrance. Edmund Gosse believed that the 'wells of human hope had been poisoned for him by some condition of which we know nothing'. And we have *Jude the Obscure*, Hardy's last novel that his wife tried to get suppressed, where pain and unhappiness suggest a spirit, in Lawrence's phrase, 'like a naked nerve on air'. 'A marriage should be dissolvable as soon as it becomes a cruelty to either of the parties,' he wrote in 1912. Some of the stories in Carl J. Weber's *Hardy of Wessex* (1940) make it hard for us to accept Weber's contention that Hardy and his first wife were not 'cruelly mismated'.

What was wrong? Much of the blame may be laid on Emma's

[1] Emma Hardy, *Some Recollections*, edited by Evelyn Hardy and Robert Gittings; together with some relevant poems by Thomas Hardy (London: OUP, 1961).

character. Her unhesitant energy, which was what had attracted
Hardy in the first place, seemed to turn as years went by into
petulance, delusions, and religious mania, and was not taken up by
children. Her husband's very uncomplaining meekness seems to
have aroused an unpleasant streak of bullying and nagging in her.
His literary renown, and patronage by Edwardian society hostesses,
inevitably relegated her to a secondary position at social functions,
making her seek compensation by implying that she herself revised
her husband's manuscripts, and that there were upstairs several
momentous works by her that he would not, out of jealousy, allow to
be published. Lastly there was the question of religion. Mrs Hardy
was the niece of a Canon of Worcester, and bitterly resented Hardy's
agnosticism and outspokenness against lip-service to conventional
morality. For this reason she sought to persuade Dr Richard Garnett
to induce Hardy to destroy *Jude the Obscure*. Since on its publication
the Bishop of Wakefield wrote to the papers saying that he had
personally burned his copy, we can see that Mrs Hardy was attuned
to the kind of opinion that Hardy hated and despised so much. She
left open Bibles about the house. In 1912 she published *Spaces*, 'an
exposition of Great Truths', giving an account of the afterlife, in a
turgid sub-Apocalyptic style.

It is possible that Hardy's own rather unnerving taste for the
macabre, his temperamental sunlessness, and his life-long intense
awareness of women, exacerbated Emma's peculiarities. Certainly he
was at a loss how to deal with her except by patience and avoiding the
occasion, as with the separate entrance. At times he thought her
delusions and fits of impatience were a kind of hereditary instability:
her father had had moods of depression and drunkenness, and
Hardy was often afraid that he could see 'the figure and visage of
madness seeking for a home'. After her sudden death he found three
manuscripts in her hand: *Some Recollections, What I Thought of My
Husband*, and *The Pleasures of Heaven and the Pains of Hell*. The last two
he burnt.

The other is what we have here. To call it surprising, when a quarter
of it has been published for over thirty years, may seem ingenuous.
Yet there is a breathless vivid innocence, a light equable sanity, about
the pages that are new to us that does not square with what we know
of Mrs Hardy; it reads like a different person altogether:

(My Father) used to argue with her that but for an accident of birth she might have been a follower of Confuscious, but my Mother did not believe in an accident of birth. She was remarkable in the healthy management of her children—hygienic—though not knowing it, or the word either. We had bathings continually in the house and out of it, dips in the open sea, and in the Royal Baths in Union Street, where I used to shiver with delighted apprehension when the high clear voice echoed through the cold passages of the bathing woman who attended, carrying bathing dresses and dry towels about, and shutting people into little dressing rooms which opened on the opposite side giving a view of a high-walled large space full of sea water deepening in the centre with a long middle rope—short ropes and steps at the rooms, and cork-floats, and shouting, laughing bathers—coolness, freshness and saltness most delightful even to remember.

This surprise is such that it takes some time to grasp what she is telling us. Her narrative in fact describes her childhood and youth as the daughter of a solicitor in Plymouth and Bodmin. Later she moved to St. Juliot in Cornwall to help her sister, who married the Rector of that parish, and here met Hardy whom she married in 1874. Despite its colourful surface, her story is not especially happy. Her father, John Attersoll Gifford, gave up his profession when his mother came to live with the family, bringing '£700 a year from the New River Company'; when the old lady died, therefore, 'we had to retrench on account of her income being divided', and they moved to Bodmin in 1860. Before long, 'on account of the dullness of home life and necessity of earning something' (not much hypocrisy here), Emma's sister went as a governess, then as a companion. Their three brothers were, respectively, a civil servant, a master at Plymouth Grammar School, and an official in the Post Office, but the eldest suffered from angina pectoris, which made 'his getting-on frustrated'. This seems to have been a factor in sending the girls to work. The sister, Helen Catherine, next became a companion to an old lady in Tintagel, where she met her future husband, but not before she had fallen from a dog-cart and suffered concussion and 'was never after the same'. On her marriage to this man 'older than herself by many years', she invited Emma to make her home with them, 'which was strange, considering that my sister had had a jealous feeling towards me ever since I had been grown up' (Hardy cut that sentence out when he printed this part in the Early Life).

At St. Juliot, Emma seems to have blossomed. For the first time an element of self-consciousness creeps into the writing: 'The whole parish . . . began to take a fervent interest in the bride's sister. . . . I had taken sedately the openly expressed admiration of "the parson's sister-in-law" by the neighbours of the parish and other odd mortals, up to this date. . . .' She was largely free to do as she liked, and spent long hours riding alone: 'An unforgettable experience to me, scampering up and down the hills on my beloved mare alone, wanting no protection, the rain going down my back often and my hair floating on the wind. I wore a soft deep dark coloured brown habit, longer than to my heels as worn then which had to be caught up to one side when walking, and thrown over the left arm gracefully and carefully. . . .' With a certain self-dramatization she portrays herself as keeping herself free 'until the one intended for me arrived'. This had been many times prophesied (Emma was superstitious). Certainly for a middle-class woman of thirty in north Cornwall in 1870 sixteen miles from the nearest railway station to get a husband some kind of divine intervention seems imperative.

And yet in the end it happened. The long-delayed restoration of the church was put in hand at last, and Mr Crickmay of Weymouth sent his assistant to direct the work. As it happened, the Rector was ill, and his wife ministering to him, when the architect arrived, and it fell to Emma to open the door. 'I thought him much older than he was,' she wrote, to which Hardy—for he of course was the visitor—added 'he being tired', thus striking his own characteristic intensely sad, intensely penetrating note to mingle with Emma's enthusiastic account of their courtship.

For enthusiastic it is. There is no hint of the 'Wicked Man' (Mrs Hardy's sobriquet for her husband, usually abbreviated in her diary to 'the W.M.'), no bitterness of a life thrown away on a social inferior, no envy or jealousy:

I rode my pretty mare Fanny and he walked by my side and I showed him some more of the neighbourhood—the cliffs, along the roads, and through the scattered hamlets, sometimes gazing down at the solemn small shores below where the seals lived, coming out of great caverns very occasionally. We sketched and talked of books: often we walked down the beautiful Vallency Valley to Boscastle harbour where we had to jump over stones and climb over a low wall by rough steps, or get through by narrow pathways to come out on great wide spaces suddenly, with a sparkling little brook going the same way, into which we once lost a tiny picnic-tumbler, and there it is to this day no doubt between two small boulders.

'Scarcely any author and his wife could have had a much more romantic meeting,' she says, and clearly the romance has stayed with her; 'a strange unearthly brilliance shines around our path,' runs the last sentence of the manuscript, 'penetrating and dispersing difficulties with its warmth and glow.' Did she really think this? How did she square it with the separate room, the beautiful titled women, the terrible remarks about marriage in *Jude*? Or was she making up a dream of what reality had been to hide what reality had become?

Whatever the explanation, the effect on Hardy was cataclysmic. In the year following his wife's death, the editors calculate he wrote fifty poems about her. These, and more particularly the group headed 'Veteris vestigia flammae' in *Satires of Circumstance* (1914), make it plain that he was overwhelmed with grief and remorse, that he thought of his late wife only 'as at first, when our day was fair', and that as soon in 1913 as he could (he was seventy-two) he went to Plymouth, St. Juliot, and all other places where he and Emma had been in the early 1870s. Some of the most affecting poems of this time ('After a Journey', 'At Castle Boterel', and others) rest on the contrast between their early meetings and his present lonely revisiting: the editors reprint these, with notes, as a kind of appendix.

Their purpose in doing this is the secondary purpose of the book: to demonstrate that in a number of Hardy's poems direct verbal parallel exists with Emma's manuscript, suggesting that Hardy was drawing not on his memory but on his wife's recollections. The impressiveness of these parallels varies. When a poem describes something both Hardys witnessed, as for example the loss of the picnic-tumbler in *Under the Waterfall*, what Hardy remembers is surely inseparable from what her manuscript brought back to his mind. When a parallel exists in a description of something he could not have witnessed, as in poems about Emma's childhood in Plymouth, the case for a borrowing is of course stronger. Best of all is when the editors use the manuscript to make clear what Hardy was referring to in contexts that have hitherto been thought unidentifiable or fictional, as when they place 'During Wind and Rain' in the Gifford family in Plymouth, even down to the pet fowl. Elsewhere the references are more tenuous. I see no reason to accept their suggestion that the woman in 'Lonely Days' was Emma Hardy.

The interest of the book does not, however, end here. If it does not tell us what went wrong with Hardy's marriage, it at least explains why it happened. Nothing in Emma's recollections suggests that she would make her husband's life a misery; rather the reverse:

> In our back garden bloomed our beloved roses, with some apple and other fruit trees and our great water-casks we had brought. A very little old woman came at regular intervals to clean and freshly tar them getting inside to do so. A miserable attempt to grow vegetables was first made but not continued, and we kept to flowers as before, a tortoise lived happily and appeared occasionally, and a tame seagull lived in the front garden. . . .
>
> The military and navy usually present, *tarlatine* dresses and book-muslin the most frequent kind of dress worn, with ribbons and flowers—and very graceful and light and airy we all looked in them. Splendid sashes and stockings and shoes also adorned us, and our hair floated about in the rush of air made by our whirlings. Never to be forgotten parties!

'How she would have loved / A party today . . .' The editors do not quote this, but it comes unbidden to the mind: 'she was so alive,' as Hardy said, and her manuscript makes this vitality clear to us. Finally, the end of the story is a telling comment on the operation of the poetic impulse in Hardy, and perhaps also in general. No poet could more truly say

> Was ich besitze, seh' ich im Weiten,
> Und was verschwand, wird mir zu Wirklichkeiten.

Not till his first wife had died could Hardy's love poetry for her be written, and then it was mixed with a flood of regret and remorse for what he had lost. This kind of paradox is inseparable from poetic creation, and indeed from life altogether. At times it almost appears a sort of basic insincerity in human affection. At others it seems a flaw built deeply into the working of the emotions, creating an inevitable bias in life towards unhappiness. Indeed, it was itself part of Hardy's subject-matter, and this edition of his wife's one surviving manuscript helps us to understand its operation.

The book contains a number of previously unpublished drawings and photographs of the greatest interest. There is a sketch by Hardy of Emma groping for the picnic-tumbler, dated 19 August 1870.

1962

The Poetry of William Barnes

It is little short of astonishing that we should have had to wait seventy-five years for the complete poems of William Barnes[1]. When he died in 1886, as old as the century, his work was known and admired by Tennyson, Patmore, Hardy, Allingham, Gosse, Palgrave and Quiller-Couch, and when Bridges made a characteristic sneer at 'the supposed emotion of peasants', his correspondent, Gerard Manley Hopkins, replied sharply: 'I hold your contemptuous opinion an unhappy mistake: [Barnes] is a perfect artist and of a most spontaneous inspiration.' Nor was his appeal limited to men of letters: 'an old Domestic Servant' wrote to him in 1869, having found his poems among some books she was dusting: 'Sir, I shook hands with you in my heart, and I laughed and cried by turns.' Nor has time devalued these tributes. Barnes's work is still acknowledged as a unique part of the variegated richness of nineteenth-century English poetry. His view of nature is clear, detailed and shining, full of exquisite pictorial miniatures: his view of human life is perceptive, compassionate and sad. Yet the time when he is read as an English and not a Dorset poet has been slow in coming—if, indeed, it has come at all.

The obstacle, of course, is the Dorset dialect. It is not so much that the eye is put off by Barnes's attempt to render it phonetically ('Lwonesome woodlands! zunny woodlands!'); nor that, once a few simple rules are grasped, it is particularly difficult to follow (not that an age so determined to make hard work out of reading poetry should mind if it were); it is rather that nowadays we are impatient of dialect as such, and regard efforts to perpetuate it as affectation, a futile attempt to deny the historical necessity of usage that a real artist turns to his own ends. We cannot see why Barnes deliberately made his poems to all intents and purposes unreadable: what prompted, in Mr Geoffrey Grigson's phrase, this 'learned perversity'.

[1] *The Poems of William Barnes*, edited by Bernard Jones, 2 vols. (London: Centaur Press, 1962).

Barnes, a schoolmaster for most of his life, was certainly learned: according to Willis D. Jacobs (*William Barnes, Linguist*, Albuquerque, N. Mex., 1952) he knew upwards of sixty languages, 'from Hindustani, Persian, and Russian, to early Saxon, Welsh, and Hebrew'. And like many a polyglot he was also a philologist, the kind that deplores the 'corruption' of English by Greek and Latin borrowings, and advocates such coinages as 'two-horned rede-ship' (dilemma) and 'pushwainling' (perambulator). His love of Dorset dialect was strong and unaffected: he saw it as a kind of Doric English, 'bold and broad', and although when Hardy made a selection of his poems in 1908 he could see this championship as an utterly lost cause, dialect may well have seemed to hold a much more impregnable position in Barnes's early lifetime, before halfpenny newspapers, the Education Act of 1870, and even the railways.

But his use of it was not a mere schoolmasterly fad. Barnes was a remarkable man, a kind of successful Jude Fawley, who began life as the son of a poor smallholder and gradually made his way from village school to town school, a B.D. at Trinity College, Cambridge, and the living of Winterborne Came, near Dorchester. It would have been easy for him to go to London—even the unambitious Hardy managed that—but he seems not to have wanted to. Nor did his education set him at odds with his environment. He liked his family, his neighbours, and the scenes that surrounded them. He saw nothing out of the way in writing poems called 'Grammer A-Crippled' and 'Uncle an' Aunt': Kilvert reports him as saying 'that there was not a line which was not inspired by love for and kindly sympathy with the things and people described'. This being so, it was natural that he should find these things and people indivisible from their own language. If he wrote of joy and sadness, it was their joy and sadness; if it was his own, it came more easily in their accents:

> Since I noo mwore do see your feäce,
>   Up steäirs or down below,
> I'll zit me in the lwonesome pleäce,
>   Where flat-bough'd beech do grow;
> Below the beeches' bough, my love,
>   Where you did never come,
> An' I don't look to meet ye now,
>   As I do look at hwome.

Barnes chose to write in dialect, in short, because it was inextricably bound up, emotionally, with the subjects that moved him to write. Not that he used it exclusively. There are in the present edition some 400 pages of poems in 'national' English against 500 pages of Dorset ones, and in many cases a version in each of the same poem. Comparison of them is interesting, because it shows that while dialect may be antipathetic to us, it carries one unexpectedly modern virtue—that of naturalness, the natural words in their natural order:

> Our minds could never yield the room for all
> Our days at once; but God is ever kind . . .

> Our minds ha' never room enough to call
> Back all sweet days at oonce, but God is kind . . .

Here the dialect is not only smoother, but has the clearer meaning. Barnes liked the colloquial, but he matched it with the artificial: as he chose narrow limits for his life, so he sought intricate stanza forms and devices of rhyme and alliteration from the Welsh and Hebrew. The result is a unique blend of nature and art:

> Aye, at that time our days wer but vew,
> An' our lim's wer but small, an' a-growen;
> An' then the feäir worold wer new,
> An' life wer all hopevul an' gaÿ;
> An' the times o' the sprouten o' leaves,
> An' the cheäk-burnen seasons o' mowen,
> An' binden o' red-headed sheaves,
> Wer all welcome seasons o' jaÿ.

> Then the housen seem'd high, that be low,
> An' the brook did seem wide that is narrow,
> An' time, that do vlee, did goo slow,
> An' veelens now feeble wer strong . . .

This is a fair sample of Barnes's most characteristic mood, for though, as Mr Jones points out, he was by no means unaware of the decline in agricultural conditions ('The Common A-Took In') nor devoid of humour, his sense of the melancholy stealth of time was almost as keen as Hardy's and took precedence. Indeed, the imaginative delicacy of his conceptions ('Woak Hill') at times was superior to Hardy's, though if his work has a deficiency, it is in lacking Hardy's bitter and ironical despair: Barnes is almost too gentle, too submissive and forgiving.

In this edition, described by its editor as 'the first part of a study of Barnes's life and work', all Barnes's poems, both published and unpublished, are brought together for the first time. This is a considerable achievement, involving much searching of columns of nineteenth-century newsprint, and Mr Jones is to be congratulated on carrying out this arduous and long overdue task. One cannot read far without coming upon fresh pieces to delight in, and the notes add much valuable background information. Mr Jones's introduction, however, communicates little of the sensitive enthusiasm Mr Grigson showed in his Muses' Library selection, and even the general reader will miss an index of titles. On a more academic level, the editor's vagueness about the precise number and location of his manuscript sources may be criticized, as may his loose ascription of poems to the *Dorset County Chronicle* without the relevant dates of issue. As this is likely to be the primary source for some time to come for scholar and general reader alike, it seems a pity that more pains were not taken to render it definitive. Finally, for a book of this price the typography is depressingly unstylish.

1962

Frivolous and Vulnerable

Finding Stevie Smith's *Not Waving but Drowning* in a bookshop one Christmas some years ago, I was sufficiently impressed by it to buy a number of copies for random distribution among friends. The surprise this caused them was partly, no doubt, due to the reaction that before the war led us to emend the celebrated cigarette advertisement 'If So-and-So [usually a well-known theatrical personality] offered you a cigarette it would be a Kensitas' by substituting for the brand name the words 'bloody miracle'. But equally they were, I think, bothered to know whether I seriously expected them to admire it. The more I insisted that I did, the more suspicious they became. An unfortunate episode.

Not that I blame them. I am not aware that Stevie Smith's poems have ever received serious critical assessment, though recently I have seen signs that this may not be far off. They are certainly presented with that hallmark of frivolity, *drawings*, and if my friends had been asked to place Miss Smith they would no doubt have put her somewhere in the uneasy marches between *humorous* and *children's*. She has also written a book about *cats*, which as far as I am concerned casts a shadow over even the most illustrious name. Nevertheless, her poems, to my mind, have two virtues: they are completely original, and now and again they are moving. These qualities alone set them above 95 per cent of present-day output.

Her mode of writing, broadly speaking, is that of the *fausse-naïve*, the 'feminine' doodler or jotter who puts down everything as it strikes her, no matter how silly or tragic, in a kind of Gertrude Stein-Daisy Ashford-Lorelei Lee way. This method derives from her novels, those strange monologues (beginning in 1936 with *Novel on Yellow Paper, or, Work It Out for Yourself*) by a girl called Pompey or Celia, who works in some office or ministry, has childhood memories of the Humber, and at times breaks out into poems that are subsequently reprinted under the name of Stevie Smith.

I must admit I cannot remember a single thing that happens in any of them, but looking at them afresh I am struck now, as then, by the ease with which they skitter from 'Phew-oops dearie, this was a facer, and a grand new opening gambit that I hadn't heard before' to 'I feel I am an instrument of God, that is not altogether the Christian God; that I am an instrument of God that must *calcine these clods*, that are at the same time stupid and vulgar, and set free this God's prisoners, that are swift, white and beautiful and very bright and flaming-fierce.' The accent of *The Holiday* (1949) is unremittingly artificial, yet the extraordinary scene at the end where Celia writes her uncle's sermon and begins to read it to him catches the attention in a way that suggests it is a key passage:

> There is little landscape where you are going and no warmth. In that landscape of harsh winter where the rivers are frozen fast, and the only sound is the crash of winter tree-branches beneath the weight of the snow that is piled on them, for the birds that might have been singing froze long ago, dropping like stone from the cold sky . . . The soul, frivolous and vulnerable, will now lie down and draw the snow over her for a blanket. Now she is terrified, look, the tears freeze as they stand in her eyes. She is naked in this desert, she has no friends, she is alone.

This is not the note of a comic writer, and it is a note that sounds throughout her work again and again.

When one turns to the 'poems and drawings' (it is not easy to get hold of *A Good Time Was Had by All* or *Tender Only to One*, the pre-war volumes), it is a toss-up whether one is too irritated by the streak of facetiousness ('Kathleen ni Houlihan / Walking down the boule-igan / Ran into a hooligan' etc.) to find the pieces which carry the unique and curious flavour for which they come to be sought. There are, to be frank, a few poems in every book that should never have got outside the family. Nor do the drawings help: a mixture of 'cute' and 'crazy', they have an amateurishness reminiscent of Lear, Waugh and Thurber without much compensating felicity. But one does not have to read far before coming on something that at first seems completely surprising (I was about to say out of place):

> From a friend's friend I taste friendship,
> From a friend's friend love,
> My spirit in confusion,
> Long years I strove,
> But now I know that never

> Nearer I shall move,
> Than a friend's friend to friendship,
> To love than a friend's love.

Or if that is too recognizably poetry, what about this:

> I shall be glad to be silent, Mother, and hear you speak,
> You encouraged me to tell too much, and my thoughts are weak,
> I shall keep them to myself for a time, and when I am older
> They will shine as a white worm shines under a green boulder.

It is typical of Miss Smith that she sees something poetic move where we do not, takes a pot-shot at it, and when she holds it up forces us to admit that there was something there, even though we have never seen anything like it before.

> Do take Muriel out
> She is looking so glum
> Do take Muriel out
> All her friends are gone.
>
> Do take Muriel out
> Although your name is death . . .

Although *Not Waving but Drowning* (1957) was very much the same kind of book as its predecessors, it seemed to me then, as it does now, more confident, surer in getting its effects, than they were. Its poems were less divided into 'serious' and 'silly': as in Lear, the silliness was part of the seriousness:

> With my looks I am bound to look simple or fast I would rather look
>   simple
> So I wear a tall hat on the back of my head that is rather a temple
> And I walk rather queerly and comb my long hair
> And people say, Don't bother about her . . .

Poem after poem begins in her peculiarly plangent way, like a hand swept across strings:

> 'Twas the voice of the sweet dove
> I heard him move
> I heard him cry
> Love, love . . .
>
> Put out that Light,

> Put out that bright Light,
> Let darkness fall . . .

Or, as in 'This is Disgraceful and Abominable', she can scold remarkably like D. H. Lawrence ('Animals are animals and have their nature / And that's enough, it is enough, leave it alone'). But she is always at her most characteristic when uttering the unexpected that once expressed is never forgotten. Her most celebrated poem, 'Not Waving but Drowning', does precisely this:

> Nobody heard him, the dead man,
> But still he lay moaning:
> I was much further out than you thought
> And not waving but drowning.
>
> Poor chap, he always loved larking
> And now he's dead
> It must have been too cold for him his heart gave way,
> They said.
>
> Oh, no no no, it was too cold always
> (Still the dead one lay moaning)
> I was much too far out all my life
> And not waving but drowning.

Looking through this volume of *Selected Poems*[1] makes it possible to form one or two conclusions about this almost unclassifiable writer. It is impossible, as the blurb says, to date any given poem even to a decade, and yet one has the feeling she is improving — not, of course, becoming more consistent, for that is not her way, but dealing with stronger themes, having less to discard. Then there is the constant preoccupation with the concepts and language of Christianity—life, death, eternity, love, sin, all these are continually recurring in different contexts and from different angles. They do not make the best poems, but Miss Smith cannot leave them alone. It is not easy to judge her attitude to them. At times her tone is prophetic:

> I walked abroad in Easter Park,
> I heard the wild dog's distant bark,
> I knew my Lord was risen again,
> Wild dog, wild dog, you bark in vain.

[1] Stevie Smith, *Selected Poems* (London: Longmans, 1962).

But at others it has a kind of Rationalist Press sunlessness:

> A god is man's doll, you ass,
> He makes him up like this on purpose.
>
> He might have made him up worse.
>
> He often has, in the past.

The language and history of the Church of England and its liturgy are in her blood, but so is doubt; in 'Edmonton, thy cemetery . . .' she writes how:

> . . . Doubt returns with dreary face
> And fills my heart with dread
> . . . .
> And I begin to sing with him
> As if Belief had never been
> Ah me, the countless dead, ah me
> The countless countless dead.

And there comes a passage at the conclusion of the 'Thoughts about the Person from Porlock' that sounds as if it is as near as imagination can get to faith:

> These thoughts are depressing I know. They are depressing,
> I wish I was more cheerful, it is more pleasant,
> Also it is a duty, we should smile as well as submitting
> To the purpose of One Above who is experimenting
> With various mixtures of human character which goes best,
> All is interesting for him it is exciting, but not for us.
> There I go again . . .

I stress this aspect of her work because it may correct the bias of general opinion towards the view that she is a light-hearted purveyor of *bizarrerie*. Of course her extraordinary jumble of cats, knights, children, Racine, Excalibur, England and so on gives some colour to that view, but the truth of the matter is that her talent is, as she translates Rimbaud's line, 'drawn by everything in turn'. Almost anything can strike her, and she will have a stab at conveying just how it made her feel—a singing cat. Cranmer, Copernicus, fourteen-year-old girls, 'The Occasional Yarrow' (a charming little poem, unaccountably missing from this collection), and thoughts and reflections that are hardly more than twists and grace-notes of the mind such as no one else would ever attempt to put into words. And her successes are not full-scale four-square poems that can be anthologized and anatomized, but occasional phrases ('not waving but drowning') or refrains ('For I love you more than ever / In the wet and stormy weather') that one finds hanging about one's mind like nursery rhymes, or folk poetry, long after one has put the book down in favour of Wallace Stevens.

Why does my Muse only speak when she is unhappy?
She does not, I only listen when I am unhappy
When I am happy I live and depise writing
For my Muse this cannot but be dispiriting.

Perhaps this explains it. For all the freaks and sports of her fancy, for all her short pieces that are like rejected *Pansies* and her long pieces that are like William Blake rewritten by Ogden Nash, Miss Smith's poems speak with the authority of sadness.

1962

The War Poet

The face of Wilfred Owen, moustached and with centre-parted hair, looks out at us eternally from 1916. The production of a new and seemingly definitive edition[1] of his poems nearly half a century later suggests that we should now be able to separate his work from the temporal accidents of his lifetime. Yet it is just these accidents that condition the nature of his achievement, and make independent critical assessment so difficult.

A 'war' poet is not one who chooses to commemorate or celebrate a war but one who reacts against having a war thrust upon him: he is chained, that is, to a historical event, and an abnormal one at that. However well he does it, however much we agree that the war happened and ought to be written about, there is still a tendency for us to withhold our highest praise on the grounds that a poet's choice of subject should seem an action, not a reaction. 'The Wreck of the Deutschland', we feel, would have been markedly inferior if Hopkins had been a survivor from the passenger list. Again, the first-rank poet should ignore the squalid accident of war: his vision should be powerful enough to disregard it. Admittedly, war might come too close for this vision to be maintained. But it is still essentially irrelevant.

In the case of Owen, not only what he wrote but how he wrote it might fairly be called historically predictable. He was part of what Dr D. S. R. Welland calls 'the Phase of Protest', the wave of sickened indignation born of the battle of the Somme and Passchendaele that produced the 'no annexations and no indemnities' peace agitations of 1917, and a new and shocking realism in art and literature:

> The place was rotten with dead: green clumsy legs
> High-booted, sprawled and grovelled along the saps
> And trunks, face downward, in the sucking mud

---

[1] *The Collected Poems of Wilfred Owen*, edited by C. Day Lewis (London: Chatto & Windus, 1963).

Wallowed like trodden sandbags loosely filled;
And naked sodden buttocks, mats of hair,
Bulged, clotted heads slept in the plastering slime . . .

He had also been anticipated, as in these lines by Siegfried Sassoon, a writer some years his senior who since 1914 had moved independently from Dr Welland's stage of Bardic Rhetorical ('And, fighting for our freedom, we are free') to one which Owen adopted almost immediately. The two men met in a war hospital in August 1917, where they were both nerve patients: Owen because he had just had three months in a bad sector on the Western Front, Sassoon because he had sent his commanding officer a letter saying: 'I believe that this war, upon which I entered as a war of defence and liberation, has now become a war of aggression and conquest.' Sassoon was already known for his war poems (or rather, anti-war poems), and Owen immediately assumed a position of admiring pupillage. They were both anxious that the war should be shown up, that the carnage, the waste, the exploitation should all be brought home to innocent non-combatants. Sassoon, whose characteristic voice was a bitter casualness ('Does it matter ?—losing your legs?'), has in *Siegfried's Journey* deprecated the notion that his own example was crucial in Owen's development: he calls it 'one of those situations where imperceptible effects are obtained by people mingling their minds at a favourable moment'. At any rate, it is hard to imagine that Owen would have written 'Smile, Smile, Smile' or 'The Dead-Beat' without this coincidental and fortunate contact.

But in fact we have very little idea of how Owen developed, whether in ideas or technique: all that seems certain is that he experienced a year and a half of intense poetic activity in 1917–18 until his death seven days before the Armistice. The present editor does not follow the vaguely chronological order of Edmund Blunden's 1931 edition (from which the memoir is reprinted): he opens with a tremendous barrage of Owen's most effective pieces, leaving the early and minor poems to follow at leisure through the gap thus torn. A sonnet, '1914', is full of foreboding ('now the Winter of the World / With perishing foul darkness closes in'), but there is little to show whether Owen's view of the war changed. In 'Exposure' (presumed to date from February 1917, though Dr Welland thinks it was extensively revised later) occurs the verse:

Since we believe not otherwise can kind fires burn;

Nor ever suns smile true on child, or field, or fruit.
For God's invincible spring our love is made afraid;
Therefore, not loath, we lie out here; therefore were born,
    For love of God seems dying.

This is very much what Sassoon's bishops were saying. But in a letter written a month or so later from hospital he adopts a very different outlook:

Already I have comprehended a light which will never filter into the dogma of any national church: namely, that one of Christ's essential commands was: Passivity at any price! Suffer dishonour and disgrace, but never resort to arms. Be bullied, be outraged, be killed, but do not kill. It may be a chimerical and an ignominious principle, but there it is. . . . Thus you see how pure Christianity will not fit in with pure patriotism.

It was the second view that prevailed. But though Owen had in fact been religiously trained (for almost two years he was a lay assistant to a vicar in Oxfordshire), his pacifism was less a Christian principle than 'the philosophy of many soldiers', a passionate conviction that anything is better than war and its annihilations:

O Life, Life, let me breathe—a dug-out rat!
Not worse than ours the existences rats lead—
Nosing along at night down some safe rut,
They find a shell-proof home before they rot.
Dead men may envy living mites in cheese . . .

There could hardly be any plainer statement that what is terrible about war is the premature death ('there was a quaking / Of the aborted life within him leaping') or disablement it brings:

'Strange friend,' I said, 'here is no cause to mourn.'
'None,' said that other, 'save the undone years . . .'

The conviction was to permeate the entire national consciousness during the next twenty years; it reached forward to Baldwin's refusal to re-arm, Dick Sheppard and the Peace Pledge Union, and Chamberlain flying to Berchtesgaden. 'It is Owen, I believe,' writes Mr C. Day Lewis in his introduction, 'whose poetry came home deepest to members of my generation, so that we could never again think of war as anything but a vile, if necessary, evil.' That 'if necessary', which would not have been there before 1939, shows that on the whole the implications of Owen's poems have been found unacceptable. We do not honour him the less for this, but it strengthens the historical limitations that attend his work.

This is not, however, the end of the story. Owen did not write 'My subject is War, and the horror of War' but 'the pity of War': both he and Sassoon rejoined their units in order to be with their comrades. While Sassoon sought to turn the insensitivity that permitted the continuance of the war into disgust, Owen tried to turn it into compassion. Sassoon concentrated on the particular ('When Dick was killed last week he looked like that, / Flapping along the firestep like a fish'); Owen deliberately discarded all but generalities:

> But cursed are dullards whom no cannon stuns,
> That they should be as stones;
> Wretched they are, and mean
> With paucity that never was simplicity.
> By choice they made themselves immune
> To pity and whatever mourns in man
> Before the last sea and the hapless stars;
> Whatever mourns when many leave these shores;
> Whatever shares
> The eternal reciprocity of tears.

'It seemed that out of battle I escaped . . .'. It was less an escape than a contrived withdrawal into mythopoeic impersonality that so far from muffling his words lent them extraordinary resonance:

> And He, picking a manner of worm, which half had hid
> Its bruises in the earth, but crawled no further,
> Showed me its feet, the feet of many men,
> And the fresh-severed head of it, my head.

For Owen ('his thick dark hair . . . already touched with white above the ears') to achieve at twenty-four this degree of imaginative identification suggests that his response had been as powerful as the stimulus was violent. 'This book', he noted, 'is about war':

> The long, forlorn, relentless tread
> From larger day to huger night.

But in the end Owen's war is not Sassoon's war but all war; not particular suffering but all suffering; not particular waste but all waste. If his verse did not cease to be valid in 1918, it is because these things continued, and the necessity for compassion with them. This makes him the only twentieth-century poet who can be read after Hardy without a sense of bathos. His secret lies in the retort he had already written when W. B. Yeats made his fatuous condemnation 'Passive suffering is not a theme for poetry': 'Above all, I am not concerned with Poetry.'

1963

Freshly Scrubbed Potato

Shortly after the publication of *The Autobiography of a Super-Tramp*, a few of Davies's friends, knowing him to be more famous than rich, arranged some small sinecure such as a librarianship to make him financially independent. They little knew their man. 'They wanted me to work,' Davies said years later in relating his rejection of this ignoble proposal. 'I have never worked in my life.' There was nothing for it, the friends realized, but a Civil List pension.

The incident is revealing. Reading Mr Stonesifer's engrossing pages[1] (I had read nearly to page 100 before I remembered I was supposed to be making notes), one encounters a personality that never swerved from its intuited object, the poetic life. Davies chose to be a tramp: his first thirty years were spent in idleness, poverty and vagrancy both here and in America, but it was an instinctive holding-off from what he did not want until such time as he could get what he did want more than any love of the open road. Back in London with a wooden leg, he devoted himself to writing poems by the light of doss-house fires, which he then recited in the street, or, as on one occasion, had printed on broadsheets which he tried, unsuccessfully, to sell. (A remarkable delicacy of feeling prevented him from trading on his disability.) After five years of this he got enough money together to print a volume: this he sent to a list of prominent literary people, compiled from *Who's Who*, asking them to send half a crown if they wished to buy it. This was the turning point in his career. Bernard Shaw bought eight copies. St. John Adcock wrote him up in the *Daily Mail*. There were reviews in the *Bookman*, the *Athenaeum* and the *Academy*, and 'Representatives of Harmsworth have been here and taken my photo in three different attitudes.' He was a literary curiosity who was destined to become a literary celebrity and finally part of literature itself.

The next fifteen years were probably the happiest in Davies's life. He became a recognized figure in Fitzrovia and Soho, and was never

[1] Richard Stonesifer, *W. H. Davies: A Critical Biography* (London: Cape, 1963).

more at home than when partying with Nina Hamnett and Augustus John or lunching with Ralph Hodgson, Gordon Bottomley, Arthur Ransome, *et al*. in Gerrard Street. One feels strongly that this was the kind of company he really liked, for which Detroit Fatty, Saginaw Slim and Harlem Baldy had been colourless, though understandable, substitutes. In fact he was more at home with artists than with writers, and amassed a fine collection of portraits of himself by Epstein, John, Sickert, Laura Knight and Nicholson, among which he used to sit, contentedly deriving inspiration. At fifty-two he married (his wife was about thirty years his junior), an age at which he was ready to exchange a measure of precious independence for love and the comfort of home life. The remainder of his life was peaceful and productive, though domestic pressure forced him to give up most of his friends and live in the country, a region which he found he rather disliked as a permanent thing. He hit back in minor ways such as neglecting the garden and waving at girls in a near-by laundry.

The critical section of Mr Stonesifer's book sets out Davies's quality as a prose writer, a humanitarian poet, a love poet and a nature poet (the categories would have fitted Hardy, and indeed Davies was always uneasily aware of the stature of the older poet), and his treatment is on the whole sensitive and just, though his parallel of Davies's world with that of Disney is not happy. It is surprising how completely all ideas of crudity and violence, such as Davies's picaresque life might suggest, have to be discarded: he looked like a realist, but his realism was that of the freshly scrubbed potato as opposed to the genuine earthy article (the image is Robert Frost's). Davies was not fastidious: he liked drinking and cheap whores, but there was an instinctive gentleness and adaptability about him that made him socially 'possible' and facilitated his patronage by London literary society. This accounts for the inoffensiveness of his prostitutes, the extraordinary language of his tramps ('Boys,' continued Fatty in a broken voice—'boys, I am no longer fit for your company'), and the, on the whole, failure of his more powerful pieces of social comment ('Oh, collier, collier, underground, / In fear of fire and gas, / What life more danger has?'). In fact, so much was his own taste for the gentler and more beautiful in life that often his harsher anecdotes seem put in to play up to the current idea of him as a romantic chronicler of the underworld.

To read through his entire poetic output, as I have just done, is a curious experience; perpetually on the edge of formula, mannerism, routine, it continually surprises by unpredictable successes that make almost every piece worth reading. His method was simple: it was, as he told Walter de la Mare, to wait till an idea came to him ('What do you mean by "an idea comes to you"?' de la Mare interrupted), and then put it down without too much soul-searching in language he did not have to look up in a dictionary and metres that had been used by centuries of poets before him. As most of his ideas concerned vague and comfortable concepts such as Beauty, Fortune, Joy, Pleasure, Wonder, Gold (but it was gold then), Content, Youth, Love and so on, and required for their expression equally comfortable properties such as dreams, butterflies, nightingales, sheep, flowers, rain and bees, there is a kind of stodgy unreality imminent (and sometimes actual) in much he did, meriting D. H. Lawrence's characteristic scolding: 'I think one ought to be downright cruel to him. . . . Then he might leave his Sevenoaks room, where he is rigged up as a rural poet, proud of his gilt mirrors and his romantic past: and he might grow his wings again. . . .'

Consistently through his poetic career, however, he had the power to rise intermittently above this level by piercingly happy moments of description and observation that carry the poems that contain them permanently into our memory—'Sheep', Strong Moments', 'The Beautiful', 'When Leaves Begin', and many more. He had a remarkable talent that he himself describes in this way:

> my Muse
> . . . .
> Will rise like that great wave that leaps and hangs
> The seaweed on a vessel's mast-top high.

That precisely describes his knack of suddenly unearthing, as it were, some hitherto unnoticed detail or irony or pleasure and extending it for our enjoyment on the end of a far-fetched metaphor or simile. The wind dragging the corn by her long hair into the dark wood, the sheep that walk up the hill and become clouds, the wet tombstones breathing in the sun, the summer spreading a green tent on the bare pole of a tree: Davies never lost the power to refresh the commonest experience. Perhaps what one cherishes most, however, is not this never-sleeping fancy (which is after all never far from whimsy), but the honest simplicity of spirit—the decency—that informs all he wrote: his tenderness for the animal world, his continual wonder and delight in natural surroundings, his love for women and children and the poor. That this in its turn could become perilously close to kindergarten banality Davies was very well aware. His response was characteristic: he could never be as bad as Masefield. (In fact Mr Stonesifer might well have had a fifth chapter, 'Davies the Ironist', for the poet could be lethally deflating under his simple exterior if he thought the occasion demanded it.) But when it was supported by sharpness of language and keenness of observation it comes out on the other side of banality, as it were, and constitutes Davies's unique contribution to literature—a steady, unecstatic celebration of natural beauty and the qualities in man that seem most allied to it.

The best that can be said of the new edition of his poems[1] is that it is clearly printed and at 616 pages for 25s good value for money. It has an introduction by Sir Osbert Sitwell, and a Foreword by Daniel George, but neither undertakes the elementary editorial responsibility of saying which poems came from which books and whether they are the text as it was first printed. Mr George proudly announces that he has persuaded the publishers to include 113 poems that Davies, in some unspecified circumstances, had suppressed, but does not say which they are. There is no bibliography. All in all, a disappointing piece of work.

1963

[1] *The Complete Poems of W. H. Davies* (London: Cape, 1963).

Wanted: Good Hardy Critic

From time to time the admirer of Hardy is bound to feel concern at the comparatively low esteem in which his author seems to be held by critics in this century. This is all the more remarkable because Hardy's reputation has not taken the accustomed posthumous dip: his books have continued to sell and to be read in schools, the principal post-Eliot poets (Auden, Betjeman, Dylan Thomas) have acknowledged his power, and there has been a continual ascent of tribute from what one might call the British Academy reservation. Yet one has to admit that those whose names come to mind as the century's principal critics have really shown little interest in him. Eliot was hostile, Leavis patronizing, Wilson, Empson, Blackmur, Trilling—none has been other than neglectful. And the roll-call on the other side—Lord David Cecil, Edmund Blunden, Lascelles Abercrombie, Webster, Guerard, Hawkins—does not on the whole have the penetration of intelligence and sensibility that would command confidence. The fact is that Hardy doesn't seem to attract the best modern critics.

This must be due to one of two reasons: either Hardy's work is not good enough to warrant their attention, or it is not of a kind that interests them. To choose the second of these as more likely, as we surely must, is not to get much further towards enlightenment. We can say that modern criticism thrives on the difficult—either on explaining the difficult or explaining that what seemed straightforward is in fact difficult—and that Hardy is simple; his work contains little in thought or reference that needs elucidation, his language is unambiguous, his themes easily comprehensible. A typical role of the modern critic is to demonstrate that the author has said something other than he intended (trust the tale and not the teller, etc.), but when this is tried on Hardy, as in the case of Dr Kettle and his celebrated contention that *Tess of the d'Urbervilles* symbolizes the decline of the peasantry, the reader feels uncomfortable rather than illuminated. Much of this, however, could be said of Dickens, a writer to whom modern critics have taken gladly, so that the dyspathy must have some other explanation. It may be that Hardy is just not the sort of writer that criticism can do much for, because the old-style approach—His Pessimism, His Female Characters—is really no more successful than the new. Or it may be that the true critic of Hardy has not so far materialized.

With this in mind, Mr Morrell's declaration on the first page of his foreword that his book[1] is the outcome of 'complete disagreement with the authorities' encourages the reader's interest. Unfortunately it is soon disappointed: the authorities are not the authors of *After Strange Gods* or *The Great Tradition*, but Dr John Holloway, whom Mr Morrell spends his first chapter in chivvying. Holloway is taken as representative of the present-day interpretation of Hardy as a pessimistic determinist with a strong commitment to Nature and the old agricultural order. This interpretation Mr Morrell is concerned with resisting: unfortunately his case is not helped by the fragmentary nature of its exposition. As Mr Morrell admits, 'it is not so much a book as a series of notes and essays.' The first chapter, 'Hardy and the Critical Confusion', is followed not by a flowing tide of personal conviction, but by five and a bit pages headed 'A Note on the Machine in *Tess of the d'Urbervilles*', then by seven pages headed 'A Note on "The President of the Immortals" '. This tends to weaken the cogency of the argument and lengthen the time that it takes to get under way. When it does, however, it is, to say the least of it, original. Its burden is that Hardy is not a pessimist and not a determinist; he sees man not as a pawn in the hands of hostile Nature but as a being who makes his own destiny, someone who has choice and free will and whose life directly depends on how he uses them. To believe otherwise, according to Mr Morrell, is 'a simple failure to read on, to read the whole book, the next chapter, the next paragraph, even the last half of a sentence'. I do not recollect that he says anywhere that Hardy is a cheerful writer, but it would be difficult to deduce from his book that he finds him a melancholy one.

Mr Morrell examines several of Hardy's novels, notably the early novels, *Far from the Madding Crowd*, *The Mayor of Casterbridge* and *Tess of the d'Urbervilles*, which he considers 'Hardy's greatest novel'. He recurs frequently to this last work, and as one goes through his chapters one gradually assembles a notion of it in the light of Mr Morrell's interpretation. Tess must be seen as a daughter of the

[1] Roy Morrell, *Thomas Hardy: The Will and the Way* (Kuala Lumpur: Univ. of Malaya / OUP, 1965).

shiftless Durbeyfields, and the inheritor of all their lack of resolution: 'If "Sir John" Durbeyfield, even with his fatty heart, had the energy to bury the carcase of his horse, he could have dug the ground to grow vegetables for his family; if Tess could bring herself to write the letter of confession, she could have made sure Angel received it; if she could endure hardships and humiliations and Flintcomb Ash, she could have risked a snub from Angel's father . . .' (p. 98). Tess is one of Hardy's gallery of 'losers' against whom is ranged a contrasting gallery of winners, the Farfraes and the Gabriel Oaks who meet reverses with increased determination and eventually master their environments. Mr Morrell does not even see Tess as 'betrayed':

> It is because she fails to control circumstances in time, that circumstances push her eventually in the direction of Trantridge and Alec. Even then Hardy does not describe Tess as hopelessly trapped; she has paid one visit to the d'Urbervilles, and knows, or has misgivings about, what she is in for. But even then if she has had even slight misgivings about Alec after her first visit, these become definite enough when Alec fetches her for the second journey and pesters her on the road. The seduction is not a sudden one; she knows what to expect; but does nothing with the reprieve. (p. 32.)

One wonders what Mr Morrell makes of passages such as this (which he does not quote):

> 'O mother, my mother!' cried the agonized girl, turning passionately upon her parent as if her poor heart would break. 'How could I be expected to know? I was a child when I left this house four months ago. Why didn't you tell me there was danger in men-folk? Why didn't you warn me?' (Chapter XII.)

Put nakedly, Mr Morrell's view of the novel is the story of someone (Tess) getting what they deserve:

> 'Some people, God help them, may still suppose', Hardy is saying, 'like Aeschylus long ago, or like Joan Durbeyfield, shifting the blame from her own shoulders, that fate can be blamed for Tess's disaster. The reader may wish to believe this too: but surely I have shown where the real blame lies.' (p. 40.)

If Mr Morrell can imagine Hardy saying this, one would think he could imagine anything. Again, what can he make of Hardy's additional preface to the 1912 edition?

Respecting the sub-title 'A Pure Woman' . . . I may add that it was appended at the last moment, after reading the final proofs, as being the estimate left in a candid mind of the heroine's character —an estimate nobody would be likely to dispute. It was disputed more than anything else in the book.

And, one feels, is still being disputed. Having reread *Tess* for the purpose of this review, I cannot believe that Hardy meant by it anything remotely resembling Mr Morrell's thesis. To me it comes over as a blend of Victorian melodrama with the older tradition of the ballad: Tess herself would be equally at home in either. The narrative is spotted with absurdity—Alec's conversion, Angel's 'eight-and-forty hours' dissipation with a stranger', Tess's proclaimed sexual ignorance—but these do not matter, any more than the inconsistencies in Shakespeare's time schemes. I am more conscious than I was, too, of an undercurrent of sensual cruelty in the writing—this seems an extraordinary thing to say of Hardy, but for all his gentleness he had a strong awareness of, and even relish for, both the macabre and the cruel—but this, again, is an ancient tradition, that of 'suffering beauty'. The story carries the reader along like an old country wives' tale: its theme is its first title, 'Too Late Beloved', and its moral is the cant music-hall cliché (which Hardy uses as the title of 'Phase the Fifth') 'the woman pays'. And she pays—Tess pays—precisely because she is *un*like her mother, and will not follow her advice to keep her early seduction secret: 'No girl would be such a Fool, especially as it is so long ago, and not your Fault at all.'

Mr Morrell's contentions, perverse as they are, none the less raise interesting speculations. His view of the shifts, self-doubts and hesitations of Hardy's characters as handicaps in the evolutionary struggle (and his belief that Hardy intended them as such) suggests that he sees Hardy as a kind of crypto-Shaw, who would have echoed the famous passage about the true joy in life that is to be found in the 'Epistle Dedicatory' to *Man and Superman*, and would link his evolutionary meliorism with the Lamarckism of Samuel Butler. Without doubt Hardy, like others of his century, was forever on the look-out for some sign that humanity was improving, and his failure to perceive one produced many occasional bitter utterances ('After two thousand years of mass / We've got as far as poison gas'), and it is curious to note that both he and Shaw see time as a necessary ingredient of man's spiritual and moral advance. Shaw's view is that we must live longer: Hardy's is rather that we must get old quicker or, like the little boy 'Father Time', be born old. Both, in their different ways, are asking man to grow up. Hardy seems at times to have believed in a 'modern man' whose greater sensibility marked him out almost visibly, as with Clym Yeobright in *The Return of the Native*:

> To one of middle age the countenance was that of a young man, though a youth might hardly have seen any necessity for the term of immaturity. But it was really one of those faces which convey less the idea of so many years as its age than of so much experience as its store . . . the age of a modern man is to be measured by the intensity of his history. (Book Second, Chapter VI.)

What is the intensely maturing experience of which Hardy's modern man is most sensible? In my view it is suffering, or sadness, and extended consideration of the centrality of suffering in Hardy's work should be the first duty of the true critic for which the work is still waiting. Mr Morrell, of course, explicitly rejects this centrality. The characteristic of Hardy he wishes to present is 'gaiety' (p. x), by which I take him to mean buoyancy, relish, toughness, all things Hardy certainly possessed in good measure. But it surely cannot be denied that the dominant emotion in Hardy is sadness. Hardy was peculiarly well equipped to perceive the melancholy, the misfortunate, the frustrating, the failing elements of life. It could be said of him as of Little Father Time that he would like the flowers very much if he didn't keep thinking they would all be withered in a few days. Any approach to his work, as to any writer's work, must seek first of all to determine what element is peculiarly his, which imaginative note he strikes most plangently, and to deny that in this case it is the sometimes gentle, sometimes ironic, sometimes bitter but always passive apprehension of suffering is, I think, wrong-headed. Having established as much, the real critic of Hardy could, I think, develop a thesis concerning the twofold value Hardy placed on suffering: first, he thought it was 'true' ('Tragedy is true guise, Comedy lies'); secondly, it could be demonstrated that Hardy associated sensitivity to suffering and awareness of the causes of pain with superior spiritual character.

It would follow, therefore, that the presence of pain in Hardy's novels is a positive, not a negative, quality—not the mechanical working out of some predetermined allegiance to pessimism or any other concept, but the continual imaginative celebration of what is both the truest and the most important element in life, most important in the sense of most necessary to spiritual development. To examine this element, his perception of it and treatment in literary terms would be the business of the proper study of Hardy which, as far as I know, has yet to be written.

As with critics, so with biographers. No one would wish to belittle the research on Hardy done by Carl J. Weber, now that his *Hardy of Wessex*[1] is the chief, if not the only, life available, but it is regrettable that he should be capable of the numerous journalistic vulgarities ('After five years in the big city, the native had returned') and lumbering facetiousnesses ('Hardy's eye, rolling (we may well believe) in an equally fine frenzy as he sat under his midnight lamp, glanced, *not* from Heaven to earth, but from this book to that'). Why doesn't Hardy attract people who can write? This extensively revised edition numbers some score of pages more than that of 1940, but lacks most of the illustrations and a good deal of the bibliographical material that Purdy has rendered unnecessary. The additional matter is mostly of a worthy yet pedestrian nature: Hardy's reading and instances of his plagiarism, and such new biographical facts as have come to light in the last twenty-five years. Some of this is undoubtedly valuable, such as the parallel between the storm descriptions in *Far from the Madding Crowd* and in Harrison Ainsworth's *Rookwood*: one is reminded of Hardy's assertion, 'I was forced to manufacture my novels: circumstances compelled me to turn them out.' Other suggestions—such as that the character of Henchard took its origin in the character of Anthony Trollope's father, as described in the former's *Autobiography*—do not always carry conviction.

Perhaps the oddest thing about contemporary Hardy criticism, however, is the way in which its mediocre perpetrators consider themselves justified in patronizing Hardy's poems. Weber, for instance, makes very merry with the early poems in general and 'Hap' in particular, which he suggests (without the slightest evidence that I can see) constitutes Hardy's reaction to having his poems sent back by magazine editors. He appears quite deaf to the enduring and original resonance of the poem's despair, as he is to the irony of 'The Temporary the All' or the pathos of 'She to Him'. Morrell, too, parrots

[1] Carl J. Weber, *Hardy of Wessex: His Life and Literary Career*, rev. edn. (London: Routledge, 1965).

the usual stuff about 'the number of Hardy's poems meriting serious attention is not large in relation to the bulk of his collected verse'. To these two gentlemen (and also to Samuel Hynes, author of *The Pattern of Hardy's Poetry*) may I trumpet the assurance that one reader at least would not wish Hardy's *Collected Poems* a single page shorter, and regards it as many times over the best body of poetic work this century so far has to show?

1966

The Poetry of Hardy[1]

I had always known Hardy as a novelist when I was young but I hadn't read his poems particularly. I'd always rather assumed with Lytton Strachey that 'the gloom was not relieved even by a little elegance of diction.' But when I was about twenty-five, I suppose, I was in some digs which faced east and the sun used to wake me very early in the morning—you know, about six. It seemed too early to get up, so I used to read, and it happened that I had Hardy's own selection of his poems, and I began to read them and was immediately struck by them. I was struck by their tunefulness and their feeling, and the sense that here was somebody writing about things I was beginning to feel myself. I don't think Hardy, as a poet, is a poet for young people. I know it sounds ridiculous to say I wasn't young at twenty-five or twenty-six, but at least I was beginning to find out what life was about, and that's precisely what I found in Hardy. In other words, I'm saying that what I like about him primarily is his temperament and the way he sees life. He's not a transcendental writer, he's not a Yeats, he's not an Eliot; his subjects are men, the life of men, time and the passing of time, love and the fading of love.

I think most poets who are well known today have loved Hardy's poems at one time or another. I think Auden has; I think Dylan Thomas did. Vernon Watkins told me that although Dylan Thomas thought Yeats was the greatest modern poet, Hardy was the one he loved. Betjeman clearly loves him; the Poet Laureate, Cecil Day Lewis, clearly does; and yet these are all very dissimilar poets. I rather think that they may have found what I found, that Hardy gave them confidence to feel in their own way. When I came to Hardy it was with the sense of relief that I didn't have to try and jack myself up to a concept of poetry that lay outside my own life—this is perhaps what I felt Yeats was trying to make me do. One could simply relapse back into one's own life and write from it. Hardy taught one to feel rather than to write—of course one has to use one's own language and one's

[1] From 'A Man Who Noticed Things' (Radio 4).

own jargon and one's own situations—and he taught one as well to have confidence in what one felt. I have come, I think, to admire him even more than I did then. Curiously enough, what I like about Hardy is what most people dislike. I like him because he wrote so much. I love the great *Collected Hardy* which runs for something like 800 pages. One can read him for years and years and still be surprised, and I think that's a marvellous thing to find in any poet.

I can't imagine why people say Hardy had no ear. In almost every Hardy poem in the 800 pages, barring one or two about the death of Edward VII and that sort of thing, there is a little spinal cord of thought and each has a little tune of its own, and this is something you can say of very few poets. Immediately you begin a Hardy poem your own inner response begins to rock in time with the poem's rhythm and I think that this is quite inimitable. There are no successful imitators of Hardy. I think Hardy's diction is often quaint—one has to concede that. I don't think it's any quainter than a good many other poets', but often in Hardy I feel that the quaintness, if it is quaintness, is a kind of striving to be accurate. He might say, 'I lipped her', when he means, 'I kissed her', but after all, that brings in the question of lips and that is how kissing's done. When Hardy says that a bower is 'roof-wrecked', I don't know whether 'roof-wrecked' is thought to be quaint but it means precisely that the roof is wrecked. It's a kind of telescoping of a couple of images. I think people are a little unfair to Hardy on that. He can often be extremely direct. 'I should go with them in the gloom hoping it might be so.' 'Not a line of her writing have I, not a thread of her hair.' Donne couldn't be more direct than that.

1968

The Apollo Bit

'I've always enjoyed that healthy serene, Apollo-golden-haired business,' wrote Rupert Brooke in 1912. 'But, my dear, our relationship's based a bit deeper!' To read some 700 pages of his letters[1] might reasonably be expected to reveal *how* deep—not, of course, only his relationship with Ka Cox, to whom he was writing, but the whole puzzling question of his reputation in general. For, undeniably, Brooke had and has a reputation: even in his lifetime he knew everybody (what happened to that Biograph picture of Barrie, Shaw, Yeats, Chesterton, Granville-Barker, Asquith and Brooke, taken at the Savoy in 1914?), and today my guess is (I deliberately haven't asked) that his *Collected Poems* far outsell those of Eliot and Auden. What is the secret? Is there one?

It seems clear that Rupert Brooke was one of those mythopoeic people whom it was necessary to know before understanding his full appeal. His present editor, Sir Geoffrey Keynes, makes it clear that this volume was set up in type in 1955, but that his fellow trustees (Sir John Sheppard, Dudley Ward and Walter de la Mare) objected to his selection on the grounds that it 'seriously misrepresented' the writer of the letters. Here at the outset is an additional problem: not only have we to decide what kind of person the letters suggest, but we must take into account that some of the people who knew him best think that this suggestion misrepresents him.

The dilemma is typical. People had ideas about Brooke; they kept his letters, they had ideas of him from which you differed at your peril. As a result, the letters were unpublished, and Christopher Hassall wrote his biography instead, having access to them and in some cases printing them more fully than they are reproduced here. One could, perhaps, protest mildly at the obtrusive selectivity that dogs these pages: Sir Geoffrey explains that the asterisks merely signify the omission of uninteresting or repetitive material, but

[1] *The Letters of Rupert Brooke*, edited by Sir Geoffrey Keynes (London: Faber, 1968).

sometimes they crop up in the middle of an emotional analysis, or where some bawdy flippancy might be expected. One would have thought that fifty years after a subject's death his letters might have been printed *in toto*, but there you are, this is Brooke.

To me they seem to divide naturally into four chronological sections. The first (1904–1909) takes us from his Rugby schooldays to his departure from Cambridge after his degree. Despite the havoc wrought by Brooke at King's College (and one might as well admit that all along the line some of his success was due to his thorough mashing of the homosexual establishment), his letters during this period are not especially interesting: their determined facetiousness and affectation remind one of several other clever self-conscious young men—Dylan Thomas to Pamela Hansford Johnson, for instance, or D. H. Lawrence to Blanche Jennings:

> A few days ago they found I was exactly—20: and congratulated me on my birthday, giving me a birthday cake, and such things. I hated them, and lost my temper. I am now in the depths of despondency because of my age. I am filled with a hysterical despair to think of fifty dull years more. I hate myself and everyone.

Despite his almost continual attempts at humour, he never achieves an epigram to equal a contemporary's 'Life's so flat that you can see your own tombstone at the other end'. Nor can one deduce his success as an undergraduate from anything he says: 'Cambridge is as ever: but now speciously arrayed in a pretence of heat and light green buds. Really, of course, it is a swollen corpse, and we buzz on it like flies. . . .' 'If you come to Cambridge at the end of the month you will see a performance of the Eumenides, in which an aged grey haired person called Rupert Brooke is wearily taking the part of the Herald. . . .' It is not so much that one doubts his intelligence or high spirits: it is more his idea of what is funny or charming that puts one off.

The second section (1909–1912) ranges from his departure from Cambridge to the collapse of his relations with Ka Cox. This is a period of stress and unhappiness, the nature of which (at least from the letters) is far from clear. It seems that to domestic misfortune (the death of his schoolmaster father) was added the awakening of sexual feelings, coupled with a certain (though not excessive) domination from his mother, and that the principal object of his attention was this Newnham student Katharine Cox. Why he liked her is uncertain, but it is obvious that the friendship brought him little satisfaction. It is, perhaps, significant, that in this period Brooke almost obsessively overworks the two adjectives 'clean' and 'dirty'. 'Stay young and clean-eyed', 'if one's clean-minded', 'the only clean-minded person in London', 'Oh, my Gwen, be clean, be clean!', 'I grow cleaner, perhaps', 'I've a sort of hunger for cleanliness', and then, conversely, 'my tight and dirty self', 'I'm ingratitude, dirty, dirty, dirty', 'the dirty abyss I am now', 'Dirt is Trumps', 'the whole world's rotten with mistakes and dirtiness', 'the world's a dirty enough place'. 'Perhaps soon to Grantchester,' he writes in 1912. 'Shall we bathe? I haven't bathed since November. There's a lot to wash off.' And again in the same letter: 'It may be that there is a herb growing at the bottom of the river just above the pool at Grantchester, & that if I dive & find it & bring it up—it will heal me.'

> Oh, is the river sweet and cool,
> Gentle and brown, above the pool?

Brooke, however, was not the kind of man to suffer when decisiveness could put an end to his suffering. Notwithstanding a new attachment (to Cathleen Nesbitt: 'Could a thousand poems repay God for your mouth?'), he waited only to get his Fellowship at King's, then bunked for America. Once there, he gave Miss Cox her *congé*: 'You *must* get right clear of me, cease to love me, love and marry somebody—and somebody worthy of you.' One is reminded rather of D. H. Lawrence and Jessie Chambers. This done, he starts to find America and Canada amusing ('One man said to me, Sir, I may tell you that in my opinion you have Mr Noyes skinned'), and by October 1913 he had reached his long-sought destination, Samoa. This is one of the high points of his life: as if in reaction from the turgid and stressful London-Cambridge scene, Brooke threw himself into the waking dream of the South Seas. 'Oh, Eddie, it's all true about the South Seas!' he wrote to Eddie Marsh:

> Heaven on earth, the ideal life, little work, dancing, singing and eating, naked people of incredible loveliness, perfect manners, and immense kindliness, a divine tropic climate, and intoxicating beauty of scenery.

The communal life reawoke his Fabianism, and sexual problems vanished in a society where a white flower behind the right ear meant 'I am looking for a sweetheart'. In those pre-Malinowski days, Brooke could none the less see that his Eden could not endure: 'I want to go

out and study them and cinematograph them before they're lost.'
When, reluctantly, he came back, he brought jars of coconut oil to rub
himself with and so prolong the illusion ('more precious than
spikenard').

This was phase three. The last part (1914–1915) is the most
interesting of the four. Brooke had changed, and knew he had
changed. 'The Game is Up, Eddie,' he wrote. 'If I've gained facts by
knocking about with Conrad characters in a Gauguin *entourage*—I've
lost a dream or two. . . . I am what I came out here to be—Hard.
Quite, quite hard.' His prospect of London, though critical, would
not have suited all his old Cambridge friends:

> London is full of 'miles of shopping women, served by men', and
> another Jew has bought a peerage, and I've a cold in my nose, and
> the ways are full of lean and vicious people, dirty, hermaphrodites
> and eunuchs, Stracheys, moral vagabonds, pitiable scum. . . .

What is he to do? His ideas seem to have a new aggressiveness: 'I
think I'll have to manage a theatre. I feel very energetic: and very
capable.' Or there is King's: 'I'm going to turn that damned hole into a
Place of Education.' The notion of marriage recurs, but, frustratingly,
without particular reference to anyone, though there is clearly no
shortage of girls ('It's so BLOODY being celibate'). And then, before he
can make his mind up, comes the war.

Or rather, his mind embraces the war. 'Swimmers into cleanness
leaping'—only Brooke's favourite image can express his feelings
adequately ('dirty songs' comes three lines further on): his idealism,
his need for action, his contempt for the life he had known ('the things
I loathe—capitalism and feminism and hermaphroditism') all found
full embodiment in joining the Royal Naval Division. Early on he saw
the sack of Antwerp, and he was passionately convinced that nothing
of the sort must happen in England; a friend (E. J. Dent), writing to
beg money to help a bronchitic friend to Los Angeles, gets a firm
rebuff: 'there's bigger things than bronchitis abroad'; any spare
money should go to help 'some of the outcast Belgian widows and
children'. 'I've never been quite so happy in my life, I think,' he writes
to Violet Asquith from camp. 'Not quite so *pervasively* happy . . .' The
end came oddly, accidentally, inappropriately, but Brooke was ready
for it. 'You've been very good to me,' he wrote to Eddie Marsh. 'I wish
I'd written more. I've been such a failure.' Less than a month later he
was dead from dysentery and blood-poisoning in Greece.

The impression one is left with is that, so far from being Mrs Cornford's Apollo, or even the most distant relation of Percy Bysshe Shelley, Rupert Brooke was a vigorous, practical and self-interested character whose short life was a continual approximation towards knowing this. If he had not moved in the heady atmosphere of Edwardian Cambridge, he would have realized it sooner. 'Personal relations' were not, in the last analysis, as important to him as doing what he wanted and thought was right. Is this the 'serious misrepresentation' his former trustees resented? Perhaps they were more romantic than Brooke himself. If he had lived, there seems small likelihood that he would have found sufficient fulfilment in writing verse. With his political ideas and good looks, he might have become leader of the Liberal Party, or even (being his mother's son) succeeded Arnold in the headmastership of Rugby.

1968

The Most Victorian Laureate

To open the complete works of Tennyson is to enter the Victorian age itself. There are the emerald-green landscapes, the dewy roses, the pearly-teethed children; the melancholy maidens, the heavy gardens; peasants, at once comic and pathetic, bob and curtsy. Then there is the tea-shop orientalism, the cardboard classicism, the sawdust Arthurianism. There are railways and geology. The silliness and sentimentality are excruciating. We see the flash of moral indignation, and hear the rumble of received opinion: the smoke of double-think drifts obscuringly across the scene. Then suddenly we are brought up sharp by a voice speaking of doubt; there is a vision of fen country on a winter evening; something robust and chuckling digs us in the ribs; finally we hear the assertive trumpets of imperial patriotism and historic endurance. We are confounded by the range, the colour, the self-confidence of it all.

This long-awaited one-volume annotated edition of the poems[1] permits us to repeat the experience *in extenso*. It is, of course, a landmark in Tennyson studies, and is, equally certainly, fortunate in its editor (Professor Ricks's seminars on his author are well known). Its design is majestic: the poems are set in chronological order of composition, as far as this is ascertainable, with substantial headnotes regarding origin and first publication, and a fringe of footnotes giving such textual variants and parallels as seem significant. In parts these are almost more interesting than the text. It is not, as Professor Ricks emphasizes, a complete edition, although it includes many poems not included in Tennyson's own final edition: the songs from the plays are here, but the plays are not (with the exception of *The Devil and the Lady*), nor are the unpublished poems and variants from the manuscripts in the care of Trinity College, Cambridge. Apparently the College allows consultation of the collection but not transcription from it, against the inclinations of the present Lord Tennyson and

[1] *The Poems of Tennyson*, edited by Christopher Ricks (London: Longman, 1969).

also of Sir Charles Tennyson (but not, presumably, those of Tennyson himself). Such an achievement naturally requires a volume of considerable dimensions: its 1,850 pages make up a book approximately the size and weight of a brick. It is, I suppose, just about usable as a reading copy; some of the type is rather small, and each page betrays the printing on its other side too distinctly for comfort. So far I have found only one error: the last line of text on page 1,108 has strayed unaccountably to the foot of page 1,109.

The one thing it does not contain is any kind of attempt to reassess Tennyson critically, and one wonders how the world of English studies regards the fact that the general reader's image of Tennyson is pretty much as Harold Nicolson left it in 1923. To be sure, there has been plenty of work at the symposium level, and in one case at least (that of Miss Valerie Pitt) a determined effort to make us think of Tennyson differently, but the fact is that no one has repeated Nicolson's persuasive readability, and this is what—deplorably, no doubt—counts. It's odd to remember that Nicolson's book was an attempt to *rehabilitate* Tennyson, to raise him from the fallen pantheon of Victorian Nobodaddies and show him to be a normal suffering human being, with the same pretensions and absurdities as ourselves. Odd because, as we can now see, it was in essence a Bloomsbury hatchet job: Nicolson, like his master Strachey, was half in love with his subject, but still couldn't forbear to mention the upset over the can of shaving water, or the poet's opinion of his own verses ('How beautiful that is!'). It was designed to prevent us from ever again looking at Tennyson with the eyes of 1859, the year of the Oxford doctorate:

> Among his colleagues in the honour were Sir De Lacy Evans and Sir John Burgoyne, fresh from the stirring exploits of the Crimea; but even patriotism, at the fever heat of war, could not command a more fervent enthusiasm for the old and gallant warriors than was evoked by the presence of Mr Tennyson.

(The writer is Mr Gladstone.) Instead, Tennyson was presented as a wild, silent, irresolute, rather silly young man of stormy ancestry who, after a youth of amatory and financial troubles, sailed into the double haven of the most Victorian of marriages and the most Victorian of laureateships, fossilizing, to use Auden's word, into a picturesque and still rather silly old man in a hat and cloak who was, underneath, the same frightened and love-needing personality that had fled to the established virtues for protection against hostile circumstance. It is now agreed that what he did best was melancholy ('there was little about melancholia that he didn't know: there was little else that he did'—Auden, again).

None the less, the picture is a sympathetic one, and it is pretty certain that the general reader would sooner be wrecked on a desert island with a complete Tennyson than with a complete Wordsworth. Here again, although the contention is not a new one (Walter Bagehot spent some time claiming that Tennyson was better than Wordsworth because he had 'a power of making fun', and had given in his works a general picture of human life), one wonders what the world of English studies would say. There has been a good deal of comparison lately of the universities with medieval monasteries (useless, parasitic, distrusted by the workers, soon to be dissolved, etc.), and another parallel might be that just as we paid the monks to offer prayers we ourselves could not be bothered to formulate, so today we pay English schools to praise authors (Spenser, Milton, Pound, etc.) whom personally we find unreadable. Hence it is likely that they rank Wordsworth higher than Tennyson: they may even find him more sympathetic. But they are not losing interest in Tennyson either.

Even the general reader, however, is bound to find a good deal of Tennyson unacceptable. His silliness, which was immediately seized on by his contemporaries, is such as one looks for in vain in both better and worse poets. It is not only the kiss-in-the-bower, tit-on-the-tree kind of silliness, but the failure to see larger absurdities, as when he follows 'Who would be / A merman bold . . . I would be a merman bold' with another poem starting 'Who would be / A mermaid fair . . . I would be' etc.; or his curious inability to know when enough is enough, as with the repeated eponym in 'The Ballad of Oriana':

> They should have stabb'd me where I lay,
>> Oriana!
> How could I rise and come away,
>> Oriana?
> How could I look upon the day?
> They should have stabb'd me where I lay,
>> Oriana—
> They should have trod me into clay,
>> Oriana.

It was Mr Robert Graves, I think, who suggested the substitution of the words 'bottom upwards' for the refrain. This is disgraceful, but it is the kind of mockery Tennyson invited.

This failing is perhaps related to the business of 'technical proficiency'. Tennyson's most enduring claim to renown is, as Eliot put it, in having 'the finest ear of any English poet since Milton'; he goes on to say that Tennyson thought he knew the quantity of the sound of every English word except 'scissors'. This concept of technique as something you can be good at without necessarily being good at poetry is quite foreign to a modern reader, who sees form and content as indissoluble, and he is not likely to be convinced he is wrong when he reads that Tennyson reckoned his best line was 'The mellow ouzel fluted in the elm'. But was Tennyson's ear invariably good? He was over-fond of those walloping George R. Sims rhythms, even when they were not especially appropriate, and without them his lines seem to hover awkwardly between speech and verse:

> O me, why have they not buried me deep enough?
> Is it kind to have made me a grave so rough,
> Me, that was never a quiet sleeper?
> Maybe still I am but half-dead;
> Then I cannot be wholly dumb;
> I will cry to the steps above my head
> And somebody, surely, some kind heart will come
> To bury me, bury me
> Ever so little deeper.

Context apart, I find it difficult to read this as anything but a lachrymose bleat, quite without inner organization. Another area, too, in which Tennyson has lost heavily is his classicism: one is reminded of Isherwood's identification of Tithonus in an American university in *A Single Man* ('Well, then, I advise you *all* to spend part of your week-end reading Graves's *Greek Myths*'). Classical references are a liability nowadays: the same with Arthurian legends.

On the other hand (and I am picking out simply the points on which the general reader of the Sixties might disagree with the accepted, or Nicolsonian, version: I take it there is no argument about the lyrics, or parts of *In Memoriam*), we are not so impatient with his role of public poet, or Laureate. Tennyson did not enter public life through backing away from personal problems: he *believed* a poet should know as much as any spokesman of his time. Not only was he a member of

those intimidating Apostles ('Is an intelligible First Cause deducible
from the phenomenon of the Universe?'), he also in his sixties
attended meetings of the Metaphysical Society along with Huxley,
Tyndall, Froude and Gladstone. The last-named, in fact, received
occasional nudges on political matters ('Steersman, be not precipitate
in thine act') without finding it funny or inappropriate. One suspects
Nicolson derided Tennyson as Laureate because he didn't agree with
him. But to read 'Should banded unions persecute / Opinion . . .' in
the age of Barbara Castle, or 'Riflemen Form!' in the age of Denis
Healey, is rather different from reading them in 1923. And if one goes
through that splendid tirade 'Locksley Hall Sixty Years After' with
which the Laureate spoilt the nation's appetite for the 1887 Jubilee,
one is bound to admit that a good deal of what he said would happen
has happened. 'Authors—essayist, atheist, novelist, realist, rhymes-
ter, play your part, / Paint the mortal shame of nature with the living
hues of Art' is not a bad description of twentieth-century literature as
far as it goes.

Lastly, the group of Tennyson's poems for which one has to make
remarkably few allowances is the anecdotal, or dialect, poems: he was
always liable to base a poem on a newspaper cutting, or a story
someone told him, and when he does so it is usually shrewd, vivid,
human and moving. Nicolson praised 'The Northern Farmer', but
'The Northern Cobbler', 'The Village Wife', 'Rizpah' and 'The
Grandmother' all come under this heading. It's hard to reconcile
'Schoolmiss Alfred' with the author of 'The Church-Warden and the
Curate':

> But Parson 'e *will* speak out, saw, now 'e be sixty-seven,
> He'll niver swap Owlby an' Scratby fur owt but the Kingdom of
>   Heaven;
> An' thou'll be 'is Curate 'ere, but, if iver tha means to git 'igher,
> Tha mun tackle the sins o' the wo'ld, an' not the faults o' the Squire.

The 'power of making fun' alluded to by Bagehot has its innings
here, but what can one say of 'The Spinster's Sweet-Arts'? This
monologue of the ageing village spinster, who has rejected all her
suitors to guard her 'two 'oonderd a-year', but has called her cats after
them, is not only amusing and touching but psychologically
penetrating too. The confusion between the men and the pets in her
talk both defines her attitude to them and gives that freaking of
oddness that characterizes such solid-based eccentricity. Hardy could

not have done it as well: it is one of the flowers of Victorian domestic poetry, and argues characteristics different from those we are in the habit of attributing to Tennyson today. If we are to do him justice, we must to sentimentality add tenderness, and to vapid onomatopoeics a gruff ability to hit the nail on the head in matters of common concern.

1969

Grub Village

Every so often there emerges a figure whose importance seems to reside not so much in his own talent as in the lesson he embodies for those who succeed him. George Gissing could be instanced as an example in the world of the novel: Mr Cooke's account[1] suggests that he might have a counterpart in Edward Thomas in the field of poetry. Both were men who, largely through their own mistakes, led miserable lives, and whose reputations seem to have arisen in spite of their efforts rather than because of them.

We may not think of Thomas in this way: indeed, not all his contemporaries saw beyond the legend of the dweller in the country idyll. Somewhere there is an anecdote told by a literary man (Walter de la Mare? Forrest Reid?) who had an appointment in a London tea-shop with Edward Thomas, whom he did not know. On arrival he saw from the door the healthy, open-air Thomas sitting with an obvious and discontented-looking poet. Advancing to greet them, he discovered that the out-of-doors man was Ralph Hodgson: Edward Thomas was the other.

The story should remind us that Thomas, like Gissing, never envisaged any way of earning a living other than that of Grub Street. He was, to put it bluntly, a hack, of a kind unknown in these softer days: by reading twenty or thirty books a week from 9 a.m. to 1 a.m. daily, as well as churning out hastily fudged-up lives of people and histories of places, it was possible to live in an insanitary cottage at minimal rates, and this was his life until he joined the Artists' Rifles in 1915: 'burning the candle at three ends,' he called it.

True, he lived in the country, and had a great and enduring love of it: the irony was that his chosen way of life forced him to make book fodder out of it. It seems extraordinary that a man with an Oxford second should not have been able to command a better existence than the savage drudgery he in fact endured: couldn't he have worked in a

[1] William Cooke, *Edward Thomas: A Critical Biography, 1878–1917* (London: Faber, 1970).

bank, like T. S. Eliot or Vernon Watkins? Apparently not. One cannot help thinking that Thomas was that unfortunate character, a 'man of letters', to whom no hardship or humiliation outweighs the romance of scraping a living from the printed word.

His second major misfortune was his marriage: like many writers, he was not suited to it. 'Try not to give any thought to this flat grey shore', he wrote to Eleanor Farjeon, 'which surprises the tide by not being accessible to it'; and to his wife:

> My eyes scarce dare meet you
> Lest they should prove
> I but respond to you
> And do not love.

Every account of his married life (Mrs Thomas's included) refers to his ungovernable fits of depression and bad temper: his frequent long absences from home seem to have been undertaken as much out of desperation as from a need for new material. No secret has ever been made of his wife-to-be's pregnancy during his second year at Lincoln College: one wonders whether the marriage may not have taken its colour from this inauspicious beginning. To some extent, the two sides of his life were intertwined, like swimmers dragging each other down: marriage meant children, children meant more hack work, hack work meant more domesticity. 'You see,' wrote his wife, 'Edward is at home all day. . . . He cannot have the quiet he needs.'

How this stalemate of temperament and circumstance suddenly produced a unique body of poems is a matter for marvelling. 'I couldn't write a poem to save my life,' he told Eleanor Farjeon, but three things happened to change all that. First, he got a room outside his own house to work in. Secondly, he met Robert Frost. Thirdly, the war came.

Since they all happened at once, it is difficult to apportion the degree of effect each one had. Mr Cooke demonstrates that Thomas began writing poems under the tutelage of Frost simply by putting passages from his prose works into verse: 'I referred him to paragraphs in his book *In Pursuit of Spring* and told him to write it in verse form in exactly the same cadence. That's all there was to it.'

As for the war, Thomas was not a war poet. He volunteered, it is true, but only after contemplating emigration to America, applying for a job in the War Office, and attending for interview for a post in a boys' school. The Army did not so much give him a subject as bring his proper subject, England, into focus. When asked what he was fighting for, he answered 'Literally, for this,' crumbling a pinch of earth between his fingers. In consequence, the England of his poems is not a Georgian dream, but the England of 1915, of farms and men 'going out', of flowers still growing because there were no boys to pick them for their girls: from his mistaken and unlucky life there arose suddenly a serene and unquestionable climax.

1970

Big Victims:
Emily Dickinson and Walter de la Mare

Some of my older readers may remember a passage in which its author asserts that, although he was a child himself once and childhood is all very well in its way, when he became a man he put away childish things. The status of this heartening sentiment today is difficult to assess. On the one hand, of course, the Freudian legacy assures us that our childhoods are with us for life: we are what they made us; we cannot lose their gains, or be compensated for their losses. On the other, children themselves have been devalued: we know them for the little beasts they are (a knowledge greatly amplified since 1945 by the forcible reintroduction of a servantless middle class to its offspring), and nobody would pretend there was anything angelic about them, so that one of the major illusions of the Romantic movement has thereby quietly disappeared, like knives and forks from a university refectory. Anyone wishing to know the full story should consult Peter Coveney's absorbing *The Image of Childhood*, which moves from Blake to J. D. Salinger with dispassionate penetration and humour.

An effect of this on literature has been to make it impossible for any writer of more than minuscule pretensions to adopt the matter of childhood, or the persona of the child, as his principal literary stock-in-trade. The enormous hobby-horse shadow has lifted from the scene. In consequence, even major writers of the pre-war period have suddenly taken a list to port, weighed down by their cargo of whimsy, while the matter-of-fact coasters round adult affairs forge distantly ahead. The situation comes home with a particularly heavy impact to a reviewer faced with 700 pages of Emily Dickinson[1] and 900 of Walter de la Mare.[2]

Emily Dickinson is the more obvious, the more striking, perhaps one might even say the more clinical example of the two. Possibly the

[1] *The Complete Poems of Emily Dickinson*, edited by Thomas H. Johnson (London: Faber, 1970).
[2] *The Complete Poems of Walter de la Mare* (London: Faber, 1969).

only photograph of her depicts a small plain face, rather like a peg-top doll or a self-portrait by Gwen John: when she died aged fifty-five she 'looked thirty, not a grey hair or wrinkle'. Should one call on her, one encountered

> a step like a pattering child's in entry . . . a little plain woman with two smooth bands of reddish hair and a face with no good feature . . . She came to me with two day-lilies, which she put in a sort of childlike way into my hand and said 'These are my introduction,' in a soft, frightened, breathless childlike voice—and added under her breath, 'Forgive me if I am frightened; I never see strangers, and hardly know what I say'—but she talked soon and thenceforward continuously—and deferentially—sometimes stopping to ask me to talk instead of her—but readily recommencing.

This diarist, Colonel T. W. Higginson, who was one of the first to see Emily's poems and was co-editor of her first posthumous collection in 1890, could not help adding: 'I am glad not to live near her.'

The picture he draws is one of disturbed, if not arrested, development. Emily was forty at the time of this encounter, and her life had been a strange one. Born in Amherst in 1830, she lived there till her death in the family house, her sister Lavinia surviving her: there is no suggestion that up to her thirtieth year she was anything but a reasonably normal product of New England puritanism (in 1856, for instance, she won second prize in the Bread Division at the local Cattle Show, and in 1858 was one of the judges). Then something cataclysmic happened. She wrote a flood of poems (over 300 in 1862 alone): at times she thought she was going mad. Her eyes troubled her; increasingly she became a recluse, dressing all in white ('Of Tribulation, these are They / Denoted by the White'), and shunning even the most casual social occasion (or the least: she refused to attend her father's funeral service, listening through an open upstairs door instead). In 1886 she died. Her epitaph might have been her own words: 'Nothing has happened but loneliness.'

Did nothing happen, really? Speculation has not been wanting. Since her poems on the theme of unrequited or unfulfilled love equal in their force the poignancy of Christina Rossetti's (almost her exact contemporary), an unhappy love affair has been postulated, with the climax coming in about 1860. There were men in her life—her 'tutors', as she called them: Benjamin Franklin Newton, who died in 1854, the Reverend Charles Wadsworth, who died in 1882, and Colonel

Higginson. Of these, the second is the favourite, but evidence is circumstantial in the extreme. True to her maxim, 'Tell the truth, but tell it slant', Emily Dickinson put it this way:

> My Life had stood—a Loaded Gun—
> In Corners—till a Day
> The Owner passed—identified—
> And carried Me away—

This is romantic love in a nutshell, but who is its object? A religious poet—and Emily was this sometimes—might even have meant God. In 'probably the worst book on Emily Dickinson yet written' (as Whicher called *The Riddle of Emily Dickinson*), Rebecca Patterson proposes a brief lesbian experience in 1860 with a friend of Emily's sister-in-law Sue. Though the contentions of this highly readable work are far from conclusive, they might be thought to suit the cryptic explosiveness of the poems better than the mild and married Wadsworth.

Whatever the cause, it seems to have precipitated Emily into a kind of pseudo-immaturity—not, of course, a genuine one, but since it lasted a quarter of a century it can be taken as fairly congenial: it also spread to her poems. Her manner on meeting has already been described: the opening of her poems is just the same, a kind of breathless bouncing of the reader's attention, thrusting something tangible and striking into his hand ('These are my introduction'):

> A Toad, can die of Light—

> When I was small, a Woman died—

> Good to hide, and hear 'em hunt!

Her forms are simple, mostly quatrains balancing antithetical sentiments against each other like New England hymns, using the bee-and-flower imagery of keepsake albums, affecting a juvenile or primitive directness somewhat reminiscent of the paintings of the Grandma Moses tradition; but somewhere within them there is a deep fracture, that chills the harmless properties into a wide and arctic plain where they are wedged together eternally to represent a life gone irrevocably wrong:

> Our interview—was transient—
> Of me, himself was shy—

> And God forbid I look behind—
> Since that appalling Day!

Through this desolate childishness comes a startling and plangent enunciation:

> I cannot live with You—
> It would be Life—
> And Life is over there—
> . . . .
> So We must meet apart—
> You there—I—here—
> With just the Door ajar
> That Oceans are—and Prayer—
> And that White Sustenance—
> Despair—

Only rarely, however, did she bring a poem to a successful conclusion: the amazing riches of originality offered by the index of her first lines is belied on the page. Richard Chase said that of all Emily's poems only fifty 'have the substance and fineness of manner which urges us to accord them equality with much . . . excellent . . . lyric poetry', and of these 'only a dozen or two' were great. This is fair enough: too often the poem expires in a teased-out and breathless obscurity. Often the imagery is both trivial and immense: is this an invitation to a walk, or a consummation with the Godhead? Perhaps it is not surprising that Emily Dickinson's other subject —apart from love—was death; not surprising, that is, if we accept the psychologists' assertion that an obsession with death conceals a fear of sex. And yet her tone is as easy and intimate as if her 1860 'experience' was as much to do with death as with love:

> To die—takes just a little while—
> They say it doesn't hurt—
> It's only fainter—by degrees—
> And then—it's out of sight—

Or, as she puts it in that astonishing poem 'I Heard a Fly Buzz When I Died':

> And then the Windows failed—and then
> I could not see to see—

Indeed, it is with death that Emily Dickinson becomes least childlike, most assured, in no way needing apologies or allowances:

> Because I could not stop for Death—
> He kindly stopped for me—
> The Carriage held but just Ourselves—
> And Immortality.
>
> We slowly drove—He knew no haste
> And I had put away
> My labor and my leisure too,
> For His Civility—
>
> . . . .
> Since then—'tis Centuries—and yet
> Feels shorter than the Day
> I first surmised the Horses' Heads
> Were toward Eternity—

Was that the day, one wonders, since when 'God forbid I look behind', the day when she realized that love was not for her, but only death? Such queries are useless. If Emily Dickinson could write 700 pages of poems and three volumes of letters without making clear the nature of her preoccupations, then we can be sure that she was determined to keep it hidden ('and hear 'em hunt!'), and that her inspiration derived in part from keeping it hidden. The price she paid was that of appearing to posterity as perpetually unfinished and wilfully eccentric.

The talent of Walter de la Mare was not, like Emily Dickinson's, crucified between childhood and maturity, unable fully to leave one or attain the other; it had emerged from childhood, not liked what it saw, and slipped back. Childhood fascinated him. Sometimes he tried to pretend, as in the introduction to *Early One Morning*, that this was because it was 'the immediate future', like the dictatorship of the proletariat, but in fact his view was pure romanticism: childhood was just brighter and more beautiful and generally more memorable than being grown up. 'Can you go back in memory to your childhood and if so, how big are you then?' he asked Russell Brain in one of their conversations. 'Can you remember putting your fingers on the edge of the table when your eyes were just level with it?' Walter de la Mare was constantly speculating on such matters: the result was a body of poems which for the most part strive to attain a highly artificial 'childlike vision' (when they were not written for children themselves), as if the eye of the child was to be sought above all things. Lines such as

> And now from the watery
> Waves amonje
> Stands slooshing herself
> With that 'normous sponge

have to be endured for the sake of

> Only the inky rook,
> Hunched cold in ruffled wings,
> Its snowy nest forsook,
> Caws of unnumbered Springs.

A great deal of his work is musical, practised, well-burnished and affecting: he is much more readable than Emily Dickinson, though incapable of her isolated 'dozen or two' peaks, and really one would not seek to compare them were it not for this odd linking aberration of childhood. Voluntarily or involuntarily, part of Emily Dickinson remained a child throughout her life, and this part largely determined how she set about the whole business of writing poems. No doubt she half mastered it: writers are usually on surprisingly affable terms with their neuroses; but it forbade her in the end to express herself unambiguously or to be a poet for whom one doesn't have to make allowances. De la Mare was different—or was he? There is nothing apparent in his life to parallel Emily's 'experience', and yet an acute reader might well pick out something of a 'figure in the carpet' from his themes: darkness, a ruin, an untended rose, a return, a ghost or an echo, a betrayal, an abiding loneliness. The difference between them is that whereas Emily Dickinson built up her childishness into a theatrical hat and cloak to be worn day in, day out, de la Mare tamed his obsession to a point at which, although it remained the key to his writing, he could pass at will backwards and forwards from childhood to maturity. If Emily Dickinson was the better poet, as she was, it was not for this reason: her successes, when one comes to think of them, are when she is at her least odd, her most controlled. This is worth remembering in an age when almost any poet who can produce evidence of medical mental care is automatically ranked higher than one who has stayed sane: 'very mad, very holy,' as the natives say in one of Evelyn Waugh's novels, and we must take care not to copy their way of thinking. Poetry is an affair of sanity, of seeing things as they are. The less a writer's work approximates to this maxim, the less claim he has on the attention of his contemporaries and of posterity.

1970

Palgrave's Last Anthology:
A. E. Housman's Copy

Among the books from the library of A. E. Housman bought by Mr John Sparrow from Blackwell's in 1936 was a copy of *The Golden Treasury: Second Series*, selected by Francis T. Palgrave. In his preface Palgrave, who died in the month of the book's publication (October 1897), admitted that this attempt to 'complete' his famous anthology had 'cost thrice the labour of the first. For nothing, it need scarcely be said, is harder than to form an estimate even remotely accurate of our own contemporary artists. . . .' Despite his stature as an anthologist and assured position in the literary world, Palgrave clearly anticipated a hostile reception for his book: 'Varieties in taste, often deeply rooted and strenuously held, will lead every reader to condemn me for omissions and inclusions: inevitably, and rightly.' Housman appears to have been one such reader, for in Mr Sparrow's copy no less than 41 poems are neatly yet decisively deleted.

The copy so marked is a first edition, which, since the book was twice reprinted in November 1897, suggests that Housman had bought it on publication. If so, he would have been thirty-eight years old, and, more importantly, would have published *A Shropshire Lad* in the previous year, a circumstance that may have rendered him especially sensitive to contemporary selections of 'the finest work of our greater Victorian poets'. His deletions take the form of a pencil line ruled vertically down the centre of the poem; in 37 instances the line extends through the whole text, but in 4 poems a stanza or part-stanza is spared. Additional minor markings, indicating misprints, unacknowledged excisions ('portions, large or small, have been omitted,' as Palgrave confesses in the first of his Notes), or other errors, suggest that he had studied the book carefully. The cancellations, as the use of a ruler implies, represent a considered judgement of Palgrave's choice.

The completely deleted poems are:

> II A. Lord Tennyson, *Cradle Song* ('What does little birdie say')

VIII C. Tennyson-Turner, *Little Sophy by the Seaside* ('Young Sophy leads a life without alloy')

XVI A. Lord Tennyson, *In the Children's Hospital* ('Our doctor had call'd in another, I had never seen him before')

XVIII G. J. Romanes, *Simply Nature* ('Be it not mine to steal the cultured flower')

XX J. Clare, *My Early Home* ('Here sparrows build upon the trees')

LI A. O'Shaughnessy, *Keeping a Heart* ('If one should give me a heart to keep')

LII G. J. Romanes, *Home at Last* ('Now more the bliss of love is felt')

LXIV R. Wilton, *On a Photograph* ('Since through the open window of the eye')

LXVII R. M. (Milnes) Lord Houghton, *The Men of Old* ('I know not that the men of old')

LXX A. H. Clough, *Sic Itur* ('As, at a railway junction, men')

LXXII A. O'Shaughnessy, *The Spectre of the Past* ('On the great day of my life—')

LXXIV R. M. (Milnes) Lord Houghton, *Strangers Yet* ('Strangers yet!')

XCI F. Tennyson, *Song of an Angel* ('At noon a shower had fallen, and the clime')

XCII A. Domett, *A Christmas Hymn*, 1837 ('It was the calm and silent night!—')

XCVI J. C. Shairp, *Lost on Schihallion* ('Oh wherefore cam ye here, Ailie?')

CI A. Lord Tennyson, *The Charge of the Light Brigade* ('Half a league, half a league')

CV S. Ferguson, *The Forging of the Anchor* ('Come, see the *Dolphin*'s anchor forged—'tis at a white heat now')

CVI A. O'Shaughnessy, *Herodias* ('Her long black hair danced round her like a snake')

CXII J. Clare, *Tell-Tale Flowers* ('And has the Spring's all glorious eye')

CXV C. Whitehead, *Night* ('An hour, and this majestic day is gone')

CXXIX A. Lord Tennyson, *'Frater Ave atque Vale'* ('Row us out from Desenzano, to your Sirmione row!')

CXXXI R. Browning, *Amphibian* ('The fancy I had today')

CXXXII R. C. Archbishop Trench, 'O life, O death, O world, O time . . .'

CXXXVI R. Browning, *Prospice* ('Fear death?—to feel the fog in my throat')

CXXXVII A. H. Clough, 'Say not, the struggle nought availeth . . .'

CXL A. O'Shaughnessy, *In Love's Eternity* ('My body was part of the sun and the dew')

CXLII R. M. (Milnes) Lord Houghton, *Half Truth* ('The words that trembled on your lips')

CXLIII R. M. (Milnes) Lord Houghton, *Nessun Maggior Dolore* . . . ('They seemed to those who saw them meet')

CLI A. O'Shaughnessy, *Greater Memory* ('In the heart there lay buried for years')

CLIX F. Tennyson, *A Dream of Autumn* ('I heard a man of many winters say')

CLXVIII R. C. Archbishop Trench, *Returning Home* ('To leave unseen so many a glorious sight')

CLXX J. Clare, *Lasciate Ogni Speranza* . . . ('I am! yet what I am who cares, or knows?')

CLXXIV A. Lord Tennyson, *The Wreck* ('Hide me, Mother! my Fathers belong'd to the church of old')

CLXXVIII J. Keble, *To——, On Her Sister's Death* ('O Thou, whose dim and tearful gaze')

CLXXXI C. Tennyson-Turner, *Anastasis* ('Tho' death met love upon thy dying smile')

CLXXXIII C. Tennyson-Turner, *Mary—A Reminiscence* ('She died in June, while yet the woodbine sprays')

CLXXXIV C. Tennyson-Turner, *Mary—continued* ('And when I seek the chamber where she dwelt')

The 4 poems partly deleted are:

XXXI A. O'Shaughnessy, *Lynmouth* ('Around my love and me the brooding hills')

XXXVII A. O'Shaughnessy, *Zuleika* ('Zuleika is fled away')

LXXXV Duke of Argyll, *Our Dead* ('Sometimes I think that those we've lost')

CXVI H. C. Kendall, *After Many Years* ('The song that once I dream'd about')

Of the 38 poets represented in the book, 18 have poems wholly or partly deleted. The chief sufferers are O'Shaughnessy (7 out of 17),

Lord Houghton (4 out of 6), Lord Tennyson (5 out of 23) and Clare (3 out of 3). Of the remaining 20 whose work was not touched, Matthew Arnold (13), William Barnes (12), E. B. Browning (9), Christina Rossetti (15) and D. G. Rossetti (12) are the principal contributors.

Housman was certainly not alone in his reaction to the book: in fact, Palgrave's forebodings were amply justified. In the words of the *Academy* (23 October 1897): '. . . you shall search in vain . . . for Mr W. E. Henley, Mr Austin Dobson, Mr Francis Thompson, Mr T. E. Brown, Mr W. B. Yeats, Mr William Watson, Mr John Davidson, Mr Frederick Myers, Mr Rudyard Kipling, Mrs Meynell—but the list is too long to be taken to its just limits.' Palgrave's taste, as exhibited in this selection, was solidly mid-Victorian: his fullest admiration goes to the Tennysons, the Brownings and the Rossettis, and he is ready to recognize the talents of subsidiary 'establishment' figures such as Archbishop Trench (one of the Apostles, and friend of Hallam), Sir Francis Doyle ('Uncle Frank', and Professor of Poetry of Oxford for two five-year terms), Alfred Domett (the original of Browning's 'Waring'—what became of him was Prime Minister of New Zealand), and Canon Wilton of Market Weighton, author of *Wood-Notes* and *Church Bells*. But he was equally prepared to include at length his personal favourites William Barnes and Arthur O'Shaughnessy, which for the *Academy* matched his sins of omission:

> The number of the Tennyson poems is twenty-three. Coventry Patmore has a representation of ten; Browning, of fourteen; Mrs Browning, of nine; Matthew Arnold, of thirteen; Rossetti, of twelve; his sister, of fifteen; William Barnes, of nine [*sic*]; Walter Savage Landor and Dobell (iniquitously), of only one; Lord Houghton, of six; and Arthur O'Shaughnessy, of seventeen! . . . The anthologist who could parley with Lord Houghton while he cuts Sydney Dobell off with a shilling, is not our anthologist; but he may, perhaps, be somebody's. But in his inclusion of Mr O'Shaughnessy, we venture to say that he is nobody's but his own.

The reviewer proceeds to dilate further on O'Shaughnessy's talent, or lack of it, in a way that explains the reference of the *Oxford Magazine* (2 March 1898) to 'the severity shown by some other critics who have preceded us'.

In registering his displeasure at Palgrave's selections, therefore, Housman was not running counter to the general critical view, and certainly the reader of three-quarters of a century later would not be disposed to quarrel with the majority of his excisions. Most of them are uninteresting poems, some bad, some laboured (Browning's 'Amphibian' and Clough's 'Sic Itur' come under this head). Another large group, which overlaps the first, may have qualified for their dismissal by reason of their Victorian sentiments: one cannot imagine Housman taking kindly to Archbishop Trench's lines:

> Yet suffering is a holy thing;
>   Without it what were we?
> (CXXXII)

But some of these poems were not bad by any means: 'The Charge of the Light Brigade', 'Prospice' and 'Say not, the struggle nought availeth' are pieces which have at any rate survived into our own time. Tennyson's 'In the Children's Hospital', while less to our taste, was praised as a contemporary record by George Orwell in his essay 'How the Poor Die', and contains a realistic sketch of an accepted pathological type, that of the pre-chloroform surgeon-sadist, even down to the traditional red hair. Housman's disapproval of the poems by Tennyson Turner and Clare may have been justified, but Palgrave represents both poets in their most mid-Victorian light, and even so Housman's deafness to 'I am! yet what I am . . .' remains curious. Of Lord Houghton's contributions, it can be said that his neo-Regency pieces have awoken in at least one reader the wish to seek out his published volumes.

One can go further, moreover, and say that Housman's critical judgement does not seem always to have operated consistently. He rejected 'The Charge of the Light Brigade' but not three pieces by Sir Francis Doyle ('The Loss of the "Birkenhead" ', 'The British Soldier in China' and 'The Red Thread of Honour') in which the theme of British military courage and honour is exploited much more blatantly. Charles Tennyson Turner's young Sophy in VIII does not seem more worthy of censure than his Letty in III. In view of the many cancellations of pieces by O'Shaughnessy, the survival of 'A Love Symphony' (LXI) is all the more remarkable: its quality may be estimated from its last stanza:

> And then I went down to the sea,
>   And heard it murmuring too,
> Part of an ancient mystery,
>   All made of me and you:
> How many a thousand years ago

I loved, and you were sweet—
Longer I could not stay, and so
I fled back to your feet.

The last stanza of the same poet's 'Zuleika' received stricter assessment: Housman struck out four of the eight lines and left the others:

And soon they will reach the shore
Of that land whereof he sings,
And love and song will be evermore
The precious, the only things;
They will live and have long delight
They two in each other's sight,
In the violet vale of the nightingale,
And the flower that blooms by night.

(xxxvii)

The modern reader may be pardoned for failing to guess which of these lines won the approval of the future author of *The Name and Nature of Poetry*.

This record of a collision between the taste of the most celebrated mid-Victorian anthologist and that of the coming great classical scholar who had already made a unique contribution to English literature is full of interest, but the result of it is not precisely what might have been expected. True, Housman disliked the book, but so did contemporary reviewers, and their dislike would be largely endorsed today. What is more surprising is his deletion of some poems which have survived, and his non-deletion of others which, both on account of their quality and in relation to his other cancellations, ought to have been condemned. In the first case extra-literary considerations may have been at work: impatience with their sentiments, or even with their authors. In the second—and this is probably the larger field—both his leniency and his inconsistency in indulging it seem uncharacteristic. Perhaps there was more of a mid-Victorian in Housman than is generally realized. Posterity's deletions, at any rate, have outnumbered his own.

I am most grateful to Mr Sparrow for drawing my attention to this particular copy, and for allowing me to examine it at leisure.

1971

It Could Only Happen in England:

A study of John Betjeman's poems for American readers[1]

The quickest way to start a punch-up between two British literary critics is to ask them what they think of the poems of Sir John Betjeman. For while their author has attained nearly every honour open to a writer of verse in this country, his work and its reputation still evoke a remarkable variety of response there.

Few at any rate would deny that the poems in this book make up the most extraordinary poetic output of our time. By extraordinary I don't necessarily mean good: good poems are surprising rather than extraordinary, keeping the power to inflict their tiny pristine shock long after they have become familiar; but good poems can seem extraordinary too at first (*Leaves of Grass*, 'The Wreck of the Deutschland'), and it is only when this extraordinariness wears off that we can see whether the surprise remains. One must admit first of all that Sir John (he was knighted in 1969) is an extraordinary man. He is not, as some might suppose, one of the landed gentry like Sir Osbert Sitwell, nor is he a member of some university, gallery or museum that provides him with a comfortable stipend. In fact his public image is that of a freelance television personality and literary journalist, the sort of person who crops up on cultural TV panel games ('Where's this? When was it built?' etc.), conducts the viewer round England's cathedrals or goes up in a balloon to point out vanished villages, and who can be relied on for an appropriate half-hour of reminiscence or anthology at Christmas. Somehow he manages to produce an occasional book, often heavily illustrated, on a topographical or architectural theme.

But this is only half the story: Sir John is at once both a more and a less serious personality than this suggests. He is a Commander of the Order of the British Empire, a Companion of Literature, A Royal Fine Art Commissioner, a governor of Pusey House, a holder of honorary

[1] Written as an introduction to the American edition of John Betjeman's enlarged *Collected Poems* (Boston: Houghton Mifflin, 1971).

doctorates from three universities. On the other hand, he is one of modern England's few upper-class licensed jesters: usually photographed roaring with laughter, he will ride a bicycle through crowded London, dress up in Henry James's morning clothes (which he seems to own), explain how much he still loves his old teddy bear Archibald. How he finds time to write poems at all is a mystery: they certainly cannot take their origin in emotion recollected in tranquillity, for (to judge by appearance) Sir John has no tranquillity. His energy is boundless.

The many contradictions of this public role are sustained by a personal charm and enthusiasm remarkable in anyone, let alone a writer. Unaffected, self-deprecating, generously tolerant of the views of whoever he is speaking to (I remember once saying to him 'Churches are all the same really', to which he replied 'Oh, I wouldn't say that', which on reflection seems the biggest understatement I have ever heard), he makes it hard for anyone to remain immune from the persuasive friendliness and honesty he radiates. Some critics, however, manage to do so, nor do they find Sir John's extraordinariness especially impressive. 'All right, suppose he does cavort round the country in a squashed hat and mackintosh, with his old teddy bear under one arm and a copy of *Crockford's Clerical Directory* under the other, suppose he does write poems about Victorian Gothic and sports girls and being afraid of death—the whole act is really only a hangover from those ghastly Twenties, isn't it? You remember, when everybody had to be "amusing"—owning pigeons and dyeing them pink and mauve, admiring people like Firbank and Angelica Kauffmann, printing facetious rubbish on private presses and playing "practical jokes" that got in the way of people doing real work. Sure enough, he saw the red light—compare the typography of *Continual Dew* in 1937 with *Old Lights for New Chancels* in 1940—but he didn't really do any more than turn himself into a woolly toy for what's left of the so-called upper classes, sucking up to the Royals and encouraging the bourgeois to snigger about saying "serviette" and poke fun at the Welfare State. Oh, it's been quite an achievement: when the rest of the boys are dead or creeping about in dark glasses like silver-haired mummies, Betjeman's got his knighthood and gold medal and all the rest of it—you've got to hand it to him. But it's the sort of thing that could only happen in England.'

American readers may like to judge the justice of this view.

'Betjeman has a mind of extraordinary originality; there is no one else remotely like him.' The speaker is Sir Maurice Bowra, as reported by the Earl of Birkenhead,[1] when both Birkenhead and Betjeman were Oxford undergraduates. The words have the ring of careful consideration, and came from a clever man: what can we infer from them? Not, at any rate, that Betjeman was a prize student: in fact he left Oxford without a degree. Nor, surely, that he was typical of his own or any other generation. What Bowra meant was that the sort of thing he heard this ex-Marlborough undergraduate say when he invited him to dinner in Wadham College was completely unlike the common talk of the day. Posterity can only conjecture what it was like: first, there was bound to be an astonishingly detailed knowledge of church architecture, furnishing and monumental sculpture, nurtured by Betjeman's preparatory schoolmaster Gerald Haynes,[2] mixed with a voluble brand of High Church camp about fiddleback chasubles and Eastern position and Low Church cocoa and so on. Then, a loving and vivid evocation of places, Cornwall, Highgate, the City of London; a gurgling celebration of little-known literature, the poems of the Reverend E. E. Bradford, the Reverend Robert Stephen Hawker, Campbell, and Arthur Machen's *The Secret Glory*; and over all a bubbling farcical affection, a self-abasing sense of ridicule, a defiant advocacy of the little, the obscure, the disregarded, all backed up with an astonishing memory and an outstanding gift for phrasing, not of the smart epigrammatic sort, but that which conjures a picture to fix whatever it is in the hearer's mind for ever. All this, coming from a toothy, somewhat baby-faced young man in a much too expensive suit and shirt and Charvet tie, was so unlike the general *blague* of the Twenties that the tough-minded Bowra knew he had picked a winner.

Betjeman was already in possession, at least in embryo, of the themes that were to make him famous, and they were resolutely opposed to the spirit of the century in two major ways: they were insular, and they were regressive. To compare Betjeman with a real figure of the Twenties, a Harold Acton, is to see immediately what a poor figure he would have cut in the Paris of Stein and Cocteau: he was not, and never has been, a cosmopolitan. To understand this we

---

[1] *John Betjeman's Collected Poems*, compiled and with an introduction by the Earl of Birkenhead (London: John Murray, 1958).
[2] *See* John Betjeman, *Summoned by Bells* (London: John Murray, 1960). ch. V.

have to realize that at Betjeman's heart lies not poetry but architecture—or, if the concepts are allowed, a poetry that embraces architecture and an architecture that embraces poetry:

I only enjoy to the full the architecture of these islands. This is not because I am deliberately insular, but because there is so much I want to know about a community, its history, its class distinctions, and its literature, when looking at its buildings, that abroad I find myself frustrated by my ignorance. Looking at places is not for me just going to the church or the castle or the 'places of interest' mentioned in the guide book, but walking along the streets and lanes as well, just as in a country house I do not like to see state rooms only, but the passage to the billiard room, where the Spy cartoons are, and the bedrooms where I note the hairbrushes of the owner and the sort of hair-oil he uses. My hunt in a town is not just for one particular thing as an antiquary might look for Romanesque tympana, an art historian for a particular phase of baroque, or an architect for Le Corbusier, but it is for the whole town. . . . I like to see the railway station, the town hall, the suburbs, the shops, the signs of local crafts being carried on in backyards. I like to be able to know for certain where to place what I am looking at. In a building I like to be sure whether that building is an original or a very good fake. This I can do in my own country but am not so sure about in someone else's.[1]

And elsewhere, more emphatically: 'For architecture means not a house, or a single building or a church, or Sir Herbert Baker, or the glass at Chartres, but your surroundings; not a town or a street, but our whole over-populated island.'[2]

What Betjeman is saying here is that his fundamental interest is human life, or human life in society, and that architecture is important in human life because a good society is one dwelling in well-proportioned surroundings. This would seem to place him with writers such as Ruskin and Morris, people for whom the appearance of things approached a morality, and in a way this is true, for with Betjeman the eye leads the spirit: he tells us that he came to the Christian religion by means of church architecture and formal ritual. But Betjeman has always mocked Morris ('Hand-woven be my wefts.

[1] John Betjeman, *The English Town in the Last Hundred Years* (Cambridge: CUP, 1956), pp. 4–5.

[2] John Betjeman, *Antiquarian Prejudice* (London: Hogarth Press, 1939), p. 5.

hand-made / My pottery for pottage'), and we shall see that it is not so much the architecture of a building that appeals to him as its relation to human use, to human scale and size, and the degree to which it reflects human life and emotions.

The quality of regressiveness I mentioned earlier might indeed be taken as no more that a latter-day version of the anti-industrialism Morris and Ruskin and their followers so vehemently professed. If the spirit of our century is onwards, outwards and upwards, the spirit of Betjeman's work is backwards, inwards and downwards. If the architecture of our day is high-rise flats, its heroes the working class, its environment motorways lit with sodium, Betjeman exalts Comper interiors, clergymen's widows and gaslight. If the age is agnostic and believes everyone is a socialist nowadays, Betjeman embraces the Christianity of the Church of England and proclaims a benevolent class system the best of all possible worlds. In a time of global concepts, Betjeman insists on the little, the forgotten, the unprofitable, the obscure; the privately-printed book of poems, the chapel behind the Corn Exchange, the local water-colours in the museum (open 2 p.m. to 4 p.m.). This, at any rate, is how the British public knows him: the man who is always trying to stop things being pulled down, or blocked in, or covered in wires or concrete railings or tarmac; the man who hates town clerks 'from north of Trent' and speculative builders, and all the modernizers and centralizers and rationalizers who are bent on making things easy for the motorist, or safe for the kiddies, or economic for the corporation cleansing department. To go for a drive with Betjeman is to enjoy a constant monologue on what he sees, a series of variations on the theme 'Gosh, how lovely' (interspersed, when he gets bored, with a flat voice that greets every fresh architectural prospect of distinction with the assurance 'We're 'avin' that down'); some idea of this may be gained from 'A Walk with Mr Betjeman', by Tom Driberg,[1] a fascinating and on the whole successful attempt to preserve a record of this highly developed and humorous sensibility in action. Of course, Betjeman is not an isolated figure: there are many societies striving to preserve both town and countryside, and they are starting to link up with all who are increasingly concerned with the nature of our environment as the century nears its poisoned end, but Sir John is their figurehead, their most original voice, the signature that appears

[1] The *New Statesman*, 6 January 1961, pp. 9–10.

most often under letters to *The Times*. In fairness one should also point out that he got in first.

All this is a necessary prelude to an understanding of Betjeman's poems, partly because a great deal of what he writes is, overtly or covertly, propaganda for what he believes, partly because his poetic aesthetic is only another version of his social aesthetic. The first thing to realize about Betjeman as a writer of verse is that he is a poet for whom the modern poetic revolution has simply not taken place. Insularity and regression rule here as there. For him there has been no symbolism, no objective correlative, no T. S. Eliot or Ezra Pound, no reinvestment in myth or casting of language as gesture, no *Seven Types* or *Some Versions*, no works of criticism with titles such as *Communication as Discipline* or *Implicit and Explicit Image-Obliquity in Sir Lewis Morris*. He addresses himself to his art in the belief that poetry is an emotional business, and that rhyme and metre are means of enhancing that emotion, just as in the days when poetry was deemed a kind of supernatural possession (I have been trying, without much success, to think of any present-day work demanding such a hypothesis); the result is that Betjeman's poems, however trivial or light-hearted their subjects, always carry a kind of primitive vivacity that sets them apart from the verses of his contemporaries and captures the reader's attention in advance of his intellectual consent:

> Miss J. Hunter Dunn, Miss J. Hunter Dunn,
> Furnish'd and burnish'd by Aldershot sun,
> What strenuous singles we played after tea,
> We in the tournament—you against me!

There lurks within him someone who weeps at Victorian ballads ('My heart finds rest, my heart finds rest in Thee') and roars out Edwardian comic songs ('There's something about a varsity man that distinguishes him from a cad'), someone to whom every poem seems to *matter* in a rare refreshing way. For Betjeman's poems, forthright, comprehensible, and couched in the marked button-holing rhythms of Praed or Tennyson, are nothing if they are not personal: they are exclusively about things that impress, amuse, excite, anger or attract him, and—and this is most important—once a subject has established its claim on his attention he never questions the legitimacy of his interest. Energy most contemporary poets put into screening their impulses for security Betjeman puts into the poem.

The result is, at first sight, a poetic corpus of extreme oddity: Betjeman, we remember, has a mind of extraordinary originality; there is no one else remotely like him. And yet his actual subjects, in so far as they are classifiable, are familiar enough: topography, religion, satire, death, love and sex, people and childhood take care of four-fifths of the pieces, and really only an occasional poem is totally eccentric (for instance, 'The Heart of Thomas Hardy'). The uniqueness lies in his approach, a blend of the direct and the round-about. The verse just quoted is the opening of a love poem, yet what could be simultaneously more personal and ironic than the first line? The passionate reiteration of the beloved's name in a form in which it would appear, say, on her visiting-card conveys that she is clearly seen by the poet in the context of the middle classes, and that this increases her attraction for him. Betjeman has told us[1] that the poem was the expression of his feelings for a superintendent in the canteen of the Ministry of Information during the war, but even in such a traditionally direct exercise he has to invent the persona of a subaltern (or junior army officer), stage an imaginary (and somewhat masochistic) tennis match in Aldershot, and follow it with the most suburban of club dances. All this apparatus is necessary before he can say what he wishes to say—and yet, we reflect, Aldershot is a military town, and even if Betjeman was never a subaltern he did marry the daughter of a field-marshal: the poem's feeling is genuine, even if the properties are fiction—yet even the properties have, perhaps, a kind of truth.

Let us look more closely at a poem such as 'Middlesex': actually a lament for the disappearance of the countryside he knew as a boy because of the expansion of suburban London, it nevertheless starts with a gaily satiric portrait of 'fair Elaine the bobby-soxer' and a two-stanza description, acute but not unfriendly, of her home life. The subsequent switch to the River Brent may seem disconcerting, but a rapid succession of rural cameos brings us (as so often) to the human element, the long-dead inhabitants of this long-lost peace, put forward under the names of minor characters from one of Betjeman's favourite books, George Grossmith's *The Diary of a Nobody*. Only then do we see fair Elaine's function, to contrast with these 'cockney anglers, cockney shooters' and represent, with her mindless

---

[1] *The Golden Treasury of John Betjeman* (Spoken Arts 710), Band 1. See also *Sunday Times Magazine*, 8 August 1965, pp. 16–21.

consumption of branded products, those who now live in this built-over ex-paradise, her ironically Tennysonian name implying the decline such a transformation has entailed.

Transition to a more direct poem, 'The Metropolitan Railway', is easy, for past inhabitants of Ruislip are again the subject: a young Edwardian married couple ('your parents'—or his?) who come to London to work and shop respectively, and meet at Baker Street Station in the evening to go back together to 'autumn-scented Middlesex again'. In this case Betjeman first fixes our attention on a light-fitting of the period that remains in the station buffet the pair would have used: slowly he 'tracks' (the cinematic metaphor is almost inevitable) to the couple's arrival and day in Edwardian ('safe hydraulic lift') London; sharply the poem 'cuts' to the poignantly brutal:

> Cancer has killed him. Heart is killing her.
> The trees are down. An Odeon flashes fire
> Where stood their villa by the murmuring fir

and its last line takes us back to the station buffet again with its hanging electrolier, the *art nouveau* of an age when 'Youth and Progress were in partnership', but now we see it with a new understanding of its place in the poem.

This kind of poetry (and I hope these few remarks have demonstrated, at least in outline, its existence and nature) has its parallel with Betjeman's kind of architecture: just as that meant 'our whole over-populated island', so the poetry means the furniture of our lives: 'The Metropolitan Railway' is about the lives of an Edwardian married couple, and by implication all married couples, but take away the early electric suburban railway, the period light-fitting, the 'sepia views of leafy lanes in Pinner', and the poem collapses. Betjeman is a true heir of Thomas Hardy, who found clouds, mists and mountains 'unimportant beside the wear on a threshold, or the print of a hand': his poems are about the threshold, but it and they would be nothing without the wear. 'For the landscape that most appeals to him', as Mr John Sparrow wrote in his perceptive essay,[1] 'is the inhabited landscape: he cannot see a place without seeing also the life that is lived in it, without becoming conscious of its

[1] *Selected Poems by John Betjeman*, chosen with a preface by John Sparrow (London: John Murray, 1948).

human associations . . . he can find matter for poetry in the least promising surroundings, provided they have an individual character and the breath of life.'

It isn't surprising, therefore, that his poems should be about people as well as places, nor that, just as places cannot be separated from people, so the people cannot be separated from their places. Each of them carries a sharply-realized background—Myfanwy and North Oxford, the clergyman's widow and the house of rest, the night-club proprietress deep in her frowzy London mews, business girls lying in rickety built-on bathrooms, even the church mouse among the long-discarded cassocks; through each of them we see a life we should never have known, in circumstances that may have already disappeared. Or, if they are not individuals, they still make up the element of humanity—the wear on the threshold—that is so essential in Betjeman's vision; the elderly Oxford dons in 'I. M. Walter Ramsden', and beyond them, like old rowing groups, the 'long-dead generations' going back beyond Ypres and the Somme to golden summers of Edward and Victoria:

> They remember, as the coffin to its final obsequations
>   Leaves the gates,
> Buzz of bees in window boxes on their summer ministrations,
>   Kitchen din,
>   Cups and plates,
> And the getting of bump suppers for the long-dead generations
>   Coming in
>   From Eights.

Time and again, with Betjeman's best poems, the reader exclaims, But this is about a place! And then the realization follows that the place is presented in terms of its human association, without which it would be insignificant: '. . . not a house, or a single building or a church . . . but your surroundings; not a town or a street, but our whole over-populated island.'

Betjeman is consistent: he has said what he believes in, whether in architecture or poetry, and it is the backbone of his verse, at once its strength and its appeal. Of course it is not always imbued with compassion; sometimes it is tinged with fun—it would be a poor account of Betjeman that didn't say he is a master of the comic and the absurd—sometimes with amorousness, sometimes with satire: for someone often accused of tenderness towards the establishment,

Betjeman spends an unusual amount of time attacking things, sometimes with quite remarkable ferocity ('Slough', 'In Westminster Abbey'). In such passages the social-history content of his verse rises sharply:

> . . . The children have a motor-bus instead,
> And in a town eleven miles away
> We train them to be 'Citizens of To-day'.
> And many a cultivated hour they pass
> In a fine school with walls of vita-glass.
> Civics, eurhythmics, economics, Marx,
> How-to-respect-wild-life-in-National-Parks;
> Plastics, gymnastics—thus they learn to scorn
> The old thatch'd cottages where they were born.
> The girls, ambitious to begin their lives
> Serving in WOOLWORTH's, rather than as wives;
> The boys, who cannot yet escape the land,
> At driving tractors lend a clumsy hand.
> An eight-hour day for all, and more than three
> Of these are occupied with making tea
> And talking over what we all agree—
> Though 'Music while you work' is now our wont,
> It's not so nice as 'Music while you don't'.

It is customary to say that Betjeman fails as a satirist; he is certainly too kind a writer to be really savage. On the other hand, most literary critics these days are on the left wing, and so are unlikely to be appreciative of a passage such as the one above. For my part, I find the last five lines not only a pertinent summary of a subject no other present-day British poet has tried to deal with, but singularly unforgettable. But politics apart, his deceptively gentle verse can move into an attack so smooth its efficiency is seen only in retrospect:

> Our lodging-house, ten minutes from the shore.
> Still unprepared to make a picnic lunch
> Except by notice on the previous day.
> Still nowhere for the children when it's wet
> Except that smelly, overcrowded lounge.
> And still no garage for the motor-car.
> Still on the bedroom wall, the list of rules:
> *Don't waste the water. It is pumped by hand.*
> *Don't throw old blades into the W.C.*

Don't keep the bathroom long and don't be late
For meals and don't hang swim-suits out on sills
(A line has been provided at the back).
Don't empty children's sand-shoes in the hall.
Don't this, Don't that. Ah, still the same, the same
As it was last year and the year before—
But rather more expensive now, of course.

But in fact Betjeman is an accepter, not a rejecter, of his time and the people he shares it with. The notion that he is a precious aesthete whose sensibilities are perpetually either quivering before Victoriana or shuddering at locutions such as 'toilet'[1] is totally misguided. On the contrary, he is a robust and responsive writer, registering 'Dear old, bloody old England' with vivacious precision and affectionate alliteration quite beyond most avowed social realists. His gusto embraces it all—the mouldy remnants of the nineteenth century, the appalling monoliths of the twentieth, the dead church, the dying peasantry, the conurbation and candy-floss and King's College, Cambridge—all the sadness and silliness and snobbery is potential Betjeman material. I have sometimes thought that this collection of Betjeman's poems would be something I should want to take with me if I were a soldier leaving England: I can't think of any other poet who has preserved so much of what I should want to remember, nor one who, to use his own words, would so easily suggest 'It is those we are fighting for, foremost of all.' This may not be an orthodox critical judgement, but I don't see why it shouldn't be taken into account.

I have every sympathy with the American reader faced with the task of arbitrating on the value of these poems. To start with, Betjeman constitutes a kind of distorting mirror in which all our critical catch-phrases appear in gross unacceptable parody. He is *committed, ambiguous,* and *ironic*; he is *conscious of literary tradition* (but quotes the wrong authors); he is a *satirist* (but on the wrong side); he has his own *White Goddess* (in blazer and shorts). And he has done all those things such as *forging a personal utterance, creating a private myth, bringing a new language and new properties to poetry,* and even (more than 100,000 copies of the first edition of his *Collected Poems* were sold) *giving back poetry to the general reader,* all equally undeniably, yet none of them in

[1] E.g. 'Are the requisites all in the toilet?' Perhaps the American equivalent would be 'bathroom'.

quite the way we meant. No wonder our keen critical tools twitch fretfully at his approach.

From this point of view alone he represents a worthwhile challenge to readers of any country. I can well imagine the American demurring, however, on the grounds that Betjeman is like cricket, something absolutely peculiar to these islands and in consequence absolutely unexportable. 'All these place-names and English products—Ruislip Gardens (how d'you pronounce Ruislip?), Windsmoor, Jacqmar, Drene, Innoxa, Brent, Wembley, Northolt . . . and what's this bona fide stuff? And this cockney (what's that?) book I haven't read: you've told me what it is, but he doesn't. . . . No, I'm sorry, this is just too private for me. I don't mind how many local cracks he puts in, that's his privilege, but he'll have to take the consequences.' Such an attitude would be understandable, but there are several points to be made in reply. First, and perhaps rather unexpectedly, an English reader would go some of the way with it. I know Brent, Wembley, Northolt and so on are in Middlesex, because Betjeman tells me so, but I've never been there and what I feel about them depends entirely on what he tells me about them: they might as well be in New York State. In 'The Metropolitan Railway' the same applies to all the place-names; I don't know what the Bromsgrove Guild was (though I can guess), and I don't know where the quotation comes from in the last stanza. Some of Betjeman's poems are completely incomprehensible to me (e.g. 'The Irish Unionist's Farewell to Greta Hellstrom in 1922') while remaining emotionally potent. In sum, the English reader is going to need an annotated Betjeman almost as soon as the American.

Secondly, it isn't outrageously novel to expect a little topographical and period background to a work of literature on the part of its reader: think of James Joyce's Dublin. The crucial point is whether the reader gets enough out of the work initially to make it worth his while solving the references to deepen his enjoyment. In the case of Betjeman there are enough universal situations ('Cancer has killed him. Heart is killing her') to make this so; at a lighter level, there is enough fun to be had from the rhymes and metres. The task would be similar to, say, picking up the Regency references ('And boroughs were bought without a test') in Winthrop Mackworth Praed.

Even if I have been underestimating the American reader, however, he still might say something like 'All right, so Betjeman's English like Joyce is Irish, but even so I can't believe these poems add

up to much: places get described, and there are a few sketches of
people (mostly ones it's too bad about), and some pretty good
evocations of the past, *eheu fugaces* and all that, and some comedy, but
all in all it seems minor to me. What are you ranking it with? Eliot?
Auden? Honestly I don't think it makes that grade. It's more like what
you were saying, you know, Twenties stuff, Bright Young Things and
so on. Not serious.' Well, in a sense this is where we started: this is
where the punch-ups begin in England.

Betjeman is serious because he has produced an original poetry of
persons and surroundings in which neither predominates: each
sustains the other, and the poetry is in the sustaining. His texture is
subtle, a constant flickering between solemn and comic, self-mockery
and self-expression; to compare him (again) with Praed brings out the
mechanical side of the latter, and the essentially *vers de société* quality
of his switches of feeling. To compare him with Housman or Hopkins
tempts one to talk in terms of poetic ballistics: they penetrate deeper,
but he makes a bigger hole, by which I mean only that while I doubt if
any of Betjeman's pieces can be advanced against 'Tell me not here',
or 'I wake and feel the fell of dark' (still less 'The Wreck of the
Deutschland'), he can claim a much greater range of theme and
manner and metre. He offers us, indeed, something we cannot find in
any other writer—a gaiety, a sense of the ridiculous, an affection for
human beings and how and where they live, a vivid and vivacious
portrait of mid-twentieth-century English social life.

To say he is unique, however ('there is no one else remotely like
him'), is not to say that he stands outside the course of poetic history. I
once wrote that Betjeman was 'one of the rare figures on whom the
aesthetic appetites of an age pivot and swing round to face an entirely
new direction'[1]: certainly it is worth noting that, forty years after he
began to publish, young men are bearded like Victorian paterfamilias
and young ladies are draped in art nouveau shifts. But it applies to
poetry as well. I have already said that he has little in common with
what we call 'modern' poetry; his remarkable popularity in England is
partly due to this. For it is as obvious as it is strenuously denied that in
this century English poetry went off on a loop-line that took it away
from the general reader. Several factors caused this. One was the
aberration of modernism, that blighted all the arts. One was the
emergence of English literature as an academic subject, and the

[1] *Listen*, vol. III, no. 2 (Spring 1959), p. 14.

consequent demand for a kind of poetry that needed elucidation. One, I am afraid, was the culture-mongering activities of the Americans Eliot and Pound. In any case, the strong connection between poetry and the reading public that had been forged by Kipling, Housman, Brooke and *Omar Khayyám* was destroyed as a result. It is arguable that Betjeman was the writer who knocked over the 'No Road Through to Real Life' signs that this new tradition had erected, and who restored direct intelligible communication to poetry, not as a pompous pseudo-military operation of literary warfare but simply by exclaiming 'Gosh, how lovely' (or 'Gosh, how awful') and roaring with laughter. He became the living contradiction of Eliot's contention that the better the poet, the more complete the separation between the man who suffers and the mind which creates.

His relation to Eliot is in fact curious. One of the more striking passages in *Summoned by Bells* describes how, as a schoolboy in Highgate, he fancied his poems were 'as good as Campbell now':

> And so I bound my verse into a book
> *The Best of Betjeman*, and handed it
> To one who, I was told, liked poetry—
> The American master, Mr Eliot.

The scene is worthy of a nineteenth-century narrative painter: 'The Infant Betjeman Offers His Verses to the Young Eliot'. For, leaving aside the question of their respective poetic statures, it was Eliot who gave the modernist poetic movement its charter in the sentence 'Poets in our civilisation, as it exists at present, must be difficult',[1] and it was Betjeman who was to bypass the whole light industry of critical exegesis that had grown up round this fatal phrase by demonstrating that a direct relation with the reading public could be established by anyone able to be moving and memorable.

This sounds as if the two were in opposition, but I am not sure that Betjeman has not a strong affinity to 'the American master'. Why must poets be 'difficult'? Because 'our civilisation comprehends great variety and complexity, and this variety and complexity, playing upon a refined sensibility, must produce various and complex results'.[2] Why should a poet bother himself with this complexity? Because: 'there is an aspect in which we can see religion as the *whole*

[1] T. S. Eliot, *Selected Essays*, 3rd edn. (London: Faber, 1951), p. 289.
[2] ibid.

way of life of a people, from birth to the grave, from morning to night and even in sleep, and that way of life is also its culture.'[1]

And what is this 'whole way of life' that a poet should (presumably) concern himself with expressing? Eliot was obliging enough to leave us a list of its properties: 'Derby Day, Henley Regatta, Cowes, the twelfth of August, a cup final, the dog races, the pin table, the dart board, Wensleydale cheese, boiled cabbage cut in sections, beetroot in vinegar, nineteenth-century gothic churches, and the music of Elgar.'[2]

Now if this passage reminds us of anyone's poetry, it is Betjeman's rather than Eliot's or anyone else's. But over and above this, what kind of response is Eliot adumbrating, if not the one I have already quoted from Betjeman? '. . . how much is embraced by the word culture. It includes all the characteristic activities and interests of a people.'[3] '. . . not a house, or a single building or a church . . . but your surroundings; not a town or street, but your whole over-populated island.'

It is, to say the least of it, notable that both writers should have chosen to emphasize the identical element of cultural inclusiveness in describing what they most value; perhaps it is a coincidence, like the fact that both of them, by their different ways, were led to Anglicanism and the Church of England. It does, however, provide another instance of Betjeman fulfilling one of our critical criteria in an unexpected and not entirely acceptable way. Can it be that, as Eliot dominated the first half of the twentieth century, the second half will derive from Betjeman? I do not think this is as completely unlikely a suggestion as it might first appear. After all, he may be unique, but he is not solitary. Behind him stand Hardy, Tennyson, Crabbe, Cowper, the Reverend Robert Stephen Hawker—all those on whom he descanted so persuasively at Sir Maurice Bowra's dinner table many years ago.

1971

---

[1] T. S. Eliot, *Notes Towards the Definition of Culture* (London: Faber, 1948), p. 31.
[2] ibid.
[3] ibid.

Mr Powell's Mural

'Jean, rather splendid in what was called "The New Look" . . .' Yes, the war is over and Nicholas Jenkins and his friends have resumed their civil round[1]; or, as Mr Powell puts it:

> The war had washed ashore all sorts of wrack. . . . Among the many individual bodies sprawled at intervals on the shingle, quite a lot resisted the receding tide. Some just carried on life where they were on the shore; others—the more determined—crawled inland.

Much of the crawling has a distinctly literary flavour. The new publishing firm of Quiggin & Craggs (possessed of the goodwill of the now defunct Boggis & Stone, not to mention the Vox Populi Press) launches a magazine named *Fission* under the editorship of one Bagshaw (an unmemorable character whose previous appearances, if any, have escaped me), and this provides a rallying point for faces old and new. Nick becomes literary editor, Widmerpool contributes an article entitled 'Affirmative Action and Negative Values', and both come in contact with a fancy-stick-carrying Fitzrovian novelist unpromisingly called X. Trapnel (X for Xavier). After two years (virtually the span of the book) the magazine folds up, not without accompanying calamities: a parody of Widmerpool by Trapnel ('Assumptions of Autarchy v. Dynamics of Adjustment'), the attempted destruction by Lady Craggs (née Gypsy Jones) of a book by Odo Stevens called *Sad Majors*, and the actual destruction of Trapnel's new novel *Profiles in String* by Pamela Flitton, now Pamela Widmerpool.

Even bearing in mind that the *Music of Time* novels read better the second time than the first (on the first reading one is looking for events, which in fact are nearly always secondary in importance to the way the events are presented), I found the literary element in this one disappointing. Bagshaw is a cipher, and though office conflicts and general snideries are occasionally referred to they are never

---

[1] Anthony Powell, *Books Do Furnish a Room* (London: Heinemann, 1971).

demonstrated convincingly: the whole thing, in fact, is wrapped up with an only just decent haste in half a dozen pages of the last chapter. Possibly the author's intention was that *Fission* should serve as a kind of maypole round which the dance could continue: it certainly does that. But no more. The most immediately rewarding sections are the portraits of Pamela Widmerpool and X. Trapnel. Mr Powell is good at horrible women: an earlier example, Mrs Maclintick, regrettably doesn't appear in these pages (she is reported to be keeping Moreland hard at work), but whereas her horribleness centred on and was mostly reserved for her husband, Pamela Widmerpool practises bitchery as a way of life. One could in fact call this a sketch of a psychopath, if such a clinical term suited Mr Powell's urbane world, but even his suave prose can't soften her edges.

Trapnel, too, is another favourite type:

> He wanted, among other things, to be a writer, a dandy, a lover, a comrade, an eccentric, a sage, a virtuoso, a good chap, a man of honour, a hard case, a spendthrift, an opportunist, a *raisonneur*; to be very rich, to be very poor, to possess a thousand mistresses, to win the heart of one love to whom he was ever faithful, to be on the best of terms with all men, to avenge savagely the slightest affront, to live to a hundred full of years and honour, to die young and unknown but recognised the following day as the most neglected genius of the age. Each of these ambitions had something to recommend it from one angle or another, with the possible exception of being poor—the only aim Trapnel achieved with unqualified mastery. . . .

Mr Powell himself makes the comparison with Roland Gwatkin, another of his studies in self-delusion, but Trapnel, apart from being a writer and therefore someone to whom such fantasies are appropriate and even useful, is a formidable bohemian of the kind that always travels in taxis because you're less likely to be served a writ in them than if you go more cheaply. He is also a skilled and ruthless cadger, and cultivates a somewhat gothic persona involving swordstick, greatcoat and so on. Even a provincial like myself can hazard a guess at his original: it's surprising that Mr Powell hasn't managed to find him a distinctive voice compared with, say, Sillery ('Brightman and I are buddies now'). I should also have wished him a better role to sustain than the latest in the line of Widmerpool-discomfiters, especially as his success is partial only, and carries a fearful retribution.

For the rest, much of the book's pleasure resides in the small reminiscential effects Mr Powell's grip on his by now enormous cast enables him to bring off (are we to assume that the junior named Akworth who appears in the school library on page 235 is the son of the Akworth described as 'shot out' for sending a note to Peter Templer in *A Question of Upbringing*, and that Akworth senior is therefore forgiven?), and of course there are the sudden uproarious jokes, such as the character who lingers in Dicky Umfraville's memory as the creator of a cocktail called 'Death Comes for the Archbishop'. The book ends without suggesting that the remaining two volumes of the sequence are likely to contain any innovations of form or content capable of upsetting the opinion we have already formed of it.

I am, I suppose, a Powell fan. Lovers of Mencken will remember how it was accepted in the editorial office of the *American Mercury* that a delivery from the bootlegger should suspend all work until the treasure had been unwrapped, fondled, and even tasted. A new Powell affects me in much the same fashion. I hang the equivalent of 'Gone Fishing' on my door, and tear at the wrapping with a connoisseur's anticipation and a schoolboy's greed. I know I shall be constantly amused—shall, indeed, laugh out loud several times—and intermittently charmed, stimulated, impressed and made to consider, and that all this will be achieved not by any sort of accident but with the utmost awareness and forethought, Mr Powell being a novelist who loves to contrive effects that depend on the reader's observation and intelligence.

But equally I am not, I hope, uncritical, and if, with this instalment, the end of the work is in sight, it might be worth considering how far it seems to be succeeding in what it set out to do, and how far its publishers are justified in using the adjective 'great' on the latest inside front cover. It's ironical, in my view, that the main element lacking in *The Music of Time* should be the sense of time itself—time passing, people getting older, the feeling of lines shortening and choice decreasing. This isn't to say that Mr Powell is careless of what might be called chronological colour: he is always ready with the period detail (though he makes a slight mess of the words of 'South of the Border' in *The Valley of Bones*). Perhaps, too, in a sequence in which the central character is only forty on the first page of volume 10 too great an emphasis on the hourglass and scythe might be out of place. But consider the well-known words from almost the opening paragraph of the whole series:

> The image of Time brought thoughts of mortality: of human beings . . . moving hand in hand in intricate measure: stepping slowly, methodically, sometimes a trifle awkwardly, in evolutions that take recognisable shape: or breaking into seemingly meaningless gyrations, while partners disappear only to reappear again, once more giving pattern to the spectacle . . . .

If this passage is taken to express Mr Powell's purpose, I think it explains why the element of 'time passing' is absent. To show life as a dance or a spectacle means concentrating on the dance-like and spectacular aspect of it, and ignoring precisely those factors which are essential if 'mortality' is to be portrayed: the drawing of characters in depth, the involvement of the reader in their fortunes, the evocation of suffering. In obedience to Mr Powell's plan, his characters come on, do their thing, disappear, return to do it once more in changed circumstances, and so it goes on. This frigid design is perfectly permissible for what is basically a comic novel, and indeed is there any comic novel in which time is felt to pass? But then most comic novels are not concerned with time.

I press the point because I believe this deliberate artificiality brings with it other qualities that give the books an ultimately superficial character. A small example is Mr Powell's habit of calling people by place-names—Isbister, Widmerpool, and now Ada Leintwardine: an accepted practice, but hostile to suspended disbelief if one knows the places, or even of them. More important is the style. A formal, slightly absurd view of life requires a matching style: Mr Powell's is Comic Mandarin, a descendant of Polysyllabic Facetiousness:

> Sillery's attitude might in this respect be compared with the late St John Clarke's, both equally appreciative of invitations from ladies of more or less renowned social status and usually mature age; 'hostesses' in short, now an extinct species, though destined to rise again like Venus from a sea of logistic impediment.

Although this is played off admirably against vernacular *oratio recta* ('Bugger off—I want to be alone with X'), it does in fact suggest that nothing it describes should be taken quite seriously; it imparts a glaze to the action, as if one were not getting it first hand, an illusion most novelists strive to preserve. The dance is not only a dance, it is performed behind gauze.

It is possible, in consequence, for Mr Powell to write at length about his characters without our ever getting to know them better. Nick Jenkins's anonymity is privileged (though I wonder sometimes how much money he has, and where it comes from), but what of Widmerpool? From being a school butt his gradual assumption of authority (via the putting-to-bed of Stringham) was fascinating and convincing, and suggested that this sort of development was one of the 'evolutions' promised in the key paragraph, but of late his 'thing' seems simply to be the pompous man who is involved with fearful women for our amusement, with an increasing loss of credibility (General Conyers's diagnosis—'intuitive extrovert—classical case'—adds little artistic weight). In fact, a developing character with whom the reader becomes involved would, as argued earlier, damage Mr Powell's plan, which really requires no more than 'characters' in the seventeenth-century sense—'humours', almost. Some of his sharpest portraits—Stringham, Uncle Giles, Mrs Maclintick—seem conceived on these lines, with corresponding success. On the other hand, a non-Theophrastian figure, such as Sir Magnus Donners or General Liddament, emerges but pallidly: compare the latter with Brigadier Ritchie-Hook, for instance.

A final and fundamental reservation, which is in fact pointed up in *Books Do Furnish a Room*, is how far we are reading a work of imagination which will attain a cathartic climax and leave us feeling we have learned something of life. At first it seemed we were, the evolution of Widmerpool being a case in point. Later books suggest that we are simply reading what happens to have happened to Nick Jenkins, with the growing suspicion that something very similar also happened to Mr Powell. The war novels began this disillusion, and now Mr Powell goes out of his way to underline the kinship by making Jenkins write a book on Robert Burton to parallel his own work on Aubrey. Imagination must, of course, select and arrange reality, but it must be for imaginative ends: all too often the role of imagination in this sequence is to funny-up events and people whose only significance (think of all the droves of boring Tollands, for instance) is that Mr Powell has experienced them.

These strictures may prompt the reflection that with a fan such as myself Mr Powell needs no detractors: not a bit of it. Mr Powell is writing an enormously long, varied, intelligent and funny narrative that will be a joy to us all for years to come, and his publishers are welcome to quote that on his next jacket if they wish. In pointing out its limitations I am not calling *The Music of Time* a failed *War and Peace*, simply saying that so far it hasn't displayed the impact, the feeling or the comedy that may be found in at least three of Mr Powell's earlier novels, *Afternoon Men*, *From a View to a Death* and *Venusberg*, a fact I think less well known than it should be. But it may be the fate of a mural to lack the concentrated effect of a single canvas.

1971

Supreme Sophisticate

Cole Porter had star quality. When Bessie Marbury told the *New Haven Evening Register* in June 1915 that this twenty-four-year-old ex-Yale man was the only one who could 'measure up to the standard set by the late Sir Arthur Sullivan', she was giving early warning of this. The latest, and probably not the last, is *Cole*,[1] a medium-sized paving stone of a book made up of two very different kinds of material: photographs and facsimiles from the Cole Porter Collections (Yale and Library of Congress), and the lyrics of a great many of his songs. Together these make up a sort of impressionistic biography, tied with snatches of narrative and quotations from other works, including Porter's own diary ('Sam Katz said to me, "You know, Cole, that song is beautiful, it's—why, it's Jewish." ')

Several strands of appeal can be disentangled. The simplest is that Cole Porter was smart, a rich boy (his grandfather was a millionaire) who made good. We all (Americans especially) are sneakingly impressed by the character in faultless clothes who can talk to French waiters and is with the best bunch on the beach, and in a way Cole was all that ever went with evening dress. He rented the Venetian palazzo in which Browning died, had the first speedboat on the Grand Canal, and married an Edwardian beauty eight years his senior who found Cole 'more fun' than her richer suitors. (She was rich, too: a young lady once had the temerity to ask if her jewels were real. 'Real *what*?' snapped Linda.) The Lido photographs, all brilliantly sunlit, evoke a round of *Tatler*ian tedium: Lady Diana Cooper, Baroness de Meyer, Lady Abdy, Billy Reardon, Countess Buccino, Elsa Maxwell and Countess di Zoppola, the former Edith Mortimer (known to her friends as Tookie), all in Twenties dress that makes men look bounders and the women freaks—how could he have borne it? He invented a couple called Mr and Mrs S. Beach Fitch whose imaginary doings were reported by society editors: Evelyn Waugh used the idea in *Vile Bodies*.

[1] *Cole: A Biographical Essay*, edited by Robert Kimball (London: Michael Joseph, 1972).

But his life was more interesting than this. From being the expatriate playboy-composer, he came back to America and conquered first Broadway and then Hollywood; then at the height of his success he had a terrible accident, a horse falling on him and smashing both his legs. For the rest of his life he was crippled and in great pain, but it made no difference to his work. Even when awaiting the ambulance he went on with the lyrics of 'You Never Know'. When callers asked him how he was, his invariable reply was 'Very well, thank you. Now tell me the dirt.' He was forty-six when this happened, and from then on a kind of patrician stoicism, coupled with his scrupulous professionalism, assumes command. Linda, to whom he remained devoted, became an invalid: when she died in 1954, he had her buried alongside his mother (who had died in 1952 at the age of ninety), and eventually he lay between them. Although he kept up an impassive front, he would never re-enter the house they had shared: eventually he had it destroyed. Meanwhile he pursued his life of lunches and dinners and first nights, interspersed with hours at the writing desk: 'My things,' he would say, and his manservant would bring a container of sharpened pencils, dictionaries, thesauruses and other books, a box of cough drops, a box of Kleenex, quantities of paper, and a Cutty Sark and soda.

For, above all, Cole was a great song writer. 'Night and Day', 'Begin the Beguine', 'I Get a Kick Out of You', 'So in Love', 'Rosalie'—the list is endless, and, what is more, he wrote them all himself: 'That's by Rodgers and Hammerstein,' he would say, 'if you can imagine it taking two men to write a song.' In fact he was Gilbert as well as Sullivan, a point Miss Marbury missed. First he got the beat, then he fitted words to the beat, then he fitted a tune to the words; but for all this his songs divide into two kinds, word-dominated and tune-dominated, the latter being an example of 'what we call footballs —whole notes', as Dick Adler said; 'he knew how to write that song that a singer can belt.' The former usually reads like a single idea repeated (with the aid of a rhyming dictionary) virtually *ad infinitum*: 'Let's Do It', 'The Physician', 'Always True to You in My Fashion '—this is Cole's Gilbertian side, which is highly amusing at a party or in a theatre, but inevitably seems artificial on repeated acquaintance. ('Let's Do It', for instance, is saved only by the buoyant, rising resolution of the theme, and the enchanting tune of the middle eight bars.) The words of tune-dominated songs were usually clichés, lifted from banality by the tunes they served:

> To live it again is past all endeavour
> Except when that tune clutches my heart,
> And there we are, swearing to love forever,
> And promising never,
> Never to part.

As a lyricist, therefore, Cole Porter was well within the comic song/drawing-room ballad tradition that persisted into the Thirties from the previous century. Whether he influenced it is doubtful; the 'Cole Porter song', that feat of rhyme and reference, was rarely copied, and for the rest one must remember that it was a highly literate decade, compared at least with much of what followed. The middle eight of 'Love is Just Around the Corner', for instance (not by Cole), ran

> The Venus de Milo
> Was noted for her charms,
> But, strictly between us,
> You're cuter than Venus,
> And—what's more—you've got arms.

I have tried, without much success, to imagine Mick Jagger singing this. No doubt those who were exposed daily to such products grew up thinking that songs (and perhaps even poems) were skilfully made things, requiring thought as well as feeling. The limitations of such a style, latterly exposed by influxes of folk, Negro and Rimbaud-type lyrics, none the less produced great successes, and for many of these Cole was responsible.

He, too, had his limitations. Writing songs was all he did: he had no ambitions as a composer, unlike Gershwin (or Sullivan), nor talent as a dramatist, unlike Noel Coward. Songs were his life. He wrote his first when he was nine, and after that he never stopped. At Yale he wrote football songs: at the end of his life they gave him an honorary doctorate. 'As Kern is the great romantic and Berlin is the great primitive,' wrote one obituary, 'Porter remains the supreme sophisticate of American song.' But a sophisticate with feeling. The football songs—in Dick Adler's sense—will always be here to prove that.

1972

The Real Wilfred

A writer's reputation is twofold: what we think of his work, and what we think of him. What's more, we expect the two halves to relate: if they don't, then one or other of our opinions alters until they do. When a writer dies young, however, this double process of critical and biographical assessment is dislocated. The work is published, and will not be added to, and we start making up our minds about it: the life, on the other hand, is guarded by widow, family, friends, trustees, and fifty years may go by before a total picture is presented. This is not to say that we have no picture in the meantime: nearly always we have, but it is put out by precisely the people (widow, family, etc.) who are standing in the way of complete documentation. There may be good human reasons for this, and in any case the interim picture will be far from false, but it will almost certainly require ultimate modification, which (again almost certainly) will come as something of a shock. It is doubtful whether the process has been fully worked out in the case of Rupert Brooke, or even Edward Thomas. Jon Stallworthy's present book[1] shows it happening in the case of Wilfred Owen.

Mr Stallworthy takes over what might be called the Wilfred Owen story at a particularly interesting point. When his poems, or a selection of them, first appeared in 1920, two years after his death, their editor, Siegfried Sassoon, made a bold and unusual bid: Owen should not have a Life: 'All that was strongest in Wilfred Owen survives in his poems; any superficial impressions of his personality, any records of his conversation, behaviour, or appearance, would be irrelevant and unseemly.'

It would be interesting to know whose idea this was, and why it was propounded. As a result, Owen's principal poems existed for some ten years in a vacuum, as if they were utterances of The Spirit of the Pities in some updated *The Dynasts*. Their reputation was slow to grow (it is hardly credible that Owen is not represented in even the

[1] Jon Stallworthy, *Wilfred Owen* (London: OUP/Chatto & Windus, 1974).

second (1953) edition of *The Oxford Dictionary of Quotations*, for instance), but once the 2,250 copies of the first edition had been sold it was clear that a more substantial collection, with a memoir, was needed, and this was undertaken by Edmund Blunden.

Blunden's memoir, published in 1931, was produced with the full consent and co-operation of Owen's family (which really meant his mother, as we shall see), and consequently with access to a great many of his letters and papers. The portrait it draws is of a Keats-loving and poetically dedicated youth, sometimes in delicate health, caught up in the holocaust of a European war; the greater part of it concentrates on Owen's army experiences from the time he first went to France with the Manchester Regiment at the beginning of 1917. Many of the now familiar passages from the then unpublished letters were included, together with the unforgettable account of Owen's death by his brother officer, Lieutenant Foulkes, who saw him moving among his men on the banks of the Sambre Canal that morning, encouraging them in their work under the heavy fire that a few minutes later killed him. It is a sober and responsible narrative as far as it goes, and the image of Owen it propounds is well suited to the poems: 'He was one of those destined beings who, without pride of self (the words of Shelley will never be excelled), "See, as from a tower, the end of all." Outwardly, he was quiet, unobtrusive, full of good sense; inwardly, he could not help regarding the world with the dignity of a seer.'

Blunden never met Owen, but he tried to give some idea of what Owen was like by printing reminiscenses of two people who had known him when he was convalescing at Craiglockhart War Hospital, near Edinburgh. One was Mrs Mary Gray, a member of a group that entertained convalescent officers, and the other Mr Frank Nicholson, Librarian of the University of Edinburgh, who met Owen at the Grays' house and subsequently began (at Owen's request) to teach him German. Both insist on Owen's awareness of the suffering the war had produced, Mrs Gray in particular emphasizing his sensitivity and sympathy (perhaps rather amusingly in view of Owen's comment to his mother that his new friend Sassoon was 'so restful . . . after Mrs Gray who gushes all over me').

Here for some thirty years Owen's life rested. To the reader of the poems, conscious of their unique element of visionary compassion, he seemed a genius of a high and extraordinary nature. To endure the Great War, and not only to endure it but to accept it in a way that made possible a mature artistic expression of it, while at the same time both passionately abhorring its horrors and winning the Military Cross—all this argued a personality at once robust and selfless, a spiritual nature both strong and deep. Above all, his modesty, his deference to literary figures destined to seem his inferiors, gave him affinity with the great negative capabilities; if Hardy or even Shakespeare had been killed in action at twenty-five, this, we felt, is how they would have been remembered.

In the Sixties, however, the well-fenced area of Owen studies was progressively flooded by a succession of volumes that swept away both Blunden's pard-like spirit and Sassoon's voice and nothing more. These were the three parts of Owen's younger brother Harold's memoirs, *Journey from Obscurity* (1963–5), and the *Collected Letters* of Owen himself, ably edited by John Bell with the help of Harold Owen, that appeared in 1967. These substantial works—*Journey from Obscurity* runs to over 800 pages, and the *Letters* to nearly 600, not counting editorial apparatus—changed the situation radically. From knowing very little about Owen, we suddenly came to know a great deal. If up till then he had seemed almost a spirit called into being by the Great War's unprecedented beastliness to assert compassion and humanity, he was now an ordinary human being whose 'conversation, behaviour [and] appearance' were if anything over-documented.

As Owen's next biographer, therefore—and indeed one might say his first biographer—Stallworthy's principal duty was to sort out this new material, put it into order, and calculate the effect it had on Owen's image as perpetuated by Blunden (minor contributions by Sassoon in 1945 and Osbert Sitwell in 1950 had necessitated no significant amendments). This task was important for several reasons. First, and astonishingly enough, the new material was hard reading. Harold Owen was a roundabout and sometimes repetitive writer, and Owen's letters, not to put too fine a point on it, were often simply dull. Secondly, however much new information was represented, it still needed to be sifted impartially on the grounds that it was supplied either by the family or by Owen himself. And thirdly, for the first time we were told that there was an Owen problem. In the final pages of his final volume Harold Owen describes how their mother devoted herself to the perpetuation of Wilfred's memory; how she kept everything he wrote or owned (even his revolver, still loaded, was found after her death); how it was she who dealt with

Sassoon and Edith Sitwell, and later with Blunden, when editions and memoirs were in progress. He also makes it clear that he was not happy about this:

> I knew without doubt that the real Wilfred had diverged very far from my mother's conception of *her* Wilfred. . . . She had built for herself an inviolable image—an image not only in the likeness of what she thought he was but one which she in her simple way so passionately wished him to be. . . .

Was Mrs Owen's Wilfred, then, Blunden's Wilfred? Was either the real Wilfred? Or was the real Wilfred simply Harold's Wilfred?

Stallworthy has performed the first of his responsibilities well. Although he sees his work as a portrait of Owen as artist, to complement the portrait in the *Letters* of Owen as eldest son and Harold Owen's portrait of Owen as elder brother, it is primarily a seamless paraphrase (interspersed with direct quotation) of his two main sources. His tone is alert, unprejudiced and vivid. Of the forty illustrations, I have noticed less than half in previous volumes, and he has had the happy idea of reproducing Owen's original manuscript where a poem needs to be cited (this alone gives the book a unique value). He has followed up references with rewarding thoroughness, and his study of Owen's own library (now preserved at Oxford) has revealed some interesting parallels of thought and phrase.

Where his book is less satisfactory is in its lack of emphases and its general suspension of judgement on the kind of person we now know Owen to have been, and how this new knowledge relates to his work. The evidence is there, but perhaps through the very scrupulousness that ensures its accurate presentation Stallworthy refrains from interpreting it. For instance, it is now quite clear that the fundamental biographic fact about Owen is that he was his mother's boy: his family situation was sufficiently like that of D. H. Lawrence for the comparison to be made. Differences in his parents' temperaments, exacerbated by poverty (and the Welsh, musical, humorous, somewhat histrionic Tom Owen is an even more sympathetic figure than Arthur Lawrence), seem to have caused a split in the family, Tom Owen siding with the second son Harold and Colin, the youngest, against Susan Owen and Wilfred and the daughter Mary. Indeed Harold Owen's motive in writing his book (subtitled 'Memoirs of the Owen Family') was partly to heal this split, to reclaim

Wilfred from their mother, and to re-establish Tom Owen and indeed himself as significant figures in Wilfred's upbringing. Mrs Owen was extremely ambitious for her son (she kept a lock of his hair marked 'the hair of Sir Wilfred Edward Salter-Owen at the age of 11½ months'—Salter was her maiden name), and this ambition was transferred to Wilfred by a sort of psychological osmosis. According to Harold, Wilfred was over-adult as a boy, and as an adolescent veered from 'too high spirits' to depression and attacks of bad temper in which he was inclined to lecture the whole family furiously for their failure to attain proper standards. Harold ascribes this to ever-present domestic stress and to self-dissatisfaction. In fact Wilfred seems to have made a fair contribution to such stress. His attitude to Harold was consistently discouraging. When the latter was going to sea at fifteen (one ambitious son in the house was enough, and Harold's wishes to study art were not taken seriously), he called to say goodbye to Wilfred, who was in bed, and who concluded the interview by calling through the closing door 'to remind me how atrocious my English still was, and barked at me that if—when we met again—he found that I had the slightest trace of a Liverpool accent, he would disown relationship for ever.'

Was he being funny? A better occasion could have been found. A less ambiguous incident concerns a time when Wilfred was acting as unofficial tutor to Harold:

> When I showed him my efforts, he would take a fiendish delight in verbally tearing them to pieces, putting on all the time a loud hooting laughter quite unnatural to him; but he enjoyed this part of it all very much and he long afterwards told me he always set the exercises for me just too high so that he could enjoy the pleasures of his destructive criticism.

It is not surprising that Owen, sealed within his mother's love and his own ambition, should have found it difficult to come to terms with the world through the usual channels of friendship, love and work. His formal education ceased when he was eighteen, but although the family could not possibly support him he took care not to commit himself to conventional employment. For over a year he was unpaid lay assistant to the Vicar of Dunsden, and when this appointment came to a rather mysterious end he went to France as an English teacher, at first at a Berlitz School, and later (when the Berlitz routine had proved too heavy) as a tutor in private families. In a letter to his father he said: 'If I have shirked the idea of Shop, or Office, or Elementary School, it is only because I am more clear-sighted than another; and see that once fixed in a low-level Rut one is ever-after straightened [sic] there;—straightened intellectually and socially as well as financially.'

The trouble with Owen's high standards (that his family failed to achieve) was that he had difficulty in reaching them himself. 'A rather ordinary young man, perceptibly provincial,' was Sassoon's first impression of him, and the *Letters* tend to bear this out. Nor was he especially clever. His matriculation was without honours (this sent him to bed for the day), and although the thought of a university degree was constantly in his mind his attempts in that direction suggest that he would have found it much more difficult than would Lawrence ('a great passer of examinations', as Huxley called him). Even his aspirations towards poetry achieved nothing that could be set up tangibly as something attempted and accomplished. All this he recognized: it lay at the root of his depression. 'I must have help,' he told Harold once, 'and I just can't get it.'

More remarkable was his apparent inability to form a significant relation with anyone outside the family—even the poetry-writing Leslie Gunston was a cousin—until he met Sassoon in 1917. 'The Lone Wolf' was his domestic nickname: in November 1914 he wrote to his mother from Bordeaux, where he was teaching: 'I begin to suffer a hunger for Intimacy. At bottom, it is that I ought to be in love and am not. Though I have abundance of acquaintance, and a thousand times more friends here than in England, (since out of the Family, I have not one in England) I lack any touch of tenderness.'

There is a terrible irony in Owen's telling his mother that he ought to be in love and is not. For what the *Letters* cry out on nearly every page is that it was she who magnetized his love, his intimacy, his tenderness. This is demonstrated not so much by the fact that, of the 673 Owen letters that survive, 631 are to her: he could have written another 600 letters to recipients who did not keep them. Even the fact that they are addressed, not to 'Dear Mother and Dad' as they so well might have been, but to 'Dearest Mother', 'My own Mother', 'My dear, dear Mother' could conceivably be explained as a childish survival. It is their frequency, their atmosphere of being written to someone who understands and appreciates everything, and above all their explicit declarations that drive the point home. Letters signed 'Mother's Son', 'Your dear-loving Child', and similar extravagances may contain assurances such as

> Still, I am quite wretched tonight, missing you much. Oh so much! Taking the world as it really is, not everybody of my years can boast (or as many would say, confess) that their Mother is absolute in their affections. But I believe it will always be so with me, always.

That was written not in adolescence, but at the age of twenty-five, within three months of his death. A year earlier he had written, 'I have *only once* since getting through the Barrage at Feyet felt such exultation. . . . The "only once" was when I saw you gliding up to me, veiled in azure, at the Caledonian Hotel. I thought you looked very very beautiful. . . .'

One is reminded of Lawrence's remark reported by Jessie Chambers: 'I've *loved* her, like a lover. That's why I could never love you.' ´

Only there was no 'you'. 'All women, without exception, *annoy* me,' Owen wrote to his mother in February 1914, and it is clear that this was something on which he and Harold did not agree. 'Of course you sailors are all heterosexual by nature,' Wilfred told him, and one of their more serious quarrels arose from a naïve yet cold-blooded attempt on his part to supply Harold with a woman when the latter visited him in camp. One would like to know more of the invitation to Canada from the mother of his pupils, Mme Léger, in August 1914 ('I am conscious that she has a considerable liking for me'), but no doubt Mme Léger would ultimately have agreed with Mrs Gray that 'personal experience and individual development can hardly be said to have existed for him.' Occasionally in his letters to his mother he hints at temptations ('If you knew what hands have been laid on my arm, in the night, along the Bordeaux streets'), but in fact there is no evidence that Owen ever achieved 'Intimity' with a woman.

Inevitably it has been asked whether he was homosexual. Stallworthy, while acknowledging the numerous references to male beauty in the early poems (and bringing to our notice one that begins 'It was a navy boy, so prim, so trim'), suggests that Owen's trouble was no more than that his mother had instilled into him the simple (and at that time common) equation 'women=unclean=bad', which presumably implied 'men=clean=good', but which he might have outgrown as his experience widened. Harold Owen insists that

Wilfred was both attractive to women and attracted by them: 'It was Wilfred himself who would not allow any attraction to develop.' This, he says, was because Wilfred's devotion to poetry was religious in its fervour, and demanded that he be celibate. Neither mentions the description of Owen as 'an idealistic homosexual with a religious background' that Robert Graves added to the American edition of *Goodbye to All That*, and then cut out at Harold Owen's request.

Admittedly there is no evidence of any practice in this direction, either, on Owen's part, but it cannot be ignored that in the last year of his life he was moving in homosexual society. Sassoon introduced him to Robert Ross, whom he met in November 1917; Ross who was reputed to be 'the first boy Oscar ever had' entertained him to luncheon on two successive days, and in May 1918 Owen was staying in the flat above Ross's in Half Moon Street. In early 1918, too, he is in a Scarborough oyster bar with 'a new friend . . . Philip Bainbrigge'; Stallworthy illuminatingly refers us to a mention of Bainbrigge in Timothy d'Arch Smith's *Love in Earnest* (1970), where he appears as the author of an 'obscene dialogue in Latin between two schoolboys', and a verse play, *Achilles in Scyros*, an extract from which leaves no doubt as to its character. The latter work was dedicated to C. K. Scott-Moncrieff, later the translator of Proust, whom Owen met in January 1918 in the company of Eddie Marsh, and who in May was trying to get Owen a post as instructor to a cadet battalion. It is only natural to wonder how long, in such company, any idealistic homosexual would have remained idealistic.

But then the last year, or eighteen months, of Owen's life was markedly different from the rest, although Stallworthy does not take this view: 'he dispels the notion', as the blurb says, 'that the shock of the trenches produced a poet of instant maturity.' At any rate it can be said that Owen's commitment to his subject—the suffering of men in battle — was slow. Despite Blunden's claim (repeated by Sitwell) that Owen did not return to England and volunteer in August 1914 because of the terms of his 'tutorial engagement', we find him ditching the importunate Mme Léger in October 1914, and taking up a fresh post in December that he held till the following summer. During this time his attitude to the war was one of detachment:

> I feel my own life all the more precious and more dear in the presence of this deflowering of Europe. While it is true that the

guns will effect a little useful weeding, I am furious with chagrin to think that the Minds which were to have excelled the civilisation of ten thousand years, are being annihilated. . . .

Nor was his sympathy with the British Expeditionary Force as keen as might have been expected: 'I regret the mortality of the English regulars less than that of the French, Belgian, or even Russian or German armies: because the former are all Tommy Atkins, poor fellows, while the continental armies are inclusive of the finest brains and temperaments of the land.'

As late as August 1915 he is toying with the notion of being 'a Munitions Worker at Birmingham, earning £5 a week'. Or 'Can't Uncle be more precise about "Good job in War Office"?' Or 'I seriously should like to join the Italian Cavalry; for reasons both aesthetic and practical.' It would be tempting to say that he had no real appreciation of the nature of the war if it were not for a letter to Harold Owen on 23 September 1914 recounting at length the wounds of men he had seen in a French hospital. This letter ('I deliberately tell you all this to educate you to the actualities of the war') foreshadows Owen's later habit of carrying photographs of war casualties for production on appropriate occasions, but it is also one more instance of his repressive attitude towards his brother, who at the time was sailing in submarine-patrolled waters and unlikely to relish such education.

None the less his first spell in the line (January to May 1917: his second was from the end of September 1918 to his death at the beginning of November) was a terrific shock. It takes an effort today to realize how completely unprepared, imaginatively, the men of 1914 and 1915 were for the horrors that awaited them: literature had said nothing of the 'hideous landscapes, vile noises . . . everything unnatural, broken, blasted' that was the Western Front, and this probably accounts for Owen's occasional sarcasms ('poets' tearful fooling'; 'Above all I am not concerned with Poetry') at conventional literature, suggesting that he felt he had been taken in. Looking at the thirty or so letters dating from this time one cannot but notice the extent to which he shares his sense of outrage with his next of kin:

I can see no excuse for deceiving you about these last 4 days. I have suffered seventh hell.
I have not been at the front.
I have been in front of it.

I held an advanced post, that is, a 'dug-out' in the middle of No Man's Land.
We have a march of 3 miles over shelled road then nearly 3 along a flooded trench [etc.]. . . .

While this passage, and the many that match it, are no doubt free from exaggeration, they contrast markedly with the tradition that the imaginations of wives or mothers should not be needlessly harrowed. When Lieutenant Kenneth Garnett wrote, after a year's war, to his mother in November 1915: 'Do you remember the fort at Sea View near the Point that the Curwens and I once built? This game is just like that, only more people are playing at it and we don't get into a row for getting our clothes messy . . .'[1] he was in all probability fooling nobody, but at least he was trying. A more usual tone was that of Christopher Isherwood's father, writing to his wife in November 1914:

> I can't think that Jackson had the impudence to tell you that I exposed myself unnecessarily. It was an absolute lie. I am most cautious. Of course one has to lead the men forward and to take risks in doing so, but I never do anything unnecessary or foolish, I can promise you that, and I have got at the back of my mind the determination to get back to see you again.[2]

Owen's letters are not hysterical; they are not even especially self-pitying. They are simply instinct with an 'awful *distaste*', as one of his aunts acutely though rather comically put it, for the whole business, a horror that men should suffer so, that he should suffer so, and he has no compunction about letting his mother know it. At the same time, they do not really prepare us for the poems. There are few, if any, traces of the feeling of 'Futility' or 'Greater Love'. Just once or twice at the end it shows through: 'I came out in order to help these boys—directly by leading them as well as an officer can; indirectly, by watching their sufferings that I may speak of them as well as a pleader can. I have done the first.'

To read Stallworthy's book, and to go back to the two works of which it is so largely an amalgam, prompts the conclusion that a number of elements in Owen's life and character, at first submerged or

[1] *Letters from the Front*, edited by John Laffin (1973), p. 7.
[2] Christopher Isherwood, *Kathleen and Frank* (1971), p. 303.

unresolved, were precipitated by the catalyst of trench warfare into realization or near-realization. This precipitation in some cases was so radical as to give the effect of total reversal. From being indifferent to the war, and to the troops fighting it, he became deeply concerned. From being an unimpressive and derivative poet, he became an original and unforgettable one. From lacking 'any touch of tenderness' he became the spokesman of a deep and unaffected compassion. From being an unlikeable youth he became a likeable and admirable man.

One cannot blame Stallworthy for failing to solve this complex problem; one can, perhaps, regret his failure to recognize it. 'All shaped him for his subject,' he maintains, implying a smooth and harmonious development, but much as one sympathizes with his impatience at the 'instant maturity' legend it remains a convenient shorthand for the evidence as we have it. It would be easy to guess: to say that service with the Manchesters gave Owen his first experience of belonging in a common enterprise and put the 'Lone Wolf' to flight for ever; to say that his encounter with Sassoon and his poems showed him how poetry could and must deal with things as they were and should not be; to say that his association with homosexuals introduced him to an emotional climate that at the time he found liberating and relevant; and to say, finally, that the three experiences were connected. But even if there could be evidence for such hypotheses, we have not got it.

Whether such considerations are the key to the real Wilfred or not, it is certain that the two-dimensional figure of Blunden's memoir is gone for good. In its place we must accept a much more complicated, and even contradictory, personality: commonplace yet uniquely gifted, compassionate yet insensitive, complacent yet diffident, characterized by the unnatural maturity of the mother-dominated yet retaining the eagerness and hilarity of extreme youth. 'This union of opposites was, I fancy, characteristic of his whole personality,' as Frank Nicholson wrote, 'and may perhaps explain his power of inspiring affection in men and women alike.' Affection is not, on the whole, what one feels for the subject of Stallworthy's narrative; even if we discount half of Harold Owen's anecdotes as the settling of a family feud, there is enough left to suggest that Wilfred Owen was on occasion a rather disagreeable young man, and far from the selfless paragon of Mrs Gray's reminiscence.

Does this new view of Owen affect our opinion of the poems? At first one thinks not. They are still there, an eternally resonant monument to one of the most dreadful corners of history. Yet in retrospect two casual sentences from a letter Robert Graves wrote to Owen seem increasingly significant: 'For God's sake cheer up and write more optimistically—The war's not ended yet but a poet should have a spirit above wars—' It is as if Graves guessed intuitively that for Owen the war was not an impersonal calamity to be got rid of as soon as possible, but a private involvement, something that seemed part of his isolation, his frustrated ambitions in poetry, his sexual hang-ups. This is not to accuse Owen of insincerity. Lines such as 'The Poetry is in the pity' and 'The eternal reciprocity of tears' will never lose their enormous impact that is utterly free from affectation. It is just that they no longer seem like utterances of The Spirit of the Pities. Somewhere behind them was a human problem that even after fifty years we are a long way from understanding.

1975

The World of Barbara Pym

The first thing a novelist must provide is a separate world. And so we have Mildred Lathbury, a thirtyish spinster, watching 'new people' move into the flat below hers in a house so very much the 'wrong' side of Victoria Station. Or rather, a new person, Mrs Napier, who wears trousers and is an anthropologist and leaves the washing-up ('I'm such a slut'), but who has a husband ('Rockingham') who collects Victoriana and is a flag lieutenant and will shortly be coming home. Well, it is something to tell the fortyish vicar, Julian Malory, who lives with his enthusiastic sister Winifred and appears vowed to celibacy; but then Rockingham arrives ('You must be Miss Lathbury') and the Malorys take as lodger a clergyman's widow glamorously named Allegra. And then . . .

All six of Barbara Pym's novels (published between 1950 and 1961) open on to this world from different angles: England in the 1950s, and the lives of youngish middle-class people, educated rather above the average and sometimes to a background of High Anglicanism, who find for the most part that the daily round, the common task, doesn't quite furnish all they at any rate do ask. As novels they exhibit no 'development'; the first is as practised as the last, the observation, the social comedy, the interplay of themes equally expert. Although each stands by itself, they are unobtrusively dependent: it is not until *Less Than Angels* (1955), for instance, that we learn what happens to Miss Lathbury of *Excellent Women* (1952), and this technique strengthens the claim of all six to be recognized as an *œuvre*.

Their narratives have the air of being picked up almost at random: the characters have usually been living for some time in the circumstances in which we meet them, and yet some small incident—new tenants in the flat below, a new curate ('but what a pity it was that his combinations showed'), new friends made at a conference of indexers and bibliographers at a girls' school in Derbyshire—serves to set off a chain of modest happenings among interrelated groups of characters, watched or even recounted by a protagonist who tempers an ironic perception of life's absurdities with a keen awareness of its ability to bruise. And so couples—such as Mrs Napier and Rockingham—break up; Prudence visits her college friend Jane who has married a vicar, and meets the local widower; four students after two research grants stay with the professor for a weekend and are put through their paces. And by the end things have changed: three of Miss Pym's heroines are, by the time we take leave of them, seemingly committed to future husbands; the sisters Harriet and Belinda (*Some Tame Gazelle*, 1950) both receive and decline proposals, with the unspoken agreement that they are better off together entertaining the occasional curate; Jane, who is not really an effective vicar's wife ('Oh, if only I had known it would be like this'), fails to find Prudence a husband, but sees her off safely into another love affair. The moral of it all seems to be, as the vicar says 'in too casual a tone to sound priggish', that 'We must accept people as we find them and do the best we can.'

The properties may sound trivial ('but those are the things that make up life, aren't they?'), yet Miss Pym's gay, confident gift invests everything it handles with an individual—comedy, is it? Certainly the reader is always on the edge of smiling: at the anthropological seminar ('*No* ceremonial devouring of human flesh?'), the self-indulgent widower walking out with the predatory lady's companion (' "Is there anything there you would like?" "All on this tray, 15s", Jessie read'), the genteel infighting of office workers ('I was actually here between ten and five to ten this morning'), but the humour is often deflationary: after a slight altercation, Jane and the vicar sit eating 'thick slices of bread spread with a paste made of prawns (and other fish)'—life, it is implied, is very much an affair of 'prawns (and other fish)'. Or more deliberately: when Allegra invites Miss Lathbury out to lunch, first to tell her that she is engaged to the celibate Malory, and secondly to persuade her to 'take on' his sister Winifred ('The room seemed suddenly very hot and I saw Mrs Gray's face rather too close to mine, her eyes wide open and penetrating, her teeth small and pointed'), Miss Lathbury, having extricated herself, tries to restore her composure by purchasing an exotic lipstick against the assistant's advice (' "Thank you, but I think I will have Hawaiian Fire," I said obstinately'). Amusement is constantly foiling more pretentious emotion.

But emotion is there all the same. Throughout the novels runs the theme that if we are to live at all we must turn, however hesitatingly and with whatever qualifications, to someone else—or, as the title-page of her first novel has it, 'Something to love, oh, something to love!' About love on the grand scale ('a large white rabbit thrust into your arms and not knowing what to do with it') Miss Pym says little. Some of her heroines are content with what they have, which is more often little than much ('For here she was sitting on the sofa with the person she had loved well and faithfully for thirty years . . . although he was now married and an archdeacon'); those who do attain a potentially satisfactory relationship do not always find it with the most immediately attractive person or by the most romantic way:

'I rang up to ask if you would come and have dinner with me in my flat this evening. I have got some meat to cook.'

I saw myself putting a small joint into the oven and preparing vegetables. I could feel my aching back bending over the sink.

'I'm afraid I can't come tonight,' I said baldly.

'Oh, I'm sorry.' His voice sounded flat and noncommittal, so that it was impossible to tell whether he really minded or not.

The most explicit affair is that of Catherine Oliphant, who writes stories for women's magazines, and the anthropologist Tom Mallow ('It did not seem to occur to Tom that they might get married. Catherine often wondered whether anthropologists became so absorbed in studying the ways of strange societies that they forgot what was the usual thing in their own'). Yet when she observes him holding hands with a young student in a restaurant, she dismisses him from her flat with a promptitude that is at once funny and moving:

'He smiled weakly. "You're so much braver than I am. I don't believe you mind all this at all." "I do mind. I was very fond of you, but we can't both be in tears."'

Love, for Miss Pym's characters, is everything from a consoling day-dream to a major step that takes them out of the novel's frame, but it can also be how we learn about others, or even reveal ourselves to them. The glamorous Allegra is shown up not only as a shameless husband-hunter but as a bad housekeeper ('Tins half used and then left, stale ends of loaves, and everything so *dirty* . . .'). It is hard to say whether Jessie Morrow, who stalks the widower Fabian in a blue velvet dress that had belonged to his wife ('Constance had a dress rather like that once. Velvet, isn't it?'), is more repulsive than Fabian himself, who puts a framed photograph of himself on his wife's grave instead of a stone. But on balance it is the men who come off worst:

grotesquely insensitive (Bishop Grote, or 'Theodore Mbawawa', on leave from Africa, assures Belinda when proposing to her that her looks don't matter: 'She is not fair to outward view. . .'); automatically stingy (William Caldecot looking at what's left in the bottle and filling his own glass but not Mildred's, Rocky Napier bringing her a bunch of chrysanthemums dragged up roughly from his own garden, not bought from a shop); or perhaps simply selfish, as when Digby and Mark land themselves on Catherine for supper ('It's so depressing cooking for one person, or so one hears'). Miss Pym's novels may look like 'women's books', but no man can read them and be quite the same again.

For conduct is important, as well as love. In the subtlest of her books, *A Glass of Blessings* (1958), Wilmet Forsyth ('rather selfish and frivolous', as the blurb says sternly: she knew Rocky Napier in the Navy) derives much light amusement from her dowdy friend Mary, the personalities of the Clergy House, her excessively sober husband Rodney and his mother, Sybil, in whose house they live; at the same time responding clandestinely to the enigmatic overtures of Piers Longridge, and probing idly into his withdrawn life-style. In the end, however, Mary marries the handsome Father Ransome; Rodney's mother remarries at sixty-nine ('we have the seventies before us, and perhaps even the eighties'), and Rodney admits to having taken Jane's friend Prudence out to dinner 'once or twice'; whereas Wilmet is left not only with the discovery that Piers is homosexual but with the acquaintance of his leechlike boy-friend Keith, who fingers the curtains in her lovely home to see if they are lined, and assures her that Piers does not really think she is 'unlovable' (something he implied at their last unfortunate meeting). Clearly she will never get rid of Keith (this is confirmed in *No Fond Return of Love*, 1961), and we leave her half realizing that love must be earned rather than idly pursued.

So there it stands, the world of Barbara Pym: what stays longest with the reader, once the amusement, the satire, the alert ear and the exact eye have all been acknowledged? Partly it is the underlying loneliness of life, the sense of *vulnerant omnes*, whatever one thinks of when turning out the light in bed ('The only real book of devotion she had . . . told her that we are strangers and pilgrims here and must endure the heart's banishment, and she felt she knew that anyway'); then partly it is the virtue of enduring this, the unpretentious adherence to the Church of England, the absence of self-pity, the scrupulousness of one's relations with others, the small blameless comforts. It is not a world likely to have held its own in the Swinging Sixties, and indeed it did not: Lady Chatterley's reign was not, regrettably, molested by the later unpublished novels. Yet those we have persist in small 'library' reprints; the sparkle they had on first acquaintance has been succeeded by the deeper brilliance of established art; they are miniatures, perhaps, but will not diminish. And when they come to be properly reprinted, as they inevitably will, what better epigraph for them than the reflection of the luckless Tom Mallow: 'He marvelled, as he had done before, at the sharpness of even the nicest women'?

1977

The Changing Face of Andrew Marvell

The celebration in 1921 of the tercentenary of Andrew Marvell's birth evoked an unexpected tribute: an essay on his work and position in English literature by T. S. Eliot. At that time Eliot was far from being the authoritative figure he later became; *Prufrock* (1917) and *The Sacred Wood* (1920) had sounded a new baffling voice, and even this sober reassessment of a familiar author could be seen as part of a campaign of subversion. He was not, he said, trying to heighten Marvell's reputation, simply to isolate his individual quality, but since by the end of his essay he had contrived to suggest that this was something that was lacking in Shelley, Wordsworth, Keats, Morris, Browning, Yeats, Hardy, and several others, it is not surprising that Marvell's standing began to alter nevertheless.

At the end of the nineteenth century the common view of Marvell as a poet was that of an author still half entangled in the artificial traditions of Cleveland and Donne on the one hand, and the political upheavals of his time on the other, but who none the less achieved a number of charming and exquisite poems in the pastoral tradition about gardens and mowers, presumably ascribable to a period spent as a tutor in the household of Lord Fairfax at Nun Appleton in Yorkshire. His political poems, furthermore, and especially 'An Horatian Ode upon Cromwell's Return from Ireland', represented the best of Puritan tradition, that could still find room for a magnanimous nod to Charles I. In the *Cambridge History of English Literature* (1910–16) Marvell is respectfully handled by the Reverend John Brown DD, who classes him with 'Herrick, Lovelace and Wither, rather than with Waller, Sedley, Dorset or Rochester', and sees 'The Garden' as having both the classical spirit of Horace's Epodes and the imaginative intensity of Shelley's 'Ode to the West Wind'. The monumental 11th edition of the *Encyclopaedia Britannica* (1910–11) (although terming him 'a great Puritan poet' and mentioning 'his exquisite "garden poetry"', plainly warms to him as a 'humorist and as a great "parliament man"', giving the greater part of its space to an account of him in these roles. The general impression is of a public figure whose poems were only one of his many claims to our attention.

Eliot's view of Marvell, in a seminal essay that was reprinted in the memorial volume published for the City of Kingston-upon-Hull in 1922, was very different. Conceding right away that 'his best poems are not very many', he nevertheless sees him as an altogether larger poet than Herrick, Lovelace and Wither. 'Marvell's best verse is the product of European, that is to say Latin, culture,' and Eliot finds in it a kind of distillation of an age's mental completeness that can be most simply labelled 'wit': a tough reasonableness beneath lyric grace, an alliance of levity and seriousness found in Gautier, Baudelaire and Laforgue, Catullus, Propertius and Ovid:

> I would
> Love you ten years before the Flood:
> And you should if you please refuse
> Till the Conversion of the *Jews*.
> My vegetable Love should grow
> Vaster than Empires, and more slow.

Marvell (Eliot goes on to claim) possesses the ability to make the familiar strange, and the strange familiar, attaining a brightness and clarity that of itself carries a poetic suggestiveness. He contrasts Marvell's 'The Nymph and the Fawn' with a poem by William Morris, finding Morris misty and vague, Marvell hard and precise in a way that gives his slight theme 'that inexhaustible and terrible nebula of emotion which surrounds all our exact and practical passions'. And he quotes:

> So weeps the wounded Balsome: so
> The holy Frankincense doth flow.
> The brotherless *Heliades*
> Melt in such Amber Tears as these.

Although one may not feel that these lines quite justify Eliot's magnificent description of them, one suspects in fact that his account of Marvell's quality is to some extent a description of his own, or what he would like his own to be. His essay, after all, was one of a number designed to draw attention to the seventeenth century (that seems 'to gather up and to digest into its art all the experience of the human mind'), for this was the period from which many aspects of his own verse derive as well as his Anglicanism and royalism, and the four lines quoted have just that easy assumption of common erudition that Eliot himself had begun to patent. The reference to 'European culture' (one must never forget that Eliot, and for that matter Pound, was American) reinforces this conclusion. In another essay he made it clear that Marvell shared with his contemporaries 'a mechanism of sensibility which could devour any kind of experience'—a mechanism we have, alas, lost. But that is another story.

Eliot's growing influence, supported at first by Pound and then by Leavis, was enough to bring Marvell to the attention of the young critics, and in the space of a remarkably few years he became one of the favourite subjects on their dissecting tables. It would, no doubt, be a gross oversimplification to say that twentieth-century criticism has been motivated by a desire to demonstrate that what looks simple is in fact complicated, that what seems to have one meaning has in fact three or four, and that works of literature are good in proportion to how far they can be shown to exhibit this, but it is impossible to read far in contemporary Marvell studies without believing that it has a sufficiency of truth. Here, for instance, is J. V. Cunningham, in *Tradition and Poetic Structure*, picking up Eliot's praise of the phrase 'vegetable love':

> [His readers] envisage some monstrous and expanding cabbage, but they do so in mere ignorance. *Vegetable* is no vegetable but an abstract and philosophical term, known as such to every educated man of Marvell's day. Its context is the doctrine of the three souls: the rational, which in man subsumes the other two; the sensitive, which men and animals have in common and which is the principle of motion and perception; and, finally, the lowest of the three, the vegetable soul, which is the only one that plants possess, and which is the principle of generation and corruption, of augmentation and decay. Marvell says, then, my love, denied the exercise of sense, but possessing the power of augmentation, will increase 'Vaster than empires.'

Possibly. Another reader might simply think that 'vegetable' was a good adjective for something that grows slowly. In *Some Versions of Pastoral* William Empson is equally illuminating on Marvell's second most famous couplet:

> Annihilating all that's made
> To a green thought in a green shade.

. . . either contemplating everything or shutting everything out. This combines the idea of the conscious mind, including everything because understanding it, and that of the unconscious animal nature, including everything because in harmony with it. Evidently the object of such a fundamental contradiction (seen in the etymology: turning all *ad nihil*, to nothing, and *to* a thought) is to deny its reality; the point is not that these two are essentially different but that they must cease to be different so far as either is to be known. So far as he has achieved his state of ecstasy he combines them, he is 'neither conscious nor not conscious', like the seventh Buddhist state of enlightenment. This gives its point, I think, to the other ambiguity, clear from the context, as to whether *all* considered was *made* in the mind of the author or the Creator; to so peculiarly 'creative' a knower there is little difference between the two.

Possibly again. And again another reader might simply think the lines a good description of the mind of someone half-asleep under the summer trees in a garden. Certainly critic quarrelled with critic on what could or should be read into Marvell's lines: Leavis with Bateson, Douglas Bush with Cleanth Brooks, Pierre Legouis with William Empson, Frank Kermode with Milton Klonsky. The whole situation was summarized by Brooks with an irony as devastating as it was unintentional: 'Marvell was too good a poet to resolve the ambiguity.'

Whether true or not, much of modern Marvell criticism has a curiously inhibiting effect on one's ability to read the poems, just as a description of a chair in terms of whizzing molecules would make one afraid to sit down on it. But whatever its excesses, it is Marvell who has provoked them, and not Herrick or Lovelace or Wither: there must be something in his work to call them forth. Possibly it is a kind of overloading:

> What wond'rous Life is this I lead!
> Ripe Apples drop about my head;
> The Lucious Clusters of the Vine
> Upon my Mouth do crush their Wine;
> The Nectaren, and curious Peach,
> Into my hands themselves do reach;
> Stumbling on Melons, as I pass,
> Insnar'd with Flow'rs, I fall on Grass.

—the paradisal lushness of the garden is made so overwhelming, with a hint of menace in the independently acting fruit, and a touch of the ludicrous in the Hulot-like figure of the speaker (conked on the head with apples, hit in the face by a bunch of grapes, and finally sprawling full length over a melon), that the reader cannot be blamed for seeking an interpretation over and above the poem's face value: that it is the Garden of Eden, for instance, replete with Apple and Fall, or that Marvell is really saying, What a life of sin and temptation I lead! The ingenuity that sees 'The Nymph and her Fawn' as an allegory of the Crucifixion, or a lamentation for lost virginity, while perhaps less understandable, arises from the same cause: an excess in the poem of manner over matter. The quality of Marvell's verse is such that the reader cannot believe that it relates only to a garden, or a pastoral conceit about a girl and her pet; there must be something else, and the reader—the academic reader—is determined to find it. The only one of the major poems where matter approximates to manner is 'To His Coy Mistress', and it is significant that no one so far has propounded a political or theological explanation of it.

Such convolutions seem all the more remarkable when we consider that for some hundred and fifty years after his death Marvell was hardly thought of as a poet at all: Johnson, for instance, a century later, did not include him in his *Lives of the Poets*. The manner of his works' survival is as extraordinary. None of the poems for which Marvell is known today was published during his lifetime: no manuscripts have survived, either holographs or copies. Possibly the Fairfax family had seen some of the Nun Appleton poems (if they really were written there), possibly the coy mistress (if she really existed) had read her ode, possibly the encomia upon Cromwell had reached their subject's austere eyes—possibly, but there is no evidence. On his death in 1678 his housekeeper, Mary Palmer, put together such pieces as she could find as did not seem treasonable and published them as *Miscellaneous Poems* in 1681, signing the preface Mary Marvell. Whether or not she had any claim to this title is one more uncertainty. Some eight years later his satiric poems (for in the latter part of his life Marvell had become a keen critic of Charles II and his court) were published in a volume called *Poems on Affairs of State*, and this was reprinted several times in the next quarter of a century, in contrast to *Miscellaneous Poems*, which was never reprinted.

It seems impossible that a poem such as 'To His Coy Mistress' should not, once printed, become widely celebrated, but again we see an age finding its own image in Marvell and no more. The eighteenth century, like the Restoration, was an age of satire, and Marvell survived as a political figure, a Commonwealth patriot who had made much dangerous fun of the restored monarchy and its public men. His prose polemic, *The Rehearsal Transpros'd* (1672), a reply to *Discourse of Ecclesiastical Polity* by Samuel Parker, was declared by Burnet to be with its successor 'the wittiest books that have appeared in this age', and Charles II is reputed to have read them 'over and over again'. Swift, in his Apology for *A Tale of a Tub* (1704), wrote 'We still read Marvell's Answer to Parker with Pleasure,' even though the substance of their quarrel had long since been forgotten. Those willing to test the truth of these recommendations are welcome to try. As a verse satirist Marvell was clearly effective in the context of his age, but he does not transcend it, as Dryden (whom he sometimes resembles) so manifestly does. The characters and events of which he writes are not preserved in the amber of poetry, or even rhetoric (as in 'An Horatian Ode'); they are roughly handled in coffee-house vernacular:

> But fresh as from the *Mint*, the *Courtiers* fine
> Salute them, smiling at their vain design;
> And *Turner* gay up to his Pearch doth march
> With Face new bleacht, smoothen'd and stiff with starch;
> Tells them he at *Whitehall* had took a turn,
> And for three days, thence moves them to adjourn.
> Not so, quoth *Tomkins*; and straight drew his Tongue,
> Trusty as Steel, that always ready hung;
> And so, proceeding in this motion warm,
> Th' army soon rais'd, he doth as soon disarm.

Few of the satires attributed to Marvell are certainly his, but this was the kind of poem he was writing in his later years. An American critic, anxious to make some sense of the change, suggests that, having brought his own particular brand of lyricism to perfection, Marvell was looking for fresh styles to conquer, but this is not convincing. Not the least of Marvell's claims to distinction is that he is the only substantial English poet to have been a Member of Parliament for eighteen years, and there is nothing more probable than that irritation with public affairs should become the mainspring for his verse.

Curiously enough, he was an exceptionally efficient Member of
Parliament. Elected to represent Kingston-upon-Hull in 1660, he
wrote every few days—whenever the post went—to the officers of
that city to report what was happening at Westminster. Mostly he
wrote of maritime business or other matters that concerned them
(such as 'the cutting of Hull from Hezle' or the duties on spirits and
tobacco), but he did not ignore national events, or even gossip ('at two
a clock some persons reported to be of great quality . . . set upon the
Watch & killd a poore Beadle'). Between two and three hundred of
these letters are preserved in the Guildhall at Hull, and are
exceptionally valuable in that they provide a record of parliamentary
business at a time when public reporting of it was prohibited. The city
in its turn was grateful, and sent him presents of ale and salmon from
the Humber. Not much is known of Marvell, and this unexpected
well-documented glimpse of him as a conscientious public servant is
attractive. Poets are not normally thought of as either efficient or
conscientious.

Even Marvell's reputation as a satirist, however, died with his
subject-matter, and a profound disregard ensued. When interest in
him began to stir again (thanks to a large extent to two essays by
Charles Lamb), his name was slow to get clear of his old associations;
Leigh Hunt thought that he 'wrote a great deal better in prose than
verse.' But FitzGerald provides a fascinating reminiscence of
Tennyson in the Forties reciting 'But at my back I always hear / Time's
winged chariot hurrying near,' with the characteristic comment, 'That
strikes me as sublime, I can hardly tell why.' It was Tennyson who
persuaded Palgrave to include at least 'An Horatian Ode' in The
Golden Treasury (Palgrave also added 'The Bermudas' and 'The
Garden'), but his growing fame is evidenced by the appearance of
Grosart's edition in 1872. 'A most rich and nervous poet,' Gerard
Manley Hopkins called him, providing yet another instance of
Marvell's work seeming something 'where each kind / Does streight
its own resemblance find,' and by this time we are within sight of the
remarkable celebrations at Hull in 1921. Anyone reading their official
record may smile at the decorated tram cars and the Lord Mayor's
designation of the poet as 'the biggest and cheapest advertisement'
Hull had ever had, but their sheer comprehensiveness—the mass
meeting of schools, the Holy Trinity service, the Grammar School's
wreath, the luncheon, the public meeting in the Guildhall, and above
all the involvement of so many leading citizens and representatives

—and even more their evident sincerity—confers great credit on a sometimes maligned city.

It is clear that during the three hundred years since his death Marvell's reputation has taken pretty well every turn it could. If his readers and critics are agreed on anything, it is his extraordinary diversity and the numerous contradictions exhibited by his work and what we know of his character. He was in fact a most ambivalent figure. His poetic manner extends from Elizabethan to Augustan, from metaphysical to classical; its subjects nature versus order, Charles I versus Cromwell, the spirit versus the senses; nor is one ever quite sure how serious he is. He seems to have been equally at home under King or Protector and to have taken easily to the devious ways of practical politics. It has never been possible to say what kind of man he was: according to his eighteenth-century editor, Thompson, 'he had no wife, and his gallantries were not known.' He was variously accused of impotence, homosexuality, and 'frenchified manners', and while such charges were common in the scurrilous pamphleteering of the day, his poem 'The Definition of Love' might bear such an interpretation as well as many another. John Aubrey reports that he was a private drinker ('he kept bottles of wine at his lodgeing, and many times he would drinke liberally by himselfe to refresh his spirits'); oddly enough, Bishop Hensley Henson picked this up at the meeting in the Hull Guildhall, saying it would be nasty if it were true, and also commented that 'the notion of a man writing intensely bitter things about his contemporaries, however much they deserved it, passing them about in manuscript and himself moving unsuspected and unconfessing among them, is unattractive. There is an element in Marvell of aloofness which has not yet been cleared up.' Nor has it. But if we ask how Marvell is regarded today, as compared with 1921 or any other time, we must acknowledge that the question has been made harder to answer by the formidable Marvell industry that has grown up in the last half-century. Certainly it has promoted his reputation far beyond those of Herrick, Lovelace and Wither among what might be called professional readers, but its growth has been in the esoteric areas of Neoplatonic symbolism, linguistic philosophy, and the history of inner literary conventions. Marvell has become the poet of enigma, of concealed meaning, of alternative explanation, of ambiguous attitude, and as such has been found a rich quarry for interpreters. On the other hand, he has not come to be thought more perceptive of human experience, or more sensitive to its pathos, or a better celebrant of its variety. For the general reader his achievement is still the witty tender elegance that informs perhaps half a dozen of his best-known pieces.

Every poet's reputation fades in so far as his language becomes unfamiliar, his assumptions outmoded, and his subject-matter historical, and despite the iron lung of academic English teaching Marvell is no exception. We no longer make much of adulatory poems, whether of national heroes or owners of big houses; the teasing of conceits, whether literary or scientific, strikes us as frigid; conventions such as pastoral now seem wan substitutes for imagination. What still compels attention to Marvell's work is the ease with which he manages the fundamental paradox of verse—the conflict of natural word usage with metre and rhyme—and marries it either to hallucinatory images within his own unique conventions or to sudden sincerities that are as convincing in our age as in his.

> But at my back I alwaies hear
> Times winged Charriot hurrying near:
> And yonder all before us lye
> Desarts of vast Eternity.
> Thy Beauty shall no more be found;
> Nor, in thy marble Vault, shall sound
> My ecchoing Song: then Worms shall try
> That long preserv'd Virginity:
> And your quaint Honour turn to dust;
> And into ashes all my Lust.
> The Grave's a fine and private place,
> But none I think do there embrace.

The sentiment is a familiar one; it has been said before, and will no doubt be said again. It will never be said better.

1978

Dull Beyond Description:

Florence and Thomas Hardy

'A subject for a short story: a world-famous writer in his sixties, married to a hostile and eccentric wife, meets a young woman who is infatuated with literature. They meet secretly, she helps him with his books. The wife dies and they marry, but the writer, tormented by remorseful memories, re-creates his former love in a sequence of poignant poems, neglecting his second wife to do so.' Certainly it is a story for Hardy rather than Trigorin, and the fact that it is Hardy's own story need not surprise us. A writer's life dictates his books: unless its pattern changes, he will ultimately seem to be re-enacting them. What is surprising is that he should so often be unaware of the fact.

But another writer had already seen the potentialities of the situation: 'I am asked to write my reminiscences of a famous novelist, a friend of my boyhood, living at W. with a common wife, very unfaithful to him. There he writes his great books. Later he marries his secretary, who guards him and makes him into a figure. My wonder whether even in old age he is not slightly restive at being made into a monument.' From this note grew Somerset Maugham's *Cakes and Ale*, the publication of which in 1930 upset the second Mrs Hardy very much.

As the present authors point out,[1] Maugham later denied that in creating Edward Driffield he was thinking of Thomas Hardy any more than of George Meredith or Anatole France: in any case, *Cakes and Ale* is primarily about literary reputation, and not the analysis of a human relationship. Nevertheless, up to the publication of Robert Gittings's two-volume life of Hardy in the Seventies the average reader's view of Hardy's marriage to his second wife was much as Carl J. Weber had portrayed it in 1940. After the antipathies of his first marriage to 'Dearest Em', Hardy had been taken over by the quietly managing Florence, who kept away unwelcome visitors ('Florence is

[1] Robert Gittings and Jo Manton, *The Second Mrs Hardy* (London: Heinemann Educational, 1979).

my chucker-out') and gave him the peace of mind to write his last five volumes of verse. It is an agreeable picture, and really not so different, except in tone, from the one Maugham drew. *The Older Hardy* revealed that the picture had been less agreeable for Florence Hardy herself.

Inevitably *The Second Mrs Hardy* repeats much material from the earlier book; and in consequence the reader tends to concentrate on areas that are new to him, or that have been left unexplained. Florence Dugdale was one of five daughters of the headmaster of a National School in Enfield who by slow and painful degrees became a teacher there. A melancholy and ailing young woman, she found teaching irksome, though she stuck it for over ten years and was popular with the young ones. She was much happier writing a children's column for the *Enfield Observer*, or talking to the Enfield Literary Union on Tennyson's *Idylls of the King*, or helping a local poet, A. H. Hyatt, compile pot-boiling anthologies: by a strange irony (the first of many), Hyatt published a selection from Hardy in 1906, and Florence received two letters from him about its preparation. Hyatt was poor and tubercular, but Florence loved him: one might say it is the only real love affair in the book. He was, she said, 'the only person who ever loved me, for I am not lovable.' When he died in 1911, she wrote that he had been 'more to me than anything in the world', and added that she would gladly have given the rest of her life for one brief half-hour with him. She was thirty-two then, and the affair must have strongly reinforced her temperamental sadness: it is said that Hardy found her agnosticism sympathetic, but her melancholy must have pleased him as much (Hardy's sister Kate said that she 'never saw two such dismal critters').

How did they meet? Here uncertainty persists. In *Young Thomas Hardy* it is said that Mrs Henniker introduced them in 1904, but in *The Older Hardy* the meeting is put 'somewhere and somehow in London in the summer of the year 1907'; in the present book this is accepted, and the authors say that Hardy introduced Florence to Mrs Henniker in 1910. Certainly Hardy was in London in the spring of 1907, working on *The Dynasts* in the British Museum; the odd thing is that Florence, who was still technically a teacher, went to London and was granted a British Museum reader's ticket in December 1906. 'The name of her sponsor is not at present available to researchers,' the authors report, which is disappointing; if it was Hardy, their meeting would most likely have been pre-arranged, with Florence cast as a

research assistant. For this is what she became, helping with Part III of
The Dynasts: 'by the summer of 1907, the great writer and the young
teacher were meeting regularly.'

The sour comedy of the next five years until Emma Hardy's death in
November 1912 is more fully related in *The Older Hardy*: the
clandestine visits to Edward Clodd's house in Aldeburgh, the
pushing of her work to amused editors, and her attempts to make a
living from journalism ('the most degrading work anybody could take
up'). Of the extraordinary meeting of Florence and Emma at the
Lyceum Club (ending with Emma inviting her to Max Gate, quite
unaware of her separate relation with Hardy) the authors do not
repeat Gittings's speculation that it was engineered by Hardy
himself. Her week's stay provided plenty of gossip to Clodd ('re
Hardy et uxor'), with whom she seems to have been independently
friendly, but thenceforward she was often there, as if 'both the
Hardys were in love with this girl, so much younger than their
withered embittered selves.' She encouraged Emma to finish *Some
Recollections*, the narrative that provided much material for Hardy's
love poems after her death.

The question, why did Florence marry Hardy, is repeated here with
greater emphasis than in *The Older Hardy*. When Emma died, Hardy
telegraphed for her, and after a short decisive battle with Emma's
niece Lilian she took charge of Max Gate in January 1913. The
following twelve months, so far from showing the inevitability of a
union, make it nearly inexplicable. Hardy, engulfed in a flood-tide of
regret and remembrance, had no time for anyone but Emma; he
talked of her, wrote of her, went in March to revisit the scenes of their
first meeting, leaving Florence alone in the remote ugly house. It was
a complete reversal of roles: now Emma was the cherished one, and
Florence left disregarded at home. And she could see what life with
Hardy was going to be like: 'All I hope is that I may not, for the rest of
his life, have to sit and listen humbly to an account of her virtues and
graces.' Her situation was delicate. Hardy would not be seen with her
in Dorchester, and the servants said she was his mistress (Emma's
personal maid, who stayed on for a month after her death, said many
years later that two hairpins were found in Hardy's bed). He showed
her a grave he had reserved for her in Stinsford churchyard, which
she interpreted as a proposal of marriage and seems to have accepted.
When Lilian reappeared for Christmas, Florence presented her

ultimatum. They were married at Enfield on 10 February 1914. Florence raised the question of a marriage settlement, 'but it seemed to annoy my husband, so I desisted.'

It would not be difficult to see Florence as a person whose only talent was to insinuate herself into people's lives and make herself indispensable. Already there had been the affair of Sir Thornley Stoker, a celebrated Dublin surgeon and brother of Bram Stoker, who needed someone to help with his mentally-afflicted wife. In 1906–7 Florence acted as secretary to Lady Stoker's nurse, reading aloud, answering letters and exercising the dogs, and she was often there until Lady Stoker's death in 1912. When Sir Thornley himself died in 1912, he left her £2,000, thereby much infuriating his relatives who called her 'that woman who got the Stoker money', although the nurse received £5,000. As Florence herself said, she was never so happy as when she had someone to take care of. It was much the same at the Hennikers' in 1911, where she typed Mrs Henniker's stories and took out the bulldogs. Her experiences of wage-earning (that newly-won women's privilege) had not been happy: what she really liked was to work for 'nice' people in their own houses. Given this, she repaid them with assiduous industry and flattering devotion.

The authors' explanation balances self-interest (security, social advancement, the still-potent romance of literature) with altruism: she was sorry for Hardy, he needed her, and for this she was willing to ignore the foretaste she had had of life in a solitary house with a stingy husband more than twice her age. As we already know, her fourteen years of marriage turned out sufficient punishment for any ambitions she may have nursed. The house had no gas or electricity, no proper drains, no bathroom, and an inadequate guest room. Before the year was out, Hardy had published *Satires of Circumstance*, with its heart-rending sequence of Emma poems; the following year Florence had to have an operation, but Hardy did not pay for it. Her own writing (she did publish *A Book of Baby Pets* in 1915) was blotted out by the immense task Hardy laid upon her of sorting and transcribing material for his mock biography, a project the authors ascribe to his desire to conceal his entire relation with Florence before Emma's death. She began to experience Hardy's susceptibility to young women ('as if a light were suddenly breaking through', as one of the maids put it); after another operation (which Hardy tried to prevent) she made a fool of herself over one of them, a young married woman who played Tess with the Hardy Players in Dorchester. And there was the constant depression of life with Hardy: he seems to have simultaneously ignored her and kept her in constant attendance on him. As she wrote to St. John Ervine (complaining to distant friends was her only relief), she had had only one clear week away from Max Gate in seven years, and that was to have an operation.

Her immediate widowhood was not much happier. Sir Sydney Cockerell, who had been a friend of Hardy since 1911, proved a managing co-executor, and with Barrie was responsible for the unwanted Abbey funeral (the local vicar suggested the gruesome dismembering). Cockerell, who was a more complex and sympathetic character than the authors suggest, was in later years dismissive about Florence:

> Mrs Hardy was dull beyond description—an inferior woman with a suburban mind, but very ambitious to be well off. I helped her a great deal in her life. Hardy left a very large estate; she found herself suddenly with £50,000 and wanted to shine. She thought Sir James Barrie would marry her. Barrie *did* propose—in a moment of emotion; but, to her great chagrin, he backed out. I regarded her as second-rate, though she started by greatly improving Hardy's comfort.

The authors find against the Barrie anecdote, but confirm that in early 1929 (barely a year after Hardy's death) Florence was nursing Barrie in London, sending eggs and flowers, and arranging tête-à-tête dinners: there seems no doubt that she hoped to be his second wife. One can only pity her, for if Hardy had been a path that led nowhere emotionally, Barrie was a veritable Lob's wood, out of which she stumbled in great distress back to Max Gate several years later. The remainder of her life up to her early death in 1937 was spent, rather surprisingly, as a woman of affairs in Dorset: she was a magistrate, a patron of Dorset General Hospital, and played a large part in a slum-clearance housing scheme in Dorchester, where (unlike Hardy) she was popular. It sounds as if, belatedly, she came to some extent into her own after the Hardy years, that had been, if not beyond description, certainly dull.

The authors withhold a final verdict, but their interim summary is just. Even though the attraction of literature as a way of life proved illusory, she remained loyal to Hardy, providing him with a decade and a half of peace in which to produce the bulk of his poetry. While at times she may have been gossipy and ingratiating, there is no evidence of her doing anything hurtful or unkind; she was undoubtedly more sinned against than sinning, if indeed she was either. In the somewhat sweeping judgement of her cook: 'He didn't want a wife. He wanted an unpaid secretary. Of all the married couples I have known I am certain that Mrs Hardy was the most unhappy of any wife.'

And what, finally, does all this add to our view of Hardy himself? Certainly this has undergone strange refraction of late. Looking in the index under 'Hardy, Thomas: Character' we find (omitting the page references) 'hypochondria, self-absorption, stinginess, luxuriating in misery, selfishness, inhospitality, susceptibility to young women, mother-fixation'. This hardly recalls the author of *Tess* and *Jude*, and one cannot help thinking that Hardy biography will eventually have to settle somewhere between the twin poles of adulation and execration. The strongest impression one gets from the present account is that Hardy could have written an equally good poem about a man who never noticed anything at all. He never noticed that Florence and Lilian were locked in bitter opposition; he saw nothing odd about publishing a sequence of love poems to his first wife within twelve months of marrying his second; he forgot Florence's birthday, as Florence said he had forgotten Emma's. 'In the sex-war, thoughtlessness is the weapon of the male, vindictiveness of the female,' as Cyril Connolly wrote, but this was not war; it was more as if the freshness and delicacy of feeling that Hardy retained into his eighties required a formidable carapace of indifference and self-absorption to protect and preserve it. It was more a kind of innocence, though of an unappealing kind. The reader is left wondering, with Somerset Maugham, whether there is a point beyond which innocence becomes culpable:

'. . . I think that when he had exhausted an emotion he took no further interest in the person who had aroused it. I should say that he had a peculiar combination of strong feeling and extreme callousness.'
  'I don't know how you can say that,' cried Roy. 'He was the kindest man I ever met.'
  Mrs Driffield looked at me steadily and then dropped her eyes.

1979

The Girls

Every so often a work of literature appears that is also an attempt to blow up some preconceived idea. *The Way of All Flesh* tried to explode filial affection; *Man and Superman* the idea that men chase women (oddly enough, both date from 1903). Their effect was minimal: children went on loving their parents; man continued to propose. Yet seventy-five years later, no doubt for quite other reasons, family ties have become psychologically suspect and women are claiming the same sexual freedom as men. The books, in some obscure way, have come true.

The four novels known collectively as *Les Jeunes Filles* (or *The Girls*)[1] written by Henry de Montherlant in the 1930s constitute a similar attempt to blow at least the capital letters off Women, Love and Marriage. 'The girls' are the half-dozen women in the life of a young novelist, Pierre Costals, but reduce themselves primarily to two: Andrée Hacquebaut, an intellectual admirer from the provinces who represents the tedium of being loved, and Solange Dandillot, the granddaughter of a public prosecutor ('that alone would have been enough to make me want her'), who embodies the hazards of loving. The narrative mixes Andrée's fantasy life of unanswered letters to Costals with his own fascinated pursuit and capture of Solange, even though he recognizes that it is sucking him nearer and nearer the whirlpool of bourgeois marriage.

Both themes are used to mount a colossal barrage against women. They are naturally inferior, haters of reality ('I don't want to think of it'); they cling and make a virtue of suffering; they get everything second-hand. Marriage is absolutely contrary to nature, both because man cannot help desiring many women and because women in any case become undesirable at twenty-six. Daily quotations for a Misogynist's Calendar appear on every page: 'The only thing a woman can do for a man is not to disturb his happiness'; 'In every

---

[1] Henry de Montherlant, *The Girls*, a tetralogy of novels, translated by Terence Kilmartin, 2 vols. (London: Weidenfeld, 1959).

woman there is a tart waiting to get out, and who does get out when she starts to sing'; 'When you are with a woman it is not a question of a thing being good but of its costing money'; 'Living together is almost wholly a business of waiting for the other.'

This kind of thing is of good sturdy lineage, akin to music-hall jokes and seaside postcards, but as in the case of Butler and Shaw it has been somewhat overtaken by events. Montherlant's principal dichotomy—men this, women that—has virtually disappeared from our unisex world. 'Mysterious Eve', that fag-end of the courtly love tradition, is no longer peddled even in romantic novels. Costals's claim that 'there is no valid reason why a woman should be treated otherwise than a man' has become an Act of Parliament. Conventions of courtship, whereby the lightest sexual relations had to be preceded by two or three wasted hours at a concert or restaurant (some of the book's funniest scenes derive from this), are now more direct. The element in marriage that frightens Costals most—its permanence—is hardly likely to frighten anyone today.

All the same, the formula of a man being pursued by one woman while pursuing another cannot help succeeding, and the contrast of Costals's pretensions (at thirty-four he is really too good to be true: eight novels and the Legion of Honour) with his uneasy interviews with his future mother-in-law, or his visits to different solicitors in search of 'automatic divorce', is rich in irony. Costals is something of a dream figure, what every man would like to be if he had the courage (he adds up how long women keep him waiting, and drops them when the total reaches five hours); he is also an agglomeration of inconsistencies held together by the force of his creator's obsessions. If he is so enviably independent with his 'necklace of young mistresses' (mainly kept off-stage: one supposes they are whores), why does he bother with Andrée and Solange at all? If the ages of chivalry (Greece, Japan and so on) in which women played 'not the least part' were so admirable, why does his male solidarity amount to no more than standing a taxi-driver a drink after an evening with Solange? Even his much-emphasized virility seems freaked at times with paedophilic ambivalence.

What remains, when all the windmills have been knocked over and the compensation fantasies acted out, is 'the constant duel that goes on in the male between his generosity and his egotism, between his blood and his sperm'. Costals is not the monster he claims ('A writer worthy of the name is always a monster'): he 'accepts' Solange when her father dies, and becomes engaged to her when her mother tells him that she is losing weight through worry about him.

He puzzles over this in his diary: 'Nothing on earth could make me feel I need her round me. . . . I marry you, not to make me personally happy, but to make you yourself happy.' His procrastination is literally 'self' preservation, an inability to immolate himself to his own generosity. Two years afterwards he writes to Solange (who by this time has married an engineer): 'One day, I preferred myself definitely to you, and from that day order was restored once more in all things. All the misfortune came from the fact that there were moments when I preferred you to myself.' This is the heart of the book, one that is likely to go on beating as long as human beings are in association at all.

But, if Costals is not always convincing, the girls are. Andrée's long accusing letters are full of the boredom of the provinces and the loneliness of hearing children's voices outside in the summer afternoon. Solange, with her plush bunny-rabbit and 'Laughing Faun' (an ornament Costals dreads her bringing to the matrimonial home), has a characterless obstinacy that makes Costals's strategic retreats all the more believable. And, convincing or not, Costals is often very funny: his hatred of his fellow writers, both the young experimentalists of 'Studio 27' and the holders of recognized jobs in 'the buffoonery of French literature' (great Catholic novelist, great Napoleonic historian—this passage was omitted from the final 1959 edition); his strokes of self-parody ('Anguish! The bristles of my clothes-brush have turned white in a night'); his vanities ('a fortnight had elapsed, and she had got no further towards developing the snaps of him she had taken'); such facets make his personality a shimmer of attraction and repulsion that is repeated in the tapestry of the book itself.

The Girls is both maddening and exhilarating, preposterous and acute, a celebration of the egotistical sublime and a mockery of it, a satire on women that is also an exposure of men, with a hero who, even as we reject him as make-believe, settles ever deeper into our consciousness.

1979

All Right When You Knew Him

It might be expected that this dispassionate and well-researched study,[1] the first book on Housman for over twenty years, would confirm or deny the accepted view of the 'acidulous but passionate bachelor don', as a recent writer described him, who, in Auden's brilliantly cruel line, 'kept tears like dirty postcards in a drawer.' Such, however, is not Mr Graves's intention. Drawing on many sources, some of them unpublished, he is for the most part content to assemble the evidence, and leave interpretation to the reader.

Minor surprises apart (who would have thought Housman was a pioneer air traveller, in the days of open cockpits?), one's first impression is that Housman's life was, if not happy, then remarkably successful and well organized. Not many people plough Greats at twenty-one and become a professor of Latin at thirty-three, supported by the leading classicists of the day.

He enjoyed academic society, helping to reform the constitution of University College London and, as secretary of the Garden Committee, directing the gardeners of Trinity College, Cambridge. His reputation as a scholar became unassailable, his fame as a poet world-wide (16,000 copies of *A Shropshire Lad* were sold in 1918 alone).

Although a bachelor, his family was large and affectionate, and he kept on good terms with its survivors: 'he always seemed', his sister-in-law wrote, 'to enjoy things and be happy.' He relished good food and wine, and indulged his sexual tastes (which were homosexual) on holidays in Italy and France; even in his seventies he was writing, 'I shall have a friend with me who would not mix with you nor you with him.' Honours, including the Order of Merit, were offered him only to be refused, although he accepted an honorary Fellowship of his Oxford college, St. John's, where the most genial of his portraits hangs in the Senior Common Room.

Then again, he seems to have been a very nice man. He was

[1] Richard Perceval Graves, *A. E. Housman: The Scholar-Poet* (London: Routledge, 1979).

unconcerned with money: in 1914 he sent 'the bulk of his savings' to the Exchequer, a gesture he repeated in 1931, and when his publisher, Grant Richards, went bankrupt he helped him to re-establish his business (he never took royalties for *A Shropshire Lad*).

Some people found him taciturn and withdrawn, but not all: the Master of Trinity's daughter remembers him pulling crackers and playing with children and their woolly animals, while John Drinkwater encountered 'nothing but charm, amiability, friendliness and responsiveness' (not that Housman thought much of Drinkwater's poems). All in all, the reader is reminded of the old music-hall song "E's all right when you know 'im, but you 'ave to know 'im fust.'

How does this square with the poems? For Housman is the poet of unhappiness; no one else has reiterated his single message so plangently:

> To stand up straight and tread the turning mill,
> To lie flat and know nothing and be still,
> Are the two trades of man; and which is worse
> I know not, but I know that both are ill.

His unhappiness had nothing to do with the Wine Committee, or the sailors and ballet dancers he met in Paris; it was buried deeply in the years before 1892 with the death of his mother on his twelfth birthday, his unrequited love for Moses Jackson, the realization that his nature made him one set apart.

And his poems were its sole expression: Housman could never have taken Hardy's random subjects, the second-hand suit, the discarded parasol. His sorrow required its own mythology, the haunting, half-realized legend of ploughing, enlisting, betrothals and betrayals and hangings, and always behind them summertime on Bredon, the wind on Wenlock Edge, and nettles blowing on graves.

Poetry for Housman was a physical thing, like tears. It might have been thought that when the 'continuous excitement' of 1895 had found its expression and died down he would write no more, reconciled to the world through recognition and success. But it was not to be: in 1922 he heard that Moses Jackson was dying, and once again verses poured forth. Between 30 March and 9 April he filled fifty-seven pages of his notebook; the resulting collection was with his publisher in June, and *Last Poems* was published in October.

To be more unhappy than unfortunate suggests some jamming of the emotions whereby they are forced to re-enact the same situation even though it no longer exists, but for Housman it did still exist. If unhappiness was the key to poetry, the key to unhappiness was Moses Jackson. It would be tempting to call this neurosis, but there is a shorter word. For as Housman himself said, anyone who thinks he has loved more than one person has simply never really loved at all.

1979

The Batman from Blades

The first pseudo-Bond novel appeared in 1968, four years after Ian Fleming's death: here, thirteen years later, is the second.[1] At first this suggests, hearteningly, that James Bond has joined that small but select club of characters who have been brought back to life after the death of their creators simply because their readers want more of them. But thirteen years is a long time, and during it there has been ample reason to fear that Bond had floated (literally at times) out of the world of fiction into that of cinematic fantasy, which is not quite the same thing. As everyone knows, the Bond novels were an adroit blend of realism and extravagance, and both were necessary: the one helped us swallow the other. Because Sir Hugo Drax had red hair, one ear larger than the other through plastic surgery, and wore a plain gold Patek Phillipe watch with a black leather strap, we accepted that his Moonraker rocket could blow London to bits. The Bond films, on the other hand, dispensed with the realism and concentrated on the extravagance, becoming exercises in camped-up absurdity. In this way there became two Bonds, book-Bond and film-Bond, each with his separate public. And a certain hostility arose between them: for the readers, the films were ludicrous and childish travesties; the viewers, if they had ever heard of the books, saw them simply as material to be guyed, perhaps deservedly. Since Gresham's Law operates in the world of entertainment as well as anywhere else, it looked as if the films were winning. But here is another novel. Is book-Bond making a come-back?

Looking at the original canon after some twenty years confirms their almost mesmeric readability. 'I ask weekly at the library for another Ian Fleming,' wrote George Lyttelton to Rupert Hart-Davis in 1957, 'but they are always out':

> How bad, and at the same time compellingly readable [his] thrillers are! The pattern of all four that I have read is identical. Bond does

[1] John Gardner, *Licence Renewed* (London: Cape / Hodder & Stoughton, 1981).

not attract me, and that man with brains on ice and pitiless eye who organises the secret service in London seems to be a monument of ineptitude. Everything about Bond and his plans is known long before he arrives anywhere. But I cannot help reading on and there are rich satisfactions. . . .

Indeed there are: the first sixty pages of *Moonraker*, culminating in the bafflement of grand-slammed Drax; the giant centipede in the bed in *Dr No*; the meeting with 'Captain Nash' on the train in *From Russia with Love*; all these and many more are vibrant triumphs of excitement. And the villains seem as grotesquely menacing as they ever did: Dr No with his metal hands, Le Chiffre with his 'obscene' Benzedrine inhaler, Mr Big and his great grey football of a head. Fleming was, in short, a natural writer with a vividly bizarre imagination and a mastery of tension. But what strikes one most about his books today is their unambiguous archaic decency. So far from being orgies of sex and sadism, as some outraged academics protested at the time, the books are nostalgic excursions into pre-Carnaby Street values, Gilbert and Sullivan as opposed to the Beatles. England is always right, foreigners are always wrong (Fleming's best villains are all foreign). Nobody, at least on our side, is a double agent, or has the remotest connection with Philby and Co. Girls are treated with kindness and consideration, lust coming a decorous third. Life's virtues are courage and loyalty, and its good things a traditional aristocracy of powerful cars, vintage wines, exclusive clubs, the old *Times*, the old five-pound note, the old Player's packet. Not for nothing did Kingsley Amis, in his affectionate, knowledgeable and perceptive study *The James Bond Dossier* (1965), class Fleming with 'those demi-giants of an earlier day, Jules Verne, Rider Haggard, Conan Doyle' (he might have added John Buchan): 'Ian Fleming has set his stamp on the story of action and intrigue, bringing it a sense of our time, a power and a flair that will win him readers when all the protests about his supposed deficiencies have been forgotten. He leaves no heirs.'

The last sentence has a double irony, for within three years Robert Markham's *Colonel Sun* was published, and Markham was Amis himself. The experiment was an interesting one: Amis was both a first-class writer and a Bond fan, and what he produced was a workmanlike job, though one reader at least blenched to find Bond drinking rosé with his cold beef, or with anything else for that matter.[1] The local colour (Greece) was well boned up, and Amis gave the politics an original twist: Bond ends by receiving congratulations and thanks from Comrade Kosygin (shades of Rosa Klebb!). But in fact Amis could no more write a genuine Bond novel than Fleming could write a genuine Amis novel: literate pastiche and respectful avoidance of parody were no substitute for Fleming's innate virtues. Nor was the experiment repeated: book-Bond was left in full retreat from film-Bond, the Batman from Blades.

The choice, now, of John Gardner to reverse the situation overtops the first irony by several miles, for, talented and experienced thriller writer though he is (and already a resurrection man: remember the Moriarty books), he came on the scene with the Boysie Oakes series, which in his own words were meant as 'an amusing counter-irritant to the excesses of 007': 'This seemed to be the way to provide an antidote to the snobby pseudo-sophistication of the Bond business. Looking back on it, that aim seems pretentious and, happily, Bond changed direction, the books becoming amusing send-ups of themselves when transferred to film.' The enormity of this statement in the present context needs no underlining. For Fleming's publishers to hand over book-Bond to a self-confessed film-Bond man is like the MCC handing over Lord's to Mr Packer. Despite the reassuring Chopping-style jacket of *Licence Renewed*, one fingers it fearfully, uncertain only as to how dreadful it is going to be.

Fortunately Mr Gardner is not as bad as his word, though he gets off to a stumbling start. Bond has, disastrously, *moved with the times* (Mr Gardner only just avoids admitting that he must be pushing fifty). The double-0 section has been *abolished* (though M only just avoids saying 'You'll always be 007 to me, James': shades of *Bond Strikes Camp*), and Bond *drinks less*, smokes cigarettes 'with a tar content slightly lower than any currently available on the market', and has abandoned the Mark II Continental Bentley for a *foreign* car with tear-gas ducts in all four wheels. On the other hand, May still reigns in the flat off the King's Road, the breakfast routine is unchanged, and press-ups and target practice are regularly observed.

Bond's adversary on this occasion is Dr Anton Murik, who is planning to justify his own rejected Ultra-Safe (it isn't) Reactor by causing six existing reactors to go wild by switching off their coolant systems. Murik, who is a Fellow of St. John's College, Cambridge and

[1] Mr Amis points out that Bond drinks rosé in *Goldfinger* (with sole *meunière*).

'not unlike . . . the late Lord Beaverbrook', is Laird of Murcaldy in Ross and Cromarty, and is helped in his fell designs by Franco, an international terrorist, and Caber, a sort of Harry-Lauder Odd-job ('I'm still behind ye, Bond, with the wee shooter'). Bond has a wrestling bout with Caber at the Murcaldy Games, and lays him out with a whiff of Halothane thoughtfully provided by Q Branch, but even before this has given him the Ganges Groin Gouge, a tactic seemingly in defiance of the Cumberland or Lancashire styles more likely to be observed there.

Q Branch also provides a girl, who seduces Bond perfunctorily ('Well, James, the bed's still there') before the story really starts. He then rejects Murik's mistress ('a trained physicist') in favour of the Laird's ward Lavender Peacock, whose face is reminiscent of Lauren Bacall and who has firm, impertinent breasts ('under the dress') in splendid proportion to the rest of her body (since she is tall and slender, splendid disproportion might have been better). Lavender, or Dilly as she likes to be called, is actually the 'wronged heiress' of Victorian fiction (Dr Anton has fiddled the Lairdship), and holds out till page 218, when she and Bond are twice 'united by passion'. Pallidly pally, as a Bond girl Lavender is a non-starter even though she does put paid to Caber at a crucial moment: she ends by going to 'one of the major agricultural colleges'.

The action is of the *Diamonds Are Forever* pattern: Bond sells himself to Murik as a potential accomplice, and learns what is going on, or going to go on, at Murik Castle before being rumbled. A vain attempt to escape is followed by torture; being carted off to Perpignan, which seems to be the nerve centre of Operation Meltdown, as the nuclear reactor project is called; and finally a 'ringside seat' at that event in Murik's giant Starlifter aircraft. It is all briskly enough done, without too many film-Bond absurdities, but the temperature obstinately refuses to rise. It is hard to see why. Mr Gardner has created a simulacrum of the Bond world with none of the threatened mockery, but despite his sincere and conscientious efforts it just will not come to life.

The obvious reason for this is that Mr Gardner is not as good a writer as Fleming. It is not so much the small illiteracies ('ravage' for ravish, 'a fine patina of flour') or the slightly larger clichés ('Bond so far had not been able to savour the views or delight in the beauties of Scotland'), not even the occasional echoes (Murik's ultimatum to the world recalls Blofeld's in *Thunderball*); it is simply that Mr Gardner cannot command that compelling readability noted by Lyttelton in 1957 and yielded to by many millions since. The foiling of Operation Meltdown is stolidly achieved; the separate fate reserved for Dr Murik has none of the satisfying ghastliness attending the demises of Dr No and Mr Big.

The trouble is that to resurrect Bond you have to be Fleming, for he *was* his creator in a way that Tarzan or Sherlock Holmes or Billy Bunter clearly weren't theirs. It was Fleming who smoked seventy cigarettes a day, wore dark blue Sea Island cotton shirts and loved scrambled eggs and double portions of orange juice for breakfast; Bond was a kind of *doppelgänger* sent out to enact what Fleming himself had never achieved (this relation is convincingly analysed in John Pearson's masterly *Life of Ian Fleming*). The ease with which Bond appeared (Fleming, forty-three, never having written a novel before, sat down and wrote *Casino Royale* in eight weeks) suggests the tapping of deep imaginative springs. And the novels that succeeded them drew on the same dark source: 'the next volume of my autobiography', he would call the book currently in progress, masking his personal involvement by mocking it. Of course the springs were not inexhaustible; by *Thunderball* (1961) Fleming admitted he had 'run out of puff', and his last five books are not as good as his first seven. But since they were instinct with a personality much more complex, much more intelligent, much more imaginative than Bond's—the personality, in short, of Fleming himself—they remain alive in a way that *Colonel Sun* and now *Licence Renewed* cannot hope to do.

Why then persist in trying to raise book-Bond from the dead, if such efforts can never succeed? The prospect, no doubt, of making money for somebody; perhaps—the ultimate grisly irony—the necessity of providing new vehicles for film-Bond. But one would like to think that there is also an element of homage, and a faint hoping-beyond-hope that one day the sorcery will really work, and we shall be rewarded with another unmistakable instalment of the latest — perhaps the last—of the Byronic heroes.

1981

The Great Gladys

There seems a movement nowadays to cast Gladys Mitchell as the last of the body-in-the-library practitioners: 'good writing, careful plotting and educated wit,' as her latest jacket says. Not so. Grant the good writing, but otherwise Miss Mitchell has always (and this[1] is her sixty-second book) stood splendidly apart from her crime-club confrères in total originality—even when, as today, there are almost none left to stand apart from.

This originality consists in blending eccentricity of subject-matter with authoritative common sense of style. One accepts that a Gladys Mitchell novel can begin with a cross-country runner being asked to help lift an ominously immobile wrapped-up invalid into a car, or with a young lady who dresses either in armour or eighteenth-century male costume on the grounds that her guardian has taken her clothes away. One of her novels even ends with three people buried up to their necks as part of a surrealist exhibition, their heads shaved and painted purple: the murderer is the one on the right. Dancing stones, water nymphs and other anthropological curiosities appear occasionally, and much use is made of impersonations, mistaken identity and identical twins. In consequence it is not impossible for the reader to finish a book without grasping not only who the murderer is, but sometimes even who has been murdered.

But all this is balanced by calm exposition in non-emotive prose (a Gladys Mitchell novel is never 'exciting' in the ordinary sense). Her tales are set in precise topographical surroundings, and often told by some eminently sane young teacher or writer (or, as in the masterly *The Devil's Elbow*, a coach-party courier) who becomes involved in alarming or mystifying events from which he has to be extricated.

The extricating is done by Dame Beatrice Adela Lestrange Bradley. If there is a sybilline tradition of detection, embracing Miss Marple, Miss Silver, and perhaps even Miss Murchison, Mrs Bradley is its presiding genius. Her status as Home Office psychiatric consultant

[1] Gladys Mitchell, *Here Lies Gloria Mundy* (London: Michael Joseph, 1982).

enables her to move easily among the deviations of behaviour and real or pretended mental disturbances with which the books abound (her examination of suspects by word-association is especially absorbing). She is never at a loss. Her nearest approach to bafflement is an enigmatic 'Time will tell, child.' Interviews that seem unproductive to the reader are full of significant omissions or misrepresentations to Mrs Bradley, who will only cackle uncooperatively when asked to name them ('Think, child'). Long ago she is supposed to have been tried for murder and acquitted—according to her, wrongfully. One of her ancestors was a witch.

While she has changed little since 1929, her encounter with the 'Amazonian' Laura Menzies in *Laurels Are Poison* (1942) greatly enhanced her resources. Introduced as a tomboyish Training College student, Laura becomes her secretary, and takes on something of the role of Archie Goodwin in the Nero Wolfe books, always ready to breeze in and ask questions where her principal might arouse suspicion. Before her marriage to Detective Inspector Gavin and eventual retreat into matronhood, Laura was equally prepared to strip off and dive for evidence or to test tides; some unregenerate readers came to value these episodes for themselves. She is of Highland descent, and claims 'the gift', which gives her an odd kinship with her eldritch employer. Her attachment to 'Mrs Croc' (Mrs Bradley's saurian appearance is constantly emphasized) is all the stronger for never being referred to.

They are a formidable and convincing pair, and *Here Lies Gloria Mundy* is a characteristic addition to the Mitchell canon. The story is told by an author who has been commissioned by an old college friend to write up a chain of hotels directed by the latter, as indeed he had been planning to write up an unexplained murder, and finds himself drawn into a series of happenings that lead back to the crime he has abandoned. The waif-like Gloria Mundy, known of old to the hotel friend, has half her hair red and half black (an ancestress was burnt as a witch), and is herself found murdered. A few weeks later she is seen working in a shop. This is the authentic Mitchell *frisson*.

One does not expect a writer to break new ground in her ninth decade, but the final dream sequence (not, I hasten to say, a substitute for a properly deduced solution) has an eeriness all its own. On page 167, too, two of the characters make love, which I don't remember in a Mitchell novel before. It is almost as if she were recalling the Dick Francis of *Risk*. Perhaps it was a mistake to have a third witchlike person in the cast, the Chaucerian Aunt Eglantine, but she and Mrs Bradley get on famously.

The best thing about the book is that it will send me back to some of the earlier masterpieces: to *When Last I Died*, with its Harry Price haunting, disturbing diary entries and general air of yellowing newspaper reports; to the serene convent of *St. Peter's Finger*, where the traumas of adolescence and a suspected bathroom geyser trouble the faithful; to the *tour de force* of *The Rising of the Moon*, in which a thirteen-year-old boy recounts in seamless and convincing prose gruesome goings-on by the river at Brentford. And I shall read them as novels. They ought to be known as such.

1982

The Traffic in the Distance

The train was five minutes late in arriving. The lights of the station burned dimly in the fog. Harold opened the door of the carriage and the girl stepped out. Rowland took down his suitcase from the rack. A porter strolled up. The traffic in the distance had a muffled sound.

That is the final paragraph of *The Senior Commoner* by Julian Hall, published in 1933. I have absolutely no expectation that it will arouse in the reader the excitement it does in me, and did over forty years ago when I first found it on the shelves of Coventry Central Library before the war (in those days I had the habit of looking at the end of a novel as well as the beginning). Nor do I especially want it to: like Flora Poste, I find the idea of other people reading my favourite books rather annoying. But its fascination remains. It is one of the few dozen books I keep in my bedroom and can read at any time.

Harold is Harold Weir. He is arriving in London just before Christmas, having finally left Ayrton College, where in his last term he has been Senior Commoner (Ayrton is plainly Eton, and he would have been Captain of the Oppidans). The novel, which by present-day standards is enormously long (384 pages), is about this term of office, with a protracted flashback to OTC camp in the preceding summer. Harold is an undistinguished young man who although far from being a typical Ayrtonian (he still doesn't understand the rules of football, and makes a comical hash of singing his verse of the leaving song) has a fierce admiration for Ayrton ('there's a tradition of careless mastery'). He has these feelings about people, too: Chatterton the Headmaster ('the man he most wished to resemble'); a boy, Frank Hathaway, who has just left ('he expressed something that in Harold's own nature was imprisoned'); and a junior boy Murray Gawthorne, about whom Harold has romantic feelings (well, perhaps not very romantic: 'there was something altogether immodest in the boy's figure').

We encounter Ayrton through Harold: on page 1 he meets King Said of Euphratia (' "*Oui, oui*," remarked Said, spitting on to the stone pavement'), and other visitors follow, such as the sceptical Labour MP Convil ('the privilege is so great and the result is so very commonplace'). He dines with the Provost and hears him read Dickens, and before long we are meeting these people without Harold's interposition. His housemaster McIsaacs and his wife entertain three bachelor masters ('the friends of one had warned him not to expect a good dinner'); another master, Massingham, has a famous pianist for a wife ('I want to go alone to Germany. If you come, I'd rather stay here'); Sawbury, the Vice-Provost, once 'a power in the land', is now aged and rather dotty on the subject of the school ('his eyes were almost startlingly blue'). Things happen: one boy is asked to leave on account of his kleptomania; the younger brother of another dies; a third asks the Headmaster to excuse him from attending chapel as he no longer feels himself a Christian. There is no story, or hardly any: the book is a huge structure of tiny episodes, designed to portray a complex institution at all levels.

As such, it is a remarkable enough achievement, but what fascinated me was the quality of the writing. Much of the book is in dialogue, but as the paragraph I have quoted shows, the narrative is laconic to the point of flatness, as if disclaiming concern or even interest. No one could write as badly as this without meaning to, and I came to the conclusion that it was intended to distract attention from the author's emotion. For the book is, indirectly, highly emotional; Harold feels strongly about people, about Ayrton, about being Senior Commoner. But as the Headmaster's wife says, 'What would Ayrton be without its tradition of showing no feeling in public?', and the style exemplifies this. After an evening at the Shakespeare Society

> Harold went slowly to his room and began undressing. He repeated to himself two lines spoken by Hermione in *The Winter's Tale*:
>> Sir, spare your threats:
>> The bug that you would fright me with I seek.
> The light went out in the room and he lit a candle. The use of it was a privilege which gave him satisfaction.

The reader can only guess at what is implied. Not so at the end, when Harold's last night at Ayrton is spent at the Headmaster's Christmas Dance. Nothing special happens ('He made an allusion to the training college in Hardy's *Jude the Obscure*. Miss Aynsworth had not read *Jude the Obscure*') until the time comes for him to go:

> Chatterton turned towards him and smiled. Harold suddenly averted his head, burst into tears and hurried away. The Cloisters and School Yard were deserted. The gate leading into the main street had been left open. He wept out loud as he walked.

This naked moment is the book's climax, which stands revealed as the record of a love affair with the school, not only on Harold's part but on the author's too.

Years later I wrote to Julian Hall to draw his attention to a reference I had made to his book that I knew he wouldn't have seen. An out-of-date *Who's Who* had told me a little about him: he was born in 1907, and had himself been Captain of the Oppidans before going to Balliol. He had written two other novels, one of which (*Two Exiles*) I had found on a market stall in Leicester and not greatly liked. He replied from the Garrick Club briefly but courteously, obviously pleased with my praise, and added that his publisher, Martin Secker, had said he liked the book 'only moderately . . . I think it's rather superficial.' When Hall died in 1974 I learned that he had succeeded to a baronetcy, and had been a well-known theatre critic. This seemed to explain the book's one unexpected theme: Lord Wrenbrook, an Old Ayrtonian and dilettante playwright, is making up to a young American actor named Will Campion, who does not really care for him but by the acquaintance gets to know some Ayrtonians ('he's got the most marvellous dark eyes') before being warned off by the Headmaster ('I shall say that I do *not* propose to put his house within bounds and that I do *not* think the notice is liable to be misunderstood'). Later still when reading Emlyn Williams's autobiography I wondered whether Campion had been suggested by Tom Douglas, the American who had made such a hit in London in the Twenties with Tallulah Bankhead. In fact the Campion scenes, besides providing a breather from Ayrton, are sharply funny and painful. Their explicitness of intention must have been quite daring for 1933.

But as well as the brittle plangency of the style, the book had an even odder quality: something one might call studied circumstantial irrelevancy. Nearly every scene is diversified with details that do not relate to it: background sights and sounds, pointless pieces of information, hints that lead nowhere. When Convil congratulates

Harold on getting a Balliol scholarship, 'Harold made a contemptuous gesture and looked away. In a room further down the passage a telephone was ringing.' A paragraph or two further on it is still ringing: no one answers it. When Wrenbrook stands up to take Campion to lunch 'the palms of his hands felt clammy. He remembered he had an appointment with his doctor on the following morning.' No more is heard of this appointment. Sometimes a whole scene is irrelevant to the action, yet seems to summarize it:

Another man came in and sat down at one of the writing-tables. The lamp would not work and he rang the bell for the waiter. He nodded to Stephens and the latter smiled.

'We're talking about Ayrton, Cyril,' said Stephens. 'Come and give us your views.'

The other pushed up his spectacles and looked to see whom Stephens was talking to.

'It all happened too long ago,' he replied. 'I can't go back as far as that.'

'You old humbug, Cyril, you're junior to me.' Stephens winked at Wrenbrook and pressed down the tobacco in his pipe.

'Junior to you, am I? But you've got a boy or a grandson or something at the place now. I haven't. I haven't got anybody. I say, I want a proper light,' he added, looking up as a waiter came over to his table.

When as an undergraduate I saw *Citizen Kane* and *The Magnificent Ambersons* I was reminded of this technique, a use of trivialities to suggest that other lives are going on simultaneously, and that even the lives we are shown have other dimensions. Later, writing a novel myself, I tried to use it, but found it too all-pervasive and abandoned the attempt, though traces of it may still remain.

Perhaps surprisingly, *The Senior Commoner* went into a second impression. Gerald Gould said it had reality, originality, and considerable literary merit. Francis Iles called it a brave adventure in an original technique. Ralph Straus used the adjective 'three-dimensional'. The *Manchester Guardian* termed it a skilful slow-motion picture. Then it was forgotten. Nevertheless, all these comments seem to me true. I have never met anyone else who has read it. Nor have I ever read another book in the least like it.

1982

Horror Poet

In this book[1] Ted Hughes has arranged Sylvia Plath's poems as far as possible in the order they were written, with about forty pages of juvenilia at the end. It is therefore possible to read them through, helped by Hughes's notes, with a fair degree of continuity. For someone hitherto largely unfamiliar with her life and work this is an extraordinary experience.

The first hundred poems (or, to be precise, the first ninety-eight) are not ultimately very interesting, except in so far as they predicate a remarkable personality. Plath was prolific and precocious. She seems to have written compulsively (her annual output between 1956 and her death in 1963 averaged thirty-two poems); when she had nothing to write about she wrote on set themes, as she had as a student at Smith College. She threw nothing away. She seems not to have gone through the apprenticeship of following different poets for their styles, unless there are models I do not recognize; her pieces are intellectually conceited, vivid and resourceful in image and vocabulary. Form was not her strong point: she rhymed and scanned when it suited her, which was less and less often as she grew older. Nor was her 'ear' good: 'Each teacher found my touch/Oddly wooden' she says of early piano lessons, and one can see what they meant; at times in 1956 her verse had the denseness of early Dylan Thomas:

> Now in the crux of their vows hang your ear,
> Still as a shell: hear what an age of glass
> These lovers prophesy to lock embrace
> Secure in museum diamond for the stare
> Of astounded generations; they wrestle
> To conquer cinder's kingdom in the stroke of an hour
> And hoard faith safe in a fossil.

They are the poems of a prize pupil, crammed with invention, lacking emotional centre. Hughes recounts illuminatingly her search

[1] Sylvia Plath, *Collected Poems*, edited by Ted Hughes (London: Faber, 1981).

for a title for her first book: it was called, successively, *The Earthenware Head*, *The Everlasting Monday*, *Full Fathom Five*, *The Bull of Bendylaw*, *The Devil of the Stairs*, and finally *The Colossus*, The effect is almost farcical.

Up till 1959 Plath's poems lack what one looks for in any writer of stature: the individual note or theme by and with which he or she will henceforth be identified. Line by line they are often remarkable: in sum they are unmemorable. But in that year a poem begins

> The day she visited the dissecting room
> They had four men laid out, black as burnt turkey,
> Already half unstrung. . . .

The shock is sudden, and the possibility that she is simply trying on another style is dispelled by the two following pieces, 'Suicide off Egg Rock' and 'The Ravaged Face'. Plath liked them for their 'forthrightness', a word suggesting the abandonment of literary fancy in favour of plainer realism, and in one sense this was true: she had found her subject-matter. It was, variously, neurosis, insanity, disease, death, horror, terror.

A note by Hughes says that at this time Plath was taken with the work of Theodore Roethke, and 'realized how he could help her'. She certainly picked up his something-nasty-in-the-greenhouse manner; she, too, could find the creepiness in things. In November of that year she wrote 'Mushrooms', a superficially gentle, even Georgian poem, but filled with menace. The following year saw the birth of her first child and a cessation of activity, but by the end of it she was writing,

> How the balconies echoed! How the sun lit up
> The skulls, the unbuckled bones facing the view!
> Space! Space! The bed linen was giving out entirely.
> Cot legs melted in terrible attitudes, and the nurses—
> Each nurse patched her soul to a wound and disappeared.

The pleasurable excitement of watching a young writer gaining command of her predestined material is nullified by the nature of that material and her involvement with it. Hughes's notes have already made it clear that she was mentally unstable; like many Americans, she had a psychiatrist, but, more individually, had also a scar across her cheek from an earlier suicide attempt. For her to exercise her unique talent for the distortions of horror and madness was to risk liberating these forces in herself. She was, to use Joseph Conrad's well-worn phrase, immersing herself in the destructive element.

At first the exercise seems deliberate, writing poems with titles such as 'Insomniac', 'Widow', 'The Surgeon at 2 a.m.' and 'Fever 103°', or about a hospital for mutilated war veterans, thalidomide children or cutting one's thumb half off. But there are others, in which neutral or even sympathetic subjects are wilfully refracted into something terrible or horrible; 'Zoo Keeper's Wife', according to the notes, came from Plath's frequent visits to Regent's Park Zoo, seemingly a harmless enough recreation, but

> How our courtship lit the tindery cages—
> Your two-horned rhinoceros opened a mouth
> Dirty as a bootsole and big as a hospital sink
> For my cube of sugar: its bog breath
> Gloved my arm to the elbow.

An even more striking example is the series of bee poems. Plath kept bees in Devon, and attended meetings of the local Beekeepers Association, activities surely not to be undertaken except in a matter-of-fact spirit, but she portrays it as a kind of mythopoeic nightmare:

> Which is the rector now, is it that man in black?
> Which is the midwife, is that her blue coat?
> Everybody is nodding a square black head, they are knights in visors,
> Breastplates of cheesecloth knotted under the armpits.
> Their smiles and their voices are changing. . . .
> . . . .
> I am exhausted, I am exhausted——
> Pillar of white in a blackout of knives.
> I am the magician's girl who does not flinch.
> The villagers are untying their disguises, they are shaking hands.
> Whose is that long white box in the grove, what have they accomplished, why am I cold.

Brilliant as this is, as if Hitchcock had filmed the church fête at the beginning of Graham Greene's *The Ministry of Fear*, the reader does not agree that, yes, it must have been terrible; rather, he wonders whether Plath is wilfully hyping up this ordinary event to make a poem, or whether this is really how she saw it, in which case Plath and the reader are about to part company. For a time one inclines to the first view. Hughes quotes an interesting remark by Plath when introducing a broadcast reading of 'Lady Lazarus' (one of her most celebrated poems, compounded of a suicide attempt, the Lazarus story and German death camps where God is the Commandant) to the effect that the speaker in the poem is Phoenix, the libertarian spirit, a woman who has the gift of being reborn: 'The only trouble is, she has to die first. . . . She is also just a good, plain, very resourceful woman.' One suspects that half the time this is what Plath was. She also sounds ambitious, competitive, compulsive, the girl most likely to succeed, ready to exploit her own traumas if they would make poems. Mad poets do not write about madness: they write about religion, sofas, the French Revolution, nature, their cat Jeoffry. Plath did: it was her subject, her *donnée* ('I do it exceptionally well'); together they played an increasingly reckless game of tag.

Of course it might have been all for the best. In 1961 she wrote her novel, *The Bell Jar*, perhaps with the idea of self-therapy and making a fresh start. Early in 1962 she had a second child. In September she and her husband separated. During this year she wrote fifty-six poems, one of them the long and apparently reconciled piece for voices, *Three Women*. Increasingly divorced from identifiable incident, they seem to enter neurosis, or insanity, and exist there in a prolonged high-pitched ecstasy like nothing else in literature. They are impossible to quote meaningfully: they must be read whole. In February 1963 she killed herself.

How far this was due to pressure from within, how far to pressure from without is hard to say. Plath may have taken on more than she could manage and been destroyed by circumstances. Or she may have been committed to such a break-up whatever she did. Or, as I have suggested, she may have indulged her own talent for following a literary fashion (Roethke, Lowell) until she lost control of it and it overwhelmed her. Considering what one takes to be their subject-matter, her poems, particularly the last ones, are curiously, even jauntily impersonal; it is hard to see how she was labelled confessional. As poems, they are to the highest degree original and scarcely less effective. How valuable they are depends on how highly we rank the expression of experience with which we can in no sense identify, and from which we can only turn with shock and sorrow.

1982

ALL WHAT JAZZ

Introduction to *All What Jazz*

I have rescued these articles from their press-cuttings book because for all their slightness and superficiality they contain occasional sentences that still amuse me or seem justified. Moreover, as I read them I discern a story which, though ordinary enough, it might be entertaining to bring out into the open.

To tell it means going back some way. Few things have given me more pleasure in life than listening to jazz. I don't claim to be original in this: for the generations that came to adolescence between the wars jazz was that unique private excitement that youth seems to demand. In another age it might have been drink or drugs, religion or poetry. Whatever it happens to be, parents are suspicious of it and it has a bad reputation. I can tell adolescents don't feel like this about jazz today. For one thing, there are so many kinds that to talk about jazz as such would leave them puzzled as well as cold. Then again, it has become respectable: there are scholarly books on it, and adult education courses; it's the kind of interest that might well be mentioned on a university entrance form. And there's so much of it: records, wireless, television, all dispense it regularly. In the Thirties it was a fugitive minority interest, a record heard by chance from a foreign station, a chorus between two vocals, one man in an otherwise dull band. No one you knew liked it.

Nevertheless, it had established itself in my life several years before I consciously heard anything that could properly be called real jazz. This happened by way of the dance band, a now vanished phenomenon of twelve or fourteen players (usually identically uniformed) that was employed by a hotel or restaurant so that its patrons could dance. Their leaders were national celebrities, and had regular time on the radio: five-fifteen to six in the afternoon, for instance, and half-past ten to midnight. They were in almost no sense 'jazz' bands, but about every sixth piece they made a 'hot' number, in which the one or two men in the band who could play jazz would be heard. The classic 'hot number' was 'Tiger Rag': it had that kind of

national-anthem status that 'When the Saints Go Marching In' had in
the Fifties. Harry Roy had a band-within-a-band called the Tiger-
Ragamuffins. Nat Gonella's stage show had a toy tiger lying on the
grand piano. Trombonists and tuba players became adept at
producing the traditional tiger growl. I found these hot numbers so
exciting that I would listen to hours of dance music in order to catch
them when they came, in this way unconsciously learning many now
forgotten lyrics. Those hot numbers! When the bands began to visit
the local Hippodrome, I was able actually to see them played, the
different sections suddenly rising to play four bars then sitting
sharply down again; the shouts of 'Yeah man', the slapped bass, the
drum breaks. It was the drummer I concentrated on, sitting as he did
on a raised platform behind a battery of cowbells, temple blocks,
cymbals, tom-toms and (usually) a Chinese gong, his drums picked
out in flashing crimson or ultramarine brilliants. Even the resident
Hippodrome drummer, a stolid man with horn-rimmed glasses,
excited me enough for me to insist that our tickets were for his side of
the house, so that I could see what he was doing. I wanted to be a
drummer. My parents bought me an elementary drum kit and a set of
tuition records by Max Abrams (that will date the anecdote), and I
battered away contentedly, spending less time on the rudiments than
in improvising an accompaniment to records.

I recount this simply to show that I was, in essence, hooked on jazz
even before I heard any, and that what got me was the rhythm. That
simple trick of the suspended beat, that had made the slaves shuffle in
Congo Square on Saturday nights, was something that never palled.
My transition to jazz was slow. The first jazz record by an *American*
band I ever owned was Ray Noble's 'Tiger Rag' (it had a drum break).
The second, rather surprisingly, was the Washboard Rhythm Kings'
'I'm Gonna Play Down by the Ohio'. The third was Louis
Armstrong's 'Ain't Misbehavin''. After that they came thick and fast.
Sitting with a friend in his bedroom that overlooked the family
tennis-court, I watched leaves drift down through long Sunday
afternoons as we took it in turn to wind the portable HMV, and those
white and coloured Americans, Bubber Miley, Frank Teschmacher,
J. C. Higginbotham, spoke immediately to our understanding. Their
rips, slurs and distortions were something we understood perfectly.
This was something we had found for ourselves, that wasn't taught at
school (what a prerequisite that is of nearly everything worthwhile!),
and having found it, we made it bear all the enthusiasm usually

directed at more established arts. There was nothing odd about this. It was happening to boys all over Europe and America. It just didn't get into the papers. It was years before I found any music as commanding as Jimmy Noone's 'The Blues Jumped a Rabbit', Armstrong's 'Knockin' a Jug' or 'Squeeze Me', Bessie Smith's 'Backwater Blues', or the Chicago Rhythm Kings' 'I Found a New Baby'.

At Oxford my education grew. I met people who knew more about jazz than I did, and had more records, and who could even parallel my ecstasies with their own. The shops, too, were full of unreturned deletions, some of which have never been reissued to this day (the Sharkey Bonano Vocalions, for instance, or Louis Prima's 'Chasin' Shadows'). I wish I could say that we could recite Black Swan matrix numbers, or knew what was available on Argentine HMV, or played instruments and formed a band, or at least had enough musical knowledge to discuss the records we played intelligently. Only one of our circle could read music: he played the saxophone, but his taste didn't really accord with mine: he was too fond of phrases such as 'not musically interesting' or 'mere rhythmic excitement'. True, our response to Fats Waller's 'Dream Man' or Rosetta Howard's 'If You're a Viper' was a grinning, jigging wordlessness, interspersed with a grunt or two at specially good bits. For us, jazz became part of the private joke of existence, rather than a public expertise: expressions such as 'combined pimp and lover' and 'eating the cheaper cuts of pork' (both from a glossary on 'Yellow Dog Blues') flecked our conversations cryptically; for some reason, Kaminsky's plaintive little introduction to 'Home Cooking' became a common signal, and any of us entering the steam-filled college bath-house would whistle it to see if it was taken up from behind any of the bolted partition doors.

If I say that on leaving Oxford I suffered a gap in my jazz life I am probably reporting a common experience. Most jazz enthusiasts found the war a compulsory hiatus in their devotion. If they were not away in the services, and their collections broken up, the American Federation of Musicians' recording ban of 1942–4 descended on them, together with the general shortage of consumer goods, including records, that hostilities brought increasingly as the war went on. For my part, I was in a series of provincial lodgings where jazz was not welcome, and when I was united with my collection in 1948 and had something to play it on there followed a period when I was content to renew acquaintance with it and to add only what amplified or extended it along existing lines—new records by old favourites, replacements of discs previously abandoned or broken. When the long-playing record was introduced in the middle Fifties, I was suspicious of it: it seemed a package deal, forcing you to buy bad tracks along with good at an unwantedly-high price. (The dubbing or remastering of 78s as LPs, too, was regarded as a damaging practice.) This deepened my isolation.

All this is not to say that I was ignorant of the changes taking place on the jazz scene. I knew, for instance, that what I had known as one music had now bifurcated into trad and mod. In Britain one heard a good deal more of the former, thanks to the revivalist boom, but I don't know that I went overboard about it; I liked Lyttelton, and later on the energetic little Barber band that could pack any concert hall between Aberdeen and Bristol. I heard it in Belfast in 1954: a thousand people squashed into the smallish Plaza dance hall, and a thousand more milled outside, the more enterprising getting in through a small square window in the men's lavatory. This was the pre-Ottilie period, when after 'Panama' and 'Chimes Blues' and 'Merrydown Rag' Lonnie Donegan would come forward with his impersonation of Leadbelly. There was no bar: I went and stood on the landing, pursued by the high nasal Glasgow-American version of some incident from transatlantic railway history. All the same, there seemed an element of slightly unreal archaism about much of the trad of the period, particularly from California, and I could never bring myself to take these grunting and quavering pastiches seriously. On the whole, therefore, I thought it best after the war to suspend judgement, out of an almost academic shyness about going into a 'new period'. For modern jazz I was even less well briefed. What I heard on the wireless seemed singularly unpromising, but I doubt if I thought it would ever secure enough popular acceptance to warrant my bothering about it.

II

What I am doing, I suppose, is demonstrating that when I was asked to write these articles I was patently unfitted to do so and should have declined. The reason I didn't was that I still thought of myself as a jazz lover, someone unquestionably on the wavelength of Congo Square, and although I knew things had been changing I didn't believe jazz itself could alter out of all recognition any more than the march or the waltz could. It was simply a question of hearing enough of the new stuff: I welcomed the chance to do so, feeling confident that once I got the feel of it all would be made clear. Secondly, I hadn't really any intention of being a jazz *critic*. In literature, I understood, there were several old whores who had grown old in the reviewing game by praising everything, and I planned to be their jazz equivalent. This isn't as venal as it sounds. Since my space was to be so limited, anything but praise would be wasteful; my readers deserved to be told of the best of all worlds, and I was the man to do it. It didn't really matter, therefore, whether I liked things at first or not, as I was going to call them all masterpieces.

But there came a hitch. When the records, in their exciting square packages, began obligingly to arrive from the companies, the eagerness with which I played them turned rapidly to astonishment, to disbelief, to alarm. I felt I was in some nightmare, in which I had confidently gone into an examination hall only to find that I couldn't make head or tail of the questions. It wasn't like listening to a kind of jazz I didn't care for—Art Tatum, shall I say, or Jelly Roll Morton's Red Hot Peppers. It wasn't like listening to jazz at all. Nearly every characteristic of the music had been neatly inverted: for instance, the jazz tone, distinguished from 'straight' practice by an almost human vibrato, had entirely disappeared, giving way to utter flaccidity. Had the most original feature of jazz been its use of collective improvisation? Banish it: let the first and last choruses be identical exercises in low-temperature unison. Was jazz instrumentation based on the hock-shop trumpets, trombones and clarinets of the returned Civil War regiments? Brace yourself for flutes, harpsichords, electronically-amplified bassoons. Had jazz been essentially a popular art, full of tunes you could whistle? Something fundamentally awful had taken place to ensure that there should be no more tunes. Had the wonderful thing about it been its happy, cake-walky syncopation that set feet tapping and shoulders jerking? Any such feelings were now regularly dispelled by random explosions from the drummer ('dropping bombs'), and the use of non-jazz tempos, 3/4, 5/8, 11/4. Above all, was jazz the music of the American Negro? Then fill it full of conga drums and sambas and all the tawdry trappings of South America, the racket of Middle East bazaars, the cobra-coaxing cacophonies of Calcutta.

But, deeper than this, the sort of emotion the music was trying to evoke seemed to have changed. Whereas the playing of Armstrong,

Bechet, Waller and the Condon groups had been relaxed and expansive, the music of the new men seemed to have developed from some of the least attractive characteristics of the late Thirties—the tight-assed little John Kirby band, for instance, or the more riff-laden Goodman units. The substitution of bloodless note-patterns for some cheerful or sentimental popular song as a basis for improvisation (I'm thinking of some of the early Parkers) was a retrograde step, but worse still was the deliberately-contrived eccentricity of the phrasing and harmonies. One of the songs I remember from my dance-music childhood was called 'I'm Nuts About Screwy Music, I'm Mad About Daffy Tempos', and I've often meant to look it up in the British Museum to see whether the rest of the lyric forecast the rise of bop with such uncanny accuracy. This new mode seemed to have originated partly out of boredom with playing ordinary jazz six nights a week (admittedly a pretty gruelling way of earning a living), and partly from a desire to wrest back the initiative in jazz from the white musician, to invent 'something they can't steal because they can't play it'. This motive is a bad basis for any art, and it isn't surprising that I found the results shallow and *voulu*. Worst of all was the pinched, unhappy, febrile, tense nature of the music. The constant pressure to be different and difficult demanded greater and greater technical virtuosity and more and more exaggerated musical *non sequiturs*. It wasn't, in a word, the music of happy men. I used to think that anyone hearing a Parker record would guess he was a drug addict, but no one hearing Beiderbecke would think he was an alcoholic, and that this summed up the distinction between the kinds of music.

What I was feeling was, no doubt, a greatly-amplified version of the surprise many European listeners felt when, after the war, records of Parker and his followers began to arrive across the Atlantic. 'America has gone mad!' wrote George Shearing on reaching New York during this period (it didn't take him long to follow suit), and whereas Shearing was (presumably) taking only Parker and Gillespie on the chin, I was taking everything up to 1961—Monk, Davis, Coltrane, Rollins, the Jazz Messengers, the lot. I was denied even the solace of liking this man and disliking that: I found them all equally off-putting. Parker himself, compulsively fast and showy, couldn't play four bars without resorting to a peculiarly irritating five-note cliché from a pre-war song called 'The Woody Woodpecker Song'. His tone, though much better than that of some of his successors, was thin and sometimes shrill.[1] The impression of mental hallucination he conveyed could also be derived from the pianist Bud Powell, who cultivated the same kind of manic virtuosity and could sometimes be stopped only by the flashing of a light in his eyes. Gillespie, on the other hand, was a more familiar type, the trumpeter-leader and entertainer, but I didn't relish his addiction to things Latin-American and I found his sense of humour rudimentary. Thelonious Monk seemed a not very successful comic, as his funny hats proclaimed: his *faux-naif* elephant-dance piano style, with its gawky intervals and absence of swing, was made doubly tedious by his limited repertoire. With Miles Davis and John Coltrane a new inhumanity emerged. Davis had several manners: the dead muzzled slow stuff, the sour yelping fast stuff, and the sonorous theatrical arranged stuff, and I disliked them all. With John Coltrane metallic and passionless nullity gave way to exercises in gigantic absurdity, great boring excursions on not especially attractive themes during which all possible changes were rung, extended investigations of oriental tedium, long-winded and portentous demonstrations of religiosity. It was with Coltrane, too, that jazz started to be *ugly on purpose*: his nasty tone would become more and more exacerbated until he was fairly screeching at you like a pair of demoniacally-possessed bagpipes. After Coltrane, of course, all was chaos, hatred and absurdity, and one was almost relieved that severance with jazz had become so complete and obvious. But this is running ahead of my story.

The awkward thing was that it was altogether too late in the day to publicize this kind of reaction. In the late Forties battle had been joined in the correspondence columns between the beret-and-dark-glasses boys and the mouldy figs; by the early Sixties, all this had died down. Setting aside a qualification or two I should like to make later, one can say only that to voice such a viewpoint in 1961 would have been journalistically impossible. By then Parker was dead and a historical figure, in young eyes probably indistinguishable from King Oliver and other founding fathers. There was nothing for it but to carry on with my original plan of undiscriminating praise, and I did so for nearly two years. During this time I blocked in the background by subscribing to *Down Beat* again (there were none of the FRISCO CHIRP'S

---

[1] I fancy, however, that Parker was improving at the time of his death, possibly as a result of meeting Bechet in France (Bechet was always ready to instruct the young).

VEGAS DEBUT headlines I remembered from my schooldays), and read a lot of books. I learned that jazz had now developed, socially and musically: the post-war Negro was better educated, more politically conscious and culturally aware than his predecessors, and in consequence the Negro jazz musician was musically more sophisticated. He knew his theory, his harmony, his composition: he had probably been to the Juilliard School of Music, and jazz was just what he didn't want to be associated with, in the sense of grinning over half a dozen chords to an audience all night. He had freed his music as a preliminary to freeing himself: jazz was catching up with the rest of music, becoming chromatic instead of diatonic (this was the something fundamentally awful), taking in other national musical characteristics as the American Negro looked beyond the confines of his own bondage. Practically everyone was agreed about all this. It was fearful. In a humanist society, art—and especially modern, or current, art—assumes great importance, and to lose touch with it is parallel to losing one's faith in a religious age. Or, in this particular case, since jazz is the music of the young, it was like losing one's potency. And yet, try as I would, I couldn't find anything to enjoy in the things I was sent, despite their increasing length—five, seven, nine minutes at a time, nothing like the brilliant three-minute cameos of the age of 78s. Something, I felt, had snapped, and I was drifting deeper into the silent shadowland of middle age. Cold death had taken his first citadel.

And yet again, there was something about the books I was now reading that seemed oddly familiar. This *development*, this *progress*, this *new language* that was more *difficult*, more *complex*, that required you to *work hard at appreciating it*, that you *couldn't expect to understand first go*, that needed *technical and professional knowledge* to evaluate it *at all levels*, this *revolutionary explosion* that *spoke for our time* while at the same time being *traditional* in the *fullest*, the *deepest* . . . . Of course! This was the language of criticism of modern painting, modern poetry, modern music. *Of course!* How glibly I had talked of modern jazz, without realizing the force of the adjective: this was *modern* jazz, and Parker was a modern jazz player just as Picasso was a modern painter and Pound a modern poet. I hadn't realized that jazz had gone from Lascaux to Jackson Pollock in fifty years, but now I realized it relief came flooding in upon me after nearly two years' despondency. I went back to my books: 'After Parker, you had to be something of a musician to follow the best jazz of the day.'[1] Of course! After Picasso! After Pound! There could hardly have been a conciser summary of what I don't believe about art.

The reader may here have the sense of having strayed into a private argument. All I am saying is that the term 'modern', when applied to art, has a more than chronological meaning: it denotes a quality of irresponsibility peculiar to this century, known sometimes as modernism, and once I had classified modern jazz under this heading I knew where I was. I am sure there are books in which the genesis of modernism is set out in full. My own theory is that it is related to an imbalance between the two tensions from which art springs: these are the tension between the artist and his material, and between the artist and his audience, and that in the last seventy-five years or so the second of these has slackened or even perished. In consequence the artist has become over-concerned with his material (hence an age of technical experiment), and, in isolation, has busied himself with the two principal themes of modernism, mystification and outrage. Piqued at being neglected, he has painted portraits with both eyes on the same side of the nose, or smothered a model with paint and rolled her over a blank canvas. He has designed a dwelling-house to be built underground. He has written poems resembling the kind of pictures typists make with their machines during the coffee break, or a novel in gibberish, or a play in which the characters sit in dustbins. He has made a six-hour film of someone asleep. He has carved human figures with large holes in them. And parallel to this activity ('every idiom has its idiot,' as an American novelist has written) there has grown up a kind of critical journalism designed to put it over. The terms and the arguments vary with circumstances, but basically the message is: Don't trust your eyes, or ears, or understanding. They'll tell you this is ridiculous, or ugly, or meaningless. Don't believe them. You've got to work at this: after all, you don't expect to understand anything as important as art straight off, do you? I mean, this is pretty complex stuff: if you want to know how complex, I'm giving a course of ninety-six lectures at the local college, starting next week, and you'd be more than welcome. The whole thing's on the rates, you won't have to pay. After all, think what asses people have made of themselves in the past by not understanding art—you don't want to be like that, do you? And so on, and so forth. Keep the suckers spending.

[1] Benny Green, *The Reluctant Art* (1962), pp. 182–3.

The tension between artist and audience in jazz slackened when the Negro stopped wanting to entertain the white man, and when the audience as a whole, with the end of the Japanese war and the beginning of television, didn't in any case particularly want to be entertained in that way any longer. The jazz band in the night club declined just as my old interest, the dance band, had declined in the restaurant and hotel: jazz moved, ominously, into the culture belt, the concert halls, university recital rooms and summer schools where the kind of criticism I have outlined has freer play. This was bound to make the re-establishment of any artist–audience nexus more difficult, for universities have long been the accepted stamping ground for the subsidized acceptance of art rather than the real purchase of it—and so, of course, for this kind of criticism, designed as it is to prevent people using their eyes and ears and under-standings to report pleasure and discomfort. In such conditions modernism is bound to flourish.

I don't know whether it is worth pursuing my identification of modern jazz with other branches of modern art any further: if I say I dislike both in what seems to me the same way I have made my point. Having made the connection, however, I soon saw how quickly jazz was passing from mystification ('Why don't you get a piano player? and what's that stuff he's playing?') to outrage. Men such as Ornette Coleman, Albert Ayler and Archie Shepp, dispensing with pitch, harmony, theme, tone, tune and rhythm, were copied by older (Rollins, Coltrane) and young players alike. And some of them gave a keener edge to what they were playing by suggesting that it had some political relation to the aspirations of the Black Power movement. From using music to entertain the white man, the Negro had moved to hating him with it. Anyone who thinks that an Archie ('America's done me a lot of wrong') Shepp record is anything but two fingers extended from a bunched fist at him personally cannot have much appreciation of what he is hearing. Or, as LeRoi Jones puts it, 'Listening to Sonny Murray, you can hear the primal needs of the new music. The heaviest emotional indentation it makes. From ghostly moans of spirit, let out full to the heroic marchspirituals and priestly celebrations of the new blackness.'

By this time I was quite certain that jazz had ceased to be produced. The society that had engendered it had gone, and would not return. Yet surely all that energy and delight could not vanish as completely as it came? Looking round, it didn't take long to discover what was delighting the youth of the Sixties as jazz had delighted their fathers; indeed, one could hardly ask the question for the deafening racket of the groups, the slamming, thudding, whanging cult of beat music that derived straight from the Negro clubs on Chicago's South Side, a music so popular that its practitioners formed a new aristocracy that was the envy of all who beheld them, supported by their own radio stations throughout the world's waking hours. Perhaps I was mistaken in thinking that jazz had died; what it had done was split into two, intelligence without beat and beat without intelligence, and it was the latter which had won the kind of youthful allegiance that had led me to hammer an accompaniment to Ray Noble's 'Tiger Rag' when I was twelve or thirteen. Beat was jazz gone to seed, just as 'modern jazz' was: B. B. King or Ornette Coleman? A difficult choice, and if I were to come down (as I should) on the side of the former, it wouldn't be under the illusion that I was listening to the latter-day equivalent of Billie Holiday and Teddy Wilson, Pee Wee Russell and Jess Stacy, or Fats Waller and his Rhythm.

III

My slow approximation through these articles to the position just stated is the story I promised lay in them, and the amusement—at least, for me—is watching truthfulness break in, despite my initial resolve. As I said, it's an ordinary tale, and perhaps hardly worth telling. On the other hand, once I had worked out to my own satisfaction what had happened to post-war jazz, I couldn't help looking round to see who, if anyone, had anticipated me. Jazz writers as a class are committed to a party line that presents jazz as one golden chain stretching from Buddy Bolden to Sun Ra, and their task is facilitated by the practice jazz magazines have of employing several reviewers (the trad man, the mod man, the blues man) to ensure that nobody ever has to write about anything they really detest. This is good for trade, lessens the amount of ill will flying about the business, and gives the impression that jazz is a happy and homogeneous whole. But was there no one among them who had realized what was going on, apart from myself?

I don't mean to suggest that there are not many knowledgeable critics to whom the party line is a sincere reality, nor to imply that they are given to mendacity. When a jazz writer says, 'You can hear Bessie in Bird', or 'Shepp's playing pure New Orleans street marches', I'm quite prepared to believe he means it, as long as I have permission to mark his mental competence below zero. I also take leave to reflect that most of them are, after all, involved with 'the scene' on a commercial day-to-day basis, and that their protestations might be compared with the strictures of a bishop on immorality: no doubt he means it, but it's also what he draws his money for saying. Would any critic seriously try to convince his hearers that jazz was dead? 'Jazz dead, you say, Mr Stickleback? Then we shan't be wanting next month's record stint, shall we? And don't bother to review "Pharaoh Saunders: Symbol and Synthesis" for the book page. And—let's see—we'd better cancel that New Wave Festival you were going to compère. Hope you make the pop scene, daddyo.' And so they soldier on at their impossible task, as if trying to persuade us that a cold bath is in some metaphysical way the same as a hot bath, instead of its exact opposite ('But don't you see the evolutionary development?').

But of course there was Hugues Panassié, the venerable Frog, who matter-of-factly refused to admit that bop or any of its modernist successors was jazz at all, simply adducing their records as evidence. It was a shock to find myself agreeing with Panassié: back in 1940 I had considered him rather an ass, chiefly because he overvalued Negro players at the expense of white ones ('the natural bad taste of the Negro' was a favourite phrase of the time), in particular the forcible-feeble Ladnier. But in appealing to the ear, rather than regurgitating the convoluted persuasions of the sleeves, he was producing the kind of criticism I liked, and I had to take back much of what I had thought of him in consequence. Then there was Brian Rust, authoritative discographer, who in his introduction to *Jazz Records 1932–1942* claimed that by 1944 'jazz had split, permanently, the followers of the bop cult demanding—and getting—music in an ever-freer form till (at least in the writer's opinion) it ceased even to be recognisable as jazz at all.' He also said that if he played Charlie Parker records to his baby it cried. And it was amusing to find Benny Green, who had made very merry with the bewilderment of old-style fans at the chromatic revolution, devoting the last pages of his book to sarcasms about Ornette Coleman and 'some nebulous lunacy called Free Form': nothing is funnier than an upstaged revolutionary. Now and then, too, a reviewer got the wrong record, as in 1961 when the editor of *Down Beat*, Don De Micheal, took off on Ornette in heart-warming style ('the resulting chaos is an insult to the listener'), ending, 'If Coleman is to be a standard of excellence in jazz, then other standards might as well be done away with.' Only once (August 1967) did I let fly in this way, and then it was like hitting the stumps with a no-ball: the piece wasn't printed.

Such examples[1] could indeed be multiplied, but might only seem added strokes to a self-portrait of the critic as ossified sensibility. To say I don't like modern jazz because it's modernist art simply raises the question of why I don't like modernist art: I have a suspicion that many readers will welcome my grouping of Parker with Picasso and Pound as one of the nicest things I could say about him. Well, to do so settles at least one question: as long as it was only Parker I didn't like, I might believe that my ears had shut up about the age of twenty-five and that jazz had left me behind. My dislike of Pound and Picasso, both of whom pre-date me by a considerable margin, can't be explained in this way. The same can be said of Henry Moore and James Joyce (a textbook case of declension from talent to absurdity). No, I dislike such things not because they are new, but because they are irresponsible exploitations of technique in contradiction of human life as we know it. This is my essential criticism of modernism, whether perpetrated by Parker, Pound or Picasso[2]: it helps us neither to enjoy nor endure. It will divert us as long as we are prepared to be mystified or outraged, but maintains its hold only by being more mystifying and more outrageous: it has no lasting power. Hence the compulsion on every modernist to wade deeper and deeper into violence and obscenity: hence the succession of Parker by Rollins and Coltrane, and of Rollins and Coltrane by Coleman, Ayler and Shepp. In a way, it's a relief: if jazz records are to be one long screech, if painting is to be a blank canvas, if a play is to be two hours of sexual intercourse performed *coram populo*, then let's get it over, the sooner the better, in the hope that human values will then be free to reassert themselves.

IV

I hope the reviews themselves (and I really can't keep them from the reader much longer) are tolerably free from such polemics. I tried in writing them to be fair and conscientious, and there was many a time

[1] To which should certainly be added Henry Pleasants, author of *Serious Music—And All That Jazz!* (1969).

[2] The reader will have guessed by now that I am using these pleasantly alliterative names to represent not only their rightful owners but every practitioner who might be said to have succeeded them.

when I substituted 'challenging' for 'insolent', 'adventurous' for 'excruciating', and 'colourful' for 'viciously absurd' in a thoroughly professional manner. Although my critical principle has been Eddie Condon's 'As it enters the ear, does it come in like broken glass or does it come in like honey?', I've generally remained aware that mine was not the only ear in the world. Above all, I hope they suggest I love jazz. I began by saying how much pleasure in life it has given me, and when I imagine how much I should have missed if, instead of being born on 9 August 1922, I had died then, I realize how great my debt is. How dreadful to have lived in the twentieth century, but died before King Oliver led his men into the Gennett studios at Richmond, Indiana, or before Frank Walker auditioned Bessie Smith ('fat and scared to death') or Bubber Miley joined Duke Ellington's Washingtonians! If I have any 'message' for my readers, it's that.

My readers . . . Sometimes I wonder whether they really exist. Truly they are remarkably tolerant, manifesting themselves only by the occasional query as to where they can buy records: just once or twice I have been clobbered by a Miles Davis fan, or taken to task by the press agent of a visiting celebrity. Sometimes I imagine them, sullen fleshy inarticulate men, stockbrokers, sellers of goods, living in thirty-year-old detached houses among the golf courses of Outer London, husbands of ageing and bitter wives they first seduced to Artie Shaw's 'Begin the Beguine' or the Squadronaires' 'The Nearness of You'; fathers of cold-eyed lascivious daughters on the pill, to whom Ramsay MacDonald is coeval with Rameses II, and cannabis-smoking jeans-and-bearded Stuart-haired sons whose oriental contempt for 'bread' is equalled only by their insatiable demand for it; men in whom a pile of scratched coverless 78s in the attic can awaken memories of vomiting blindly from small Tudor windows to Muggsy Spanier's 'Sister Kate', or winding up a gramophone in a punt to play Armstrong's 'Body and Soul'; men whose first coronary is coming like Christmas; who drift, loaded helplessly with commitments and obligations and necessary observances, into the darkening avenues of age and incapacity, deserted by everything that once made life sweet. These I have tried to remind of the excitement of jazz, and tell where it may still be found.

1970

Just a Little While

Whatever one thought of the clarinet playing of George Lewis, it is impossible to avoid sadness at his death. This small, gentle, 98 lb. man, who did not so much achieve greatness as have it thrust upon him, became the idol of the post-war revivalist generation in Britain. It is not too much to say that he replaced Louis Armstrong in the hearts of jazz enthusiasts as their emblem of genuine grass-roots jazz.

His life was appropriate to this legend. Born in the same year and city as Louis (1900, New Orleans), he taught himself to play the clarinet (though never to read music) and lived that odd semi-professional life common to so many New Orleans musicians till well after his fortieth birthday. He played at weddings, picnics and funerals, not to mention dances, and when no work was to be had he worked as a stevedore.

In 1929 he played his first gigs with Bunk Johnson, and when Johnson ('This ain't bunk—Bunk taught Louis,' as *Down Beat* headlined it) was discovered in 1942, he asked that Lewis should be found for the clarinet chair. The band went straight to the top. It was not a happy association, but when Bunk died in 1949 the way back to genuine New Orleans had been well and truly beaten, and Lewis was free to carry on with his unsophisticated contemporaries and their simple, heart-felt repertoire.

So they played. In San Francisco, New York, London, Berlin, Copenhagen, it was always the same: unschooled, even somewhat incompetent ensembles, perhaps a little repetitive, perhaps a trifle off pitch, but singing out over a bouncing rhythm in a way that gladdened the heart, the George Lewis band became the emblem of uncommercial jazz purity.

Chris Barber, Ken Colyer, Monty Sunshine, Acker Bilk, Keith Smith—two decades of men who wanted to play jazz as it originally sounded took Lewis as their model. What did they find in his music? Many answers might be given, but mine would be excitement without tension.

So much jazz of the Thirties had been based on the crescendo of feeling, the killer-diller, jam-session pseudo-orgasmic pattern of the ten-inch record; in George Lewis's music there was a different method, that of genial co-operation in recounting the tunes that had become deeply ingrained in the New Orleans Negro's way of life: 'Just a Little While To Stay Here', 'Bye and Bye', 'Old Rugged Cross', and the love songs of the beginning of the century such as 'When You Wore a Tulip', sounded even better in the twentieth chorus than in the first.

And that was really the beginning and the end of George Lewis's music. There were no tremendous finishes, astounding solos, murderous build-ups; just this happy, jogging polyphony, a gay-painted musical merry-go-round made up of numerous simple yet sensitive voices, a group of men playing with the complete conviction of performers at the heart of an unquestioned tradition.

It is just the nature of this tradition that makes it hard to assess Lewis finally as 'a clarinettist'. A George Lewis solo is really no more than the other horns resting while George goes on playing what he would have played in an ensemble—a careful, zig-zagging embellishment of the theme, in no way designed to draw attention to himself. But this was New Orleans.

'In the old days, it was always *our* band,' Whitney Balliett reports the New Orleans jazz musicologist Bill Russell saying rebukingly. 'Now one or another of the trumpet players is always resting, and sometimes the drums stop altogether. And there are strings of solos, like an Eddie Condon jam session.' Clearly the cult of personality was as unwelcome here as elsewhere.

But George Lewis did have a solo, a slow blues, usually called 'Burgundy Street Blues', that earned him from Bunk Johnson the mocking appellation of 'the composer'. It was slow, tremulous, formal, rather over-sweet, like 'a Victorian valentine' and seems to show something of the heart of the man, which, according to *Call Him George*, Jay Allison Stuart's readable though somewhat sentimentalized biography (1961), had few of the 'mean' qualities of the indigenous New Orleans musician.

Like many successful men, Lewis had a remarkable mother, Mrs Alice Zeno, who lived to be ninety-six and instilled into him a religious attitude to his life and playing. 'Remember that, son,' she would say. 'George Lewis does nothing. It is God does it.' Again, this is not new in the New Orleans context: we remember Joe Oliver, ill and poor and bandless, writing to his sister: 'I've got a lot to thank

God for, because I eat and sleep. . . .' And even Jelly Roll Morton, on that long, last mortal drive west in 1940, telling his wife: 'The blessed mother really taken care of me.' All the same it explains a lot in George Lewis's playing: the resilience, the modesty, the happiness, the decency.

1 January 1969

Coverage

Recently I added up the number of jazz records that had been reviewed in the previous four numbers of *The Gramophone*, and found that out of a possible 53 I had actually heard 22. Interested, I repeated the experiment in terms of *Jazz Journal*. Here I had heard 48 out of a possible 183.

I recount this anecdote partly to exemplify the difficulties a reviewer works under and partly to dispel the notion that my choice of the month's best records is absolute and unchallengeable. A great many records today are issued on cheap and comparatively fugitive labels, or are in fact imported from abroad on a strictly commercial basis, so that free distribution of review copies (unless a review is guaranteed) is out of the question. 'I seem to hear fewer and fewer LPs,' one pundit grumbled, when asked to select the best records of 1968.

But another factor is the excessive volatility of the jazz record world. A frequent phenomenon is the arrival of a chatty letter from (say) Mike Stickleback, announcing that he is now Jazz Press Release Officer for Hi-Note, Mahogany, Windy City, Extreme, Second Line and Old Man Blues labels and that my slightest wish with regard to any items they cover, past, present or future, will be instantly gratified if only I will ring Marble Arch something-or-other.

In a few weeks I send Mike a courteous note asking for perhaps three new releases; no response. I ring up; Mr Stickleback is no longer with us and in any case Hi-Note, Windy City and Second Line are now part of Megasaurus Enterprises, Mahogany and Extreme are distributed by Oafmark and Old Man Blues has packed up: and usually they aren't as polite as that, treating my request for Mr Stickleback as a subtle form of commercial leg-pulling, or equivalent to a proposal to raise the spirit of William Ewart Gladstone.

Well, it's a difficult business, suggesting that jazz lovers, like book lovers, should scan more than one source of information. For my part I shall go on pursuing the elusive Mr Stickleback.

8 February 1969

Blues Bash

I am getting rather tired of the blues boom. Having for thirty years known the blues as a kind of jazz that calls forth a particular sincerity from the player ('Yeah, he's all right, but can he play the *blues*?'), or as a muttering, plangent *lingua franca* of the southern American Negro, it gives me no pleasure to hear it banged out in unvarying fortissimo by an indistinguishable series of groups and individuals of both races and nations. Moreover, we may be killing the goose that lays the golden eggs. The blues is tough, resilient, basic, ubiquitous. But it is not indestructible, and if we go on like this the day will come when the whole genre will be as tedious as, say, the Harry Lime theme.

However, the records keep rolling in: 'Sonny Boy Williamson Vol. 2' (Blues Classics 20) presents fourteen sides from 1937 to 1945 by the original bearer of this name, accompanied by various sidekicks including Broonzy, Big Maceo, Tampa Red, Eddie Boyd and so on. This is light, agreeable music, the querulous harmonica blending nicely with the lacework of piano and guitar. 'Hand Me Down My Old Walking Stick' by Big Joe Williams (Liberty LBL 83207) is a much richer job, recorded last year, on which Big Joe's tremendous orchestra of a guitar (nine strings) pounds out music for dancing as well as accompanying his strong voice. Liberty is also issuing some anthologies: 'Rural Blues, 1 & 2' (LBL 83213–4) gives a conspectus of the post-war country styles. Lil' Son Jackson, Lightnin' Hopkins and others, moving into the era of amplification (Slim Harpo. J. D. Edwards) and—to my mind—coarsening. 'Urban Blues 1' (LBL 83215) is a parallel group offering early Fats Domino, T-Bone Walker, Joe Turner and others.

Such obituaries of Pee Wee Russell as have come my way have not seemed to do justice to this extraordinary white clarinet player who died last month at the age of sixty-two. I have referred before to the trio of great white eccentrics, Beiderbecke, Russell and Wild Bill Davison—three players who achieved completely individual styles —and it seems to me that the unique quality of each was the product of conscious and consummate artistry. I don't accept the suggestion that Russell didn't know what he was doing. Listen to his solo on Bud Freeman's 'Muskrat Ramble', for instance, where he deliberately repeats that typical squeak at the beginning of two successive phrases; hear him on the Mound City Blue Blowers' 'One Hour', or the Louisiana Rhythm Kings' 'Basin Street Blues', or the Rhythmakers' 'Spider Crawl'—all beautifully shaped statements; try Condon's 'It's Right Here for You', where Russell shatters the record with half a chorus of murderous musical agnosticism, or the last eight bars of Spanier's 'Sweet Lorraine', where he homes in like a talked-down jet. Such a prolific recorder was bound to have his dull days; admittedly he clowned for the drunks at Nick's; but on his day between, say, 1930 and 1945, when his talent was really blossoming and dancing, he had no peers.

8 March 1969

Law

If I were to frame Larkin's Law of Reissues, it would say that anything you haven't got already probably isn't worth bothering about. In other words, if someone tries to persuade you to buy a limited edition of the 1924–5 sessions by Paraffin Joe and his Nitelites, keep your pockets buttoned up; if they were any good, you'd have heard them at school, as you did King Oliver, and have laid out your earliest pocket money on them.

Everything worthwhile gets reissued about every five years.

13 April 1969

Basie

The golden rule in any art is: once you have made your name, keep in there punching. For the public is not so much endlessly gullible as endlessly hopeful: after twenty years, after forty years even, it still half expects your next book or film or play to reproduce that first fine careless rapture, however clearly you have demonstrated that whatever talent you once possessed has long since degenerated into repetition, platitude or frivolity.

A commonplace in the more established arts, it is true of jazz also.

It is perhaps ungenerous to write such a preamble to 'Count Basie Plays Neal Hefti and Quincy Jones' (Verve, SVSP 39/40). These must have been two of the earliest Basie Verve LPs, 1962/3, and each shows the band put through its paces by a first-class arranger; personally I prefer the Jones session, as it seems to stay closer to the well-tried Basie formula 'brass, reeds and rhythm, four to the bar and no messing'.

The two blues 'Count 'Em' and 'Kansas City Wrinkles' have feeling and power; in the Hefti group, Thad Jones's work on 'The Long Night' is good, and Al Aarons, another trumpet, takes the honours on 'Ain't That Right?' and 'Together Again'.

All the same, no one really believes—do they?—that the Newmans and Fosters of the Sixties equal Clayton, Edison, Young and Evans, and even the celebrated Basie beat seems to have suffered by the separation of amplified bass from over-loud drums. *The Encyclopaedia of Jazz in the Sixties* speaks of 'a sharp deterioration in the musical interest', and Whitney Balliett of 'a smooth, heavyset machine that never falters and never surprises'. If Basie has kept his reputation, it is only by remorseless application of my golden rule.

18 October 1969

Moment of Truth

I don't read as much jazz journalism as I should, but of what I did read in 1969 it is *Down Beat*'s account of the Rutgers Jazz Festival that has stayed with me most vividly.

Down Beat, as you know, is the principal magazine of the American jazz music profession; it has been going thirty-five years, and has correspondents in every land from Denmark to Japan. Its policy is a comfortable, middle-of-the-road tolerance: whatever is, generally speaking, is right. And the man they sent to Rutgers was clearly cast in the same mould: let 'em all come, Dizzy, Herbie Mann, Jethro Tull, B. B. King, the Adderley Brothers—the more the merrier. He sat patiently in his seat and tried to hear good in everything, even sermons from Stones had they been present, and on the whole he succeeded, though there is the occasional wince ('I was beginning to wish I wore a hearing aid so I could turn it down').

The flashpoint, if one can call it that, came on the Sunday evening. Our man arrived late, to find the Miles Davis group launched into what proved their final number, or, as he puts it, 'in the throes of what I most deplore, a free-form free-for-all' that 'degenerated into a musical catfight.' One must salute his honesty: here was one of the groups he was most anxious to hear, and it was terrible, and he admits it was terrible. But then—and this is the point—there followed the Newport All Stars; Braff, Norvo, Tad Farlow, and good old George Wein on piano, and the reporter's relief was so enormous that his encomia became almost pathetic in their hyperbole. Braff and his friends were sparkling spring water, they were *Macbeth* and *David Copperfield*, they were incomparable, they were as eternal as sex and sunlight: 'man, this is what it's all about.' In his enthusiasm he asked a seventeen-year-old girl what she thought of them. She said: 'It's music to go shopping at Klein's by.'

Now the point of this anecdote is twofold: first, all kinds of jazz are not equally good, no matter what editorial policy may be; some of it is ravishingly exciting, and some a musical catfight scored for broken glass and bagpipes, and you have only to hear the two in succession to grab the one and reject the other. Secondly, jazz (that is, the form of Afro-American popular music that flourished between 1925 and 1945) means nothing to the young. This should strengthen us in our devotion to it. True, we must give up any notion we may have been cherishing that beneath our hoar exteriors lurk hearts of May: we may dig jazz, but the kids want something else. Our passion for this extraordinary and ecstatic musical phenomenon that lasted a mere twenty or thirty years in the first half of our century must now take its place alongside similar passions for Hilliard miniatures or plain-chant.

10 January 1970

Wells or Gibbon?

'Every man', wrote Schopenhauer, 'mistakes the limits of his vision for the limits of the world,' a quelling sentiment that came to my mind when I was pasting up a recent bunch of press cuttings. For, however they buttered their words with subsidiary praise, there was no doubt that this was what even the friendliest of my reviewers was saying. 'A pity he had to spoil things', one of them wrote, 'by holding back history.'

The book in question, a collection of my writings on this page through the Sixties, had advanced the view that 'modern' jazz (I attached a special, non-chronological meaning to the adjective) was no more jazz than modern painting was painting or modern poetry, etc. I even hinted that in jazz we had witnessed a capsule history of all arts—the generation from tribal function, the efflorescence into public and conscious entertainment, and the degeneration into private and subsidized absurdity.

What the reviewers said was that it was not jazz that had degenerated, but Larkin; I was simply one more example of the regrettable fact that our ears grow old and sometimes shut up altogether (a sign that we should do likewise).

Well, jazz writers are either Wells or Gibbon, onwards and upwards or decline and fall: where did we differ? After much thought, I selected a contention by another reviewer as a kind of test case: 'Men like Parker and Sonny Rollins . . . inherited most of the old jazz virtues, and anyone attuned to jazz should not take long to recognize them.'

This is the party line of the Wellses. Assuming it means that 'most of the old jazz virtues' are to be found in Parker and Rollins (it doesn't actually say so), then I and the rest of the Gibbons reject it. The wonderful music that swept the world during the first half of this century, so wonderful that it sang songs about itself ('Everybody's Doing It', 'It Don't Mean a Thing If it Ain't Got That Swing'), was of limited appeal, but that appeal was new and definite: a certain area of musical and rhythmic sensibility was being played on for the first time. It could, perhaps, be defined, but its provocation was so strong and blatant that this was felt to be unnecessary (Fats Waller: 'Lady, if you has to ask,' etc.). It originated from Negro folk music and is with us now, in an infinitely vulgarized form, in beat music, rock and roll, rhythm and blues.

When Parker and the rest started bopping, therefore, their aim was to sell something as unlike jazz as possible to jazz audiences. They did this partly because they wished to recapture the lead, so to speak, by playing something the white men couldn't, but mostly, I should say, because the jazz nerve had been overstimulated. They were intelligent men, musically, and jazz bored them. What they produced, therefore, was the conscious opposite of jazz—dead tone, no collective improvisation, no 'good old good ones' (or rather different g.o.g. ones), a kind of anti-syncopated klook-mop rhythm, and of course chromatic harmonies rather than the familiar diatonic of all the lullabies, love songs, hymns, and national anthems that lie at the base of every nation's musical consciousness.

Now I am a simple soul. If someone offers me salt instead of sugar, or a waltz instead of a march, or bop instead of jazz, then I can't help pointing out that there's been some mistake. This is all I was doing: why did my critics object?

Our difference may be a semantic one. I am sure we both agree that there is a discernible basic difference between, say, Muggsy Spanier and Freddie Hubbard. What I am saying is that in consequence the word used to describe what Spanier plays should not be used to describe Hubbard. What they are saying is that the word used for Spanier should be extended to include Hubbard. Which is right?

Behind this confrontation, I fancy, lie a number of opposed prejudices. The Wellses want to extend terms, to stretch points, to see things change. The Gibbons want words to keep their meanings, to be definite, to see things stay the same. Whitney Balliett, in a recent number of the *New Yorker*, reports Duke Ellington as saying that he wants to drop the term jazz in favour of something wider. 'Afro-American music' or something like that. Duke is a Wells. Louis Armstrong, on the other hand, has talked about 'that modern malice . . . you got no tune to remember and no beat to dance to.' Louis is a Gibbon.

Well, either camp has a pretty good leader. All I would say to my critics is that the jazz that conquered the world (and me) was the jazz of Armstrong, Ellington, Bix and the Chicagoans. What Parker,

Monk, Miles and the Jazz Misanthropes are playing can be Afro-American music for all I care, but it isn't jazz. Jazz is dying with its practitioners, Red Allen, Pee Wee Russell, Johnny Hodges. Not to admit this is . . . well, holding back history.

15 August 1970

Minority Interest

Reviewing jazz records in January might be described as scraping the barrelhouse: there certainly don't seem to be many around. But is it only January? When, in search of Christmas presents (that annual conversion of one's indifference to others into active hatred), I wandered into a few 'record departments', I was shocked to see how little of the stock therein could be called jazz.

Rank on rank of shiny LP covers all depicted the same thing: a bunch of young people, mostly male, with clothes and faces appropriate to criminal vagrancy, stood scowling at me in attitudes eloquent of 'We're gonna do you, Dad.' Their names, so far from implying any national, family or artistic kinship, were phrases or even single words chosen at random in a kind of imagist or even surreal poetry—The Light Brigade, Deuteronomy, Lace, Pale Ways, The Low Foreheads. Only in a far corner did I find a small rack labelled 'Jazz' that contained the sleeves of some dozen LPs by Ellington, Basie, Ella Fitzgerald, Jacques Loussier and Ambrose.

Now of course one knew that this sort of transformation had taken place; one had watched jazz magazines fold up or turn into rock organs; one had seen (or had it been only a nightmare?) Jimi Hendrix elected by the fans to a jazz pantheon instead of Johnny Hodges; nevertheless, to see it expressed in concrete palpable terms did rather bring home one or two disagreeable truths that may be formulated thus:

(1) No jazz today is popular;
(2) The least unpopular jazz is reissues;
(3) Hence, the only jazz issues from the big companies today are reissues, few and far between;
(4) Current jazz comes on obscure, imported, highly expensive labels, and the ordinary public never sees or hears it.

Well, perhaps I am simplifying: Christmas always upsets me.

25 January 1971

Vocals

Some years ago it started to be a form of approbation of a jazz singer to say he (or she—usually she) 'used his voice like an instrument'. I was never very happy about it; to start with, it ran counter to the accepted theory that the basis of jazz instrumental intonation was using your instrument like a voice, and a Negro voice at that—widevibrato, thick, rasping, and so on.

Secondly, it seemed an attempt to devalue the *words* of a song: if the object of a singer of the words 'I love you' was not to make you think she (or he) loved you, but rather to skitter around the notes on which these words were scored, then something had gone wrong with jazz singing. One remembered, too, Lester Young's dictum that the best way to improvise on a song was to think of its words while you were doing so.

12 June 1971

What Armstrong Did

'Whereas Louis Armstrong by his artistry has through the universal language of music brought comfort, pleasure and understanding to people throughout the world. . . .' The quotation is from a 1958 citation in the Massachusetts House of Representatives at the State House in Boston, and demonstrates that the recent acclamation of Armstrong in the press and on radio and television was not something it took death to evoke. Long before his end, Louis had conquered the world, even America.

For his fans, throughout whose lives Armstrong had been something inexhaustible and unchanging like the sun, this universal endorsement of him as a great artist and a good man was some small consolation. We had given him our allegiance in the teeth of our elders' contempt: 'Jungle music . . . and why doesn't he clear his throat?' Now we were shown to be right. Armstrong was an artist of world stature, an American Negro slum child who spoke to the heart of Greenlander and Japanese alike. At the same time he was a humble, hard-working man who night after night set out to do no more than 'please the people', to earn his fee, to pay back the audience for coming.

The plaudits will continue for some while yet. But the sift of time is unceasing: soon we shall be looking at Louis over a gap of five years, then ten. The books will come out (how about a selection of his letters?); the wilful tide of taste will turn. Armstrong will become as distant as Oliver. What will the twenty-first century say of him?

It is only by imagining such a perspective that one can organize one's thoughts. As an artist, Louis was first of all inclusive; he was the deep river into which flowed all the tributaries of jazz. He was never original in the sense that Parker was original: he simply did what everyone else was doing twenty times better. Nevertheless, he outdistanced them. From playing with a band he changed to playing in front of a band: it played the tune, he sang the words, then blasted the roof off with his golden obbligato. He listened to what the audience applauded, and tried to give it to them.

There is no doubt that in the Thirties he went through a period of exhibitionism that was as tedious as it was astonishing. To think of all that inventiveness, all that power, going into hitting 350 high Cs on 'Shine' is heart-breaking, yet that was all America encouraged Louis to do. Why wasn't it Armstrong who brought about the New Orleans revival? He had the youth, the knowledge, the stature—but he was as much in the grip of his managers as his slave grandparents had been in the grip of theirs. When it came, and he was sent out on the road with the All Stars, his playing could not meld with them. Ten years older, Bunk Johnson could sway like a reed among reeds: Armstrong was an alp among villages. So the All Stars dropped away: Teagarden and Bigard became Young and Hucko, then Big Chief Russell Moore and Joe Darensbourg. Only Armstrong remained, like a great chef putting on the same meal every night.

Yet the greatness was slow to fade. When after a severe bout of emphysema the trumpet could no longer maintain even the 'straight lead' Louis so advocated, his singing—perfectly pitched, perfectly timed—could bring tears to the eyes. The all-inclusive talent had hardened, and narrowed, and grown isolated, but it still contained the essence of jazz. The records are there to prove it. Let us be thankful for their permanence.

In the great ironical takeover of western popular music by the American Negro (and remember the saying 'Let me write a nation's songs, and anyone you like may write its laws'), Armstrong stands with Ellington and Waller as one of the Trojan horses that brought it about. Mick Jagger at Altamont in 1969 is the logical outcome of Louis bringing the house down with 'Ain't Misbehavin'' in 1929, and the process isn't finished yet. When it is, the chances are that Armstrong will be remembered as much as an agent for replacing one culture with another as an individual artist. If so, it won't be his fault: nothing, in this line, is ever anyone's fault.

21 August 1971